ATLANTIS
AND OTHER LOST WORLDS

ATLANTIS
AND OTHER LOST WORLDS

FRANK JOSEPH

ARCTURUS

To Brad Steiger, whose Atlantis Rising *sparked my search
for the lost civilization a quarter-of-a-century ago.*

This edition published in 2014 by Arcturus Publishing Limited
26/27 Bickels Yard, 151–153 Bermondsey Street,
London SE1 3HA

AD003880EN

Printed in the UK

CONTENTS

INTRODUCTION
NEW DISCLOSURES REVEAL ANCIENT SECRETS

'IN THE EARTHQUAKE OF
ANCIENT PEOPLES NEW
SPRINGS BREAK FORTH.'
FRIEDRICH NIETZSCHE, *THUS SPAKE ZARATHUSTRA*

I n March 2003, an American psychologist Dr Gregory Little and his wife, Lora, were trying to verify a strange sighting made thirty-four years earlier. They had heard tales of a hulking, prehistoric wall-like structure lurking below a metre of water in the Atlantic Ocean. The sunken enigma was said to lie near Andros Island, 240 kilometres south-east of Miami, Florida. About 170 kilometres long and 57 kilometres across at it widest point, with an area of 3,703 square kilometres, Andros is not only the largest island of the Bahamas, but also the greatest tract of unexplored land in the Western Hemisphere, thanks to its profuse, often impenetrable mangrove swamps.

The Littles were following up on the claims of a local dive operator, Dino Keller. In 1992, he claimed to have navigated his tour boat over a shallow coral reef, where he observed the underwater 'wall', while cruising Nicolls Town Bay off the extreme north-east end of the island. His observation was all the more remarkable because archaeologists insist that Andros remained uninhabited until the 17th century, when former slaves from West Africa were stranded on the island. Today's 10,000 inhabitants, residing mostly in small towns along its eastern coast, are the descendants of these hapless castaways.

PLATFORM UNDER THE SEA

Following Keller's directions, Dr Little snorkelled about 600 metres from shore to find a 458-metre-long, 50-metre-wide arrangement of massive blocks in three, well-ordered sloping tiers, interspersed by two bands of smaller stones. Although standing 3 metres beneath the surface, its top section was more than 1 metre deep, just as described by Keller. Large stones comprising the tiers average 5 by 6 metres, and 1 metre thick. Each of the three tiers was 17 metres wide. The Littles also found a ramp leading from the floor of the harbour lagoon to the top of the platform.

The feature's regular appearance and almost uniformly square-cut blocks argue persuasively for a man-made identity, which, given its location at a natural harbour in the North Atlantic Current, may have been a quay, breakwater or port facility of some kind. Underscoring this characterization, together with the ramp, is a number of rectangles 13 centimetres wide and deep, and resembling post holes, cut into some of the cyclopean stones just below the uppermost tier. These holes may have held mooring pylons used to tie up docked ships. Most if not all of the blocks themselves appear to have been quarried from local beach rock and deliberately set in place, a marine construction practice that was common throughout the ancient Old World.

But who could have built such a massive project at a time when territory now covered by the ocean was dry land? And was the Andros Platform the only structure of its kind in the vicinity or merely part of a much larger complex yet to be found?

Dr Little's discovery won the endorsement of fellow investigators from the United States' Association for Research and Enlightenment, Edgar Cayce's organization, in Virginia Beach, Virginia. Together, over the next four years, they expanded their exploration of the waters around Andros to make some extraordinary discoveries. Following clues provided by local traditions of another massive formation being located underwater about 10 kilometres north of the island, Dr Little and company dove in an uninhabited chain of territory known as the Joulter Cays. There they found a stone wall at least several hundred metres long.

Although its uppermost tier rose to within just 2 metres of the water surface, 'the lowest tier of stones revealed more limestone blocks under the visible portion. How far down it extends [into the sea bed],' Dr Little stated, 'is unknown.' The blocks themselves had been cut into rectangles and squares, 1 to 2 metres wide and about 1 metre thick, though a few, less typical specimens were larger. Only sections of the wall stood intact, but its man-made nature was evident throughout in the regularity of the stonework and the unnatural placement of one block upon another. The entire site was obviously some large public-works project built many thousands of years ago by an utterly unknown civilization.

The Andros Platform has six alternating bands of stone. Six was the sacred numeral of Atlantis, whose city planners incorporated the holy number in the capital's alternating stone walls, according to Plato's description of the sunken civilization.

THE CAPRICORN CONNECTION

Precise dating of the sunken structure is problematical, but Dr Little believes the apparently related Andros Platform dates prior to 10,000BC. Sea levels were low enough then for its creation on dry land. His supposition is underscored by some very provocative parallels: 12,000 years ago, the Andros Platform lay on the Tropic of Capricorn, a circle defining the apparent journey of the sun around the earth at about 23.5 degrees north of the equator. Following it eastwards across the Atlantic Ocean and North Africa, the Tropic of Capricorn at that time intersected Philae, ancient Egypt's Temple of P-aaleq, or the 'Remote Place', regarded by dynastic Nile river dwellers as the 'Island in the Time of Ra', and therefore among the oldest ceremonial centres above the First Cataract.

The Tropic of Capricorn simultaneously connected with India's earliest port city, in the Gulf of Khambhat (Cambay). Lothal's gigantic harbour facilities included long stone jetties and sheltered quaysides for large oceangoing vessels.

Running further east still, the Tropic of Capricorn crossed Chia-shu Island, where archaeologists unearthed China's oldest Palaeolithic artefacts. These were largely harpoon points, net weights, and other, maritime objects used by an unknown seafaring people.

Moving into the Pacific Ocean, the Tropic of Capricorn passed over another island, Japan's Yonaguni, where divers discovered a huge 'citadel' 30 metres beneath the surface of the sea. This discovery is described at length in Chapter 14, but its intriguing relationship to the Tropic of Capricorn is worth mentioning here. Yonaguni's underwater ruin shares the same base length – 160 metres – as Philae's Temple of P-aaleq on the other side of the world, in the Upper Nile Valley.

It seems beyond coincidence that the Bahamian Andros, Egypt's 'Remote Place', ancient India's Lothal, China's Chia-shu Island, and Japan's Yonaguni should all have occupied the Tropic of Capricorn at the same time. These five sites – which formerly rode the northernmost passage of the sun around our planet – connected the Pacific realm with Southeast Asia, the Indian subcontinent, Africa and the Atlantic Ocean, thereby suggesting a global culture that flourished more than 12,000 years ago.

But who could have operated such a global phenomenon at a time when, according to conventional archaeologists, human beings were still millennia away from creating even the barest rudiments of the first organized societies? Clearly, mainstream assumptions about the origins of civilization and the true depth of its prehistory are in need of radical revision. Nowhere is this more especially true than in the Atlantis Controversy. Establishment scholars have long dismissed the sunken city as nothing more than a utopian fantasy. Quantum leaps in scientific technology since the end of the Second World War, however, have progressively made the deep seas of the world ever more transparent, to reveal a very different story.

THE HORSESHOE SEAMOUNTS

As early as the first sonar investigation of the Atlantic Ocean in 1949, indications of a lost civilization came to light. Some 418 kilometres due west from the Straits of Gibraltar, Dr Maurice Ewing, aboard the National Geographic research vessel *Glomar Challenger*, found a formation on the ocean floor since referred to as the Horseshoe Seamounts, comprising a large island ringed by a range of high mountains. The Columbia University geology professor determined that its highest peak, dubbed Mt Ampere, was a volcano that collapsed beneath the sea within the past 12,000 years. So, too, the fourth century BC philosopher Plato characterized Atlantis as a large island beyond Gibraltar and surrounded by a great ring of mountains overwhelmed by a natural catastrophe 11,500 years ago. Core samples taken from the ocean floor more than 3 kilometres deep came up with prodigious amounts of beach sand – physical evidence for a former shoreline that had been subject to untold centuries of wave action at sea level. This was proof that the deep-ocean landmass had at one time in the recent geological past been dry territory above sea level, and for a very long time.

Moreover, the estimated dimensions of the Horseshoe Seamounts – 515 kilometres from west to east by 310 kilometres from north to south – loosely complement the dimensions Plato gives in the *Kritias* for the island of Atlantis: 588 kilometres from west to east by 365 kilometres from north to south. Both sets of measurements are, of course, approximate, leaving room for a compromised medium that suggests commonality.

Did the *Glomar Challenger*'s early sonar investigation of the ocean depths actually find Atlantis? At least a few prominent professional researchers who followed in its wake seemed to confirm as much. Less than ten years after Dr Ewing's first discovery of Mt Ampere, Stockholm's Riksmuseum launched a Swedish deep-sea expedition under the command of Dr René Malaise, aboard the research vessel Albatross. From the ocean floor about 2 kilometres beneath the surface of the Atlantic, the scientists brought aboard fossilized remains of several thousand diatoms – small algae that flourished over the past 12,000 years. Dr Malaise's palaeobiologist colleague R.W. Kolbe went on to catalogue more than 60 freshwater diatom species at 1-kilometre depths and deeper across the mid-Atlantic. Such an unexpected abundance of retrieved algae plants proved that they once grew in far-spreading freshwater lakes on what could only have been a former stretch of dry-land territory located in the vastness of today's open sea.

Kolbe's conclusion was supported by additional evidence uncovered in 1963 by an oceanographer for the Soviet Academy of Sciences. While investigating an area of the Horseshoe Seamounts from the *Mikhail Lomonsov*'s deck, Dr Maria Klinova's robotic devices scooped up several unusual rocks from the sea floor. Laboratory testing showed that the specimens had not been formed at the 1.6-kilometre depths where they were found, but on dry land about 10,000 years ago.

Revelations such as these have convinced marine scientists that a large mountainous landmass somewhat smaller in area than Portugal (about 90,000 square kilometres) did in fact occupy the mid-Atlantic Ocean within the past 10,000 years. They are not sure, however, that the Horseshoe Seamounts, for all their appropriate setting and physical resemblance to Atlantis, comprise the same sunken island described by the great Athenian philosopher Plato, twenty-three centuries ago, in two dialogues – the *Timaeus* and *Kritias*. Sceptics argue that no archaeological evidence has so far been recovered from the sea floor.

PLATO'S ATLANTIS

Some have dismissed the entire question as nothing more than a misunderstanding of Thera, the ancient Greek name for modern Santorini, a small Aegean island north of Crete, synonymous in the minds of some conventional archaeologists with Atlantis.

They argue that a volcanic eruption experienced by Thera during the Middle Bronze Age was garbled in Plato's account and subsequently remembered, imperfectly, as the fate of the lost civilization. While a Minoan settlement was indeed located on Thera, it was too small to exert any significant cultural or economic – much less military – influence in the region. And the volcanic event it experienced in 1628BC, while powerful, did not, as archaeologists now recognize, snuff out civilization in the eastern Mediterranean after all. Thera or sometimes nearby Crete are still occasionally used by critics of Plato to explain away Atlantis, but they represent a dwindling voice shunned even by most mainstream scholars. Despite the scepticism shown by some, physical proof for the sunken capital may have come to light in early 1974, just where Plato implied it existed.

His *Kritias* mentions that once elephants abounded on the island of Atlantis. Critics have long scoffed at Plato for including this fantastically out-of-place pachyderm in the middle of the ocean, hundreds of kilometres beyond the nearest landfall, and further still from the animal's African and Asian homeland. But in 1960, oceanographers dredging the sea bottom of the Atlantic some 322 kilometres off the Portuguese coast unexpectedly hauled up literally hundreds of elephant bones from more than forty different locations. Scientists concluded that the creatures had anciently wandered across a now submerged land bridge, extending from the Atlantic shores of Morocco into formerly dry land long since sunk beneath the sea. Their discovery gave special credence not only to Plato, but also to his modern-day subscribers. Yet more unlooked-for evidence of Atlantis was yet to come.

COLD WAR PHOTOGRAPHY

During the course of an otherwise routine topographic survey of the sea floor 420 kilometres west of Gibraltar, Russian investigators stumbled upon a controversial surprise. Their discovery was suppressed in the climate of paranoia that pervaded the Soviet Union during the Cold War, until word leaked out to the West more than four years later. In late 1978, the director of the Fleet Department of the Institute of Oceanography, Alexander Nesterenko, told an Associated Press conference that photographs of 'what might be ruins' had indeed been made on the bottom of the near-Atlantic. He was seconded by Andrei Aksyonov, deputy director of the Institute of Oceanography of the

Soviet Academy of Sciences. Professor Aksyonov confirmed that the structures 'once stood on the surface of land, above sea level', although he stopped short of identifying them as remnants of Atlantis.

Early the following year, details of the Russian find were disclosed by Dr Sofia Stepanovna Barinova, among the Soviet Union's most prominent scholars at the Institute of Biology in the Soviet Academy of Sciences. In his article for the popular science magazine *Znanie-Sila* (Knowledge Is Power) (no. 8, 1979), Dr Barinova revealed that, during March 1974, geologists and his fellow biologists aboard a Soviet research vessel, the *Academician Petrovsky*, probed the shallow waters off northern Moroccan coasts, with special interest in the topographical features of submerged mountain peaks, where unknown species of marine life were expected to flourish. Their investigations were mostly conducted by sonar sweeps operating in tandem with subsurface photography.

As the *Academician Petrovsky* cruised further west over the Horseshoe Seamounts, deep-sea cameras inadvertently captured a series of images resembling the partial remains of a ruined city. Ivanovich Marakuev, an underwater-photography specialist aboard ship, confirmed that they resulted from neither film nor instrument anomalies or malfunctions, nor were the unusual targets natural geological formations mistaken for artificial structures. Most appeared around the peak of Mt Ampere, the volcano that Dr Ewing determined had collapsed into the sea within the past 12,000 years.

THE MOUNT AMPERE DISCOVERIES

Although the base of Mt Ampere plummets more than 3,000 metres, its plateau-like summit is a mere 65 metres beneath the surface of the ocean. It was here, according to the *Znanie-Sila* article, that Russian scientists found most of the man-made features. These included a wall 75 centimetres wide, 1.5 metres high and slightly longer in length. Other masonry consisted of five broad steps ascending to an expansive platform connected to another monumental staircase. If, as Dr Barinova speculated, all the visually documented structures protruded through a layer of silt perhaps 30 or more metres thick, Marakuev's photographic evidence revealed only a fraction of their uppermost portions.

Several return voyages to Mt Ampere undertaken by the *Academician Petrovsky* throughout the 1980s reconfirmed and even expanded the underwater discoveries. They were greeted with cautious interest in the West, where suspicion of all things Soviet ran high until the collapse of the Soviet Union at the end of the decade. Since then, post-Communist Russia has lacked the financial wherewithal to renew its investigation of man-made structures in the near-Atlantic, while Western archaeologists are sceptical of claims by Dr Barinova and his colleagues, who are still reluctant to share everything they found at the Horseshoe Seamounts.

In his *Znanie-Sila* article, Barinova cited the immense mantle of silt that lies over the ruins like an obscuring cloak, concealing virtually every trace of physical evidence. It is this constant deposition which has gradually but continuously descended over the ruins, not for centuries, but for millennia, making their detection difficult in the extreme. To locate and reveal them, modern research instruments would need to make kilometres of ocean transparent, and probe through amounts of sedimentary silt sufficient to hide a building or even a city. Enthusiasts expecting to find Atlantis sitting intact on the sea bottom deceive themselves. The Russians may have found faint traces of Plato's drowned capital, but it still awaits the generous funding and especially future technology necessary to overcome the special, thus far unsurmounted challenges of deep-sea archaeology.

THE KUNIE CONCRETE SHAFTS

Happily, no such challenges prevented the discovery of an immense 'citadel' standing under 30 metres of ocean off a small Japanese island. The crystal-clear waters surrounding Yonaguni almost showcase the sunken 'monument' – a wonderfully preserved counterpart to Atlantis in the Pacific, and the outpost of another 'lost' civilization, once referred to as the Motherland of Mankind, Mu, or Lemuria.

Strangely, perhaps, far more hard evidence for the previous existence of this tropical civilization has surfaced than Atlantologists have so far been able to muster for their own sunken city. Twenty-four years prior to the underwater ruin's discovery near Yonaguni in 1985, scholars were deeply puzzled by an entirely different kind of mystery at Kunie (pronounced 'Koonya'), or Îles des Pins, a far more obscure location in New Caledonia. No larger than 13 by 16 kilometres, the island is dotted by several hundred mounds of sand ranging in size from 61 centimetres to 92 centimetres across, and varying in length from 1 to 3 metres.

Kunie's 1,500 Melanesian inhabitants knew nothing about the structures, which were professionally excavated for the first time in 1961 by a Museum of New Caledonia archaeologist. Expecting to unearth human burial remains or grave goods, Luc Chevalier was startled to find inside one mound a concrete drum made of an extremely hard homogeneous lime-mortar. It contained innumerable bits of shell, its exterior speckled with silica and iron gravel fragments that appeared to have hardened the mortar as it set. A narrow shaft had been sunk vertically into the top of the mound, which was then filled with liquid lime-mortar, and hardened in position.

Assuming the curious feature must have been the incomprehensible handiwork of some modern visitor, Dr Chevalier dug into the next structure, only to find an identical concrete shaft. He excavated the remainder of Kunie's 400 hillocks, all of which concealed the same kind of lime-mortar arrangement. They contained not a single bone, artefact or piece of burnt charcoal to suggest their use for burial, habitation or ceremonial practices. Returning with samples from his digs to the New Caledonian capital at Nouméa, 65 kilometres away, Chevalier subjected them to scientific testing and was astounded by the results: the cylinders were unquestionably man-made between 10,950BC and 5120BC. This date span was subsequently reconfirmed via additional radiocarbon examinations of the same material by laboratory technicians at Yale University in the United States.

History records that the Romans first invented concrete-making little more than 2,000 years ago. Yet, the evidence from Kunie proves that someone on an obscure little island in the Pacific Ocean had mastered the process millennia before the official beginning of civilization itself. But for what purpose? While Chevalier and his fellow archaeologists were baffled by the lime-mortar cylinders, mechanical engineers have often commented on their resemblance to electrical devices or components, particularly storage batteries.

A TONGAN FLOOD HERO

Although nothing like New Caledonia's unaccountably advanced concrete cylinders has been found anywhere else in the Pacific, the ocean vastness between Asia and the Americas is studded with radically different but no less disturbing enigmas. On the island of Tonga, 22,530 kilometres east of Kunie, stands a 5-metre-high arch weighing more than 110 tonnes. The 4-metre-wide trilithon has been known to countless generations of islanders as the Ha'amonga a Maui, or 'Burden of Maui'. In a collection of Polynesian myths, *The Lore of the Wharewananga*, Maui is portrayed as a Hercules-like hero who separates the gods of earthquake and tempest endeavouring to tear apart and sink a long stretch of primeval territory. Although he prevents its total inundation, the ancient archipelago is reduced to a string of islands. This tradition is the folk memory of a former landmass broken up and partially sunk into the sea by seismic violence, a theme coursing through the traditions of virtually every native people across the Pacific. The Tongan islanders lay no claim to the monumental Ha'amonga a Maui, but associate its construction with their flood hero.

They also point to the prodigious Tauhala as a remnant of antediluvian times. Just one of this pyramidal platform's stone blocks is more than 7 metres in length, weighing an estimated 40 tonnes. With an engineering skill that defies belief, especially for a pre-industrial people, it was somehow lifted and inserted into a wall 333 metres long. The pre-deluge chiefs responsible for the Tauhala are still remembered as the Mu'a, literally, 'Men from Mu'. A more obvious allusion to a lost motherland seems impossible.

PREHISTORIC MONUMENTS IN THE PACIFIC

In the Mariana Islands, 5,934 kilometres northwest of Tonga, are found the mushroom-like monuments of Guam, Tinian, Saipan and Rota. Known as Lat'te Stones from the native *latde* for 'houses of the Old People', the name refers not to elderly islanders, but to the *taotaomona*, or 'Spirits of the Before-Time People', ascribed by the indigenous

Chamoro as foreign builders who arrived from over the sea during the ancient past. Archaeologists believe that human habitation on the Mariana Islands goes back to c.3000BC.

Hewn from a rough metamorphosed coral, the Lat'te are composed of the *haligi*, a truncated pyramidal pedestal that is surmounted by an inverted hemispherical capstone, known as the tasa, 2.5 metres high and 3 metres across. The monuments average almost 3 metres high, and weigh about 30.5 tonnes, although examples discovered at the As Nieves quarry, on Rota, are the largest known specimens at more than 6 metres and in excess of 50 tonnes. Wherever found, the Lat'te are mostly lined up in double rows of half a dozen to a dozen or more specimens, usually along river banks or on the shoreline to commemorate the 'Spirits of the Before-Time People'. Basing their estimates on the remains of the fallen megaliths and those still erect, researchers think that as many as 100 or more Lat'te may have originally populated the Marianas. They are found nowhere else on earth. Their significance and purposes are utterly unknown.

The prehistoric ruins of other megalithic structures, including pyramids and immense harbour works, are scattered across the Pacific, from Samoa and Palauli to Tahiti and Savai'i. While the towering statues of Easter Island are well known, how these 15-tonne *moai* were transported from their quarried origins to just above the coast, where they were lifted atop great platforms known as *ahus*, is beyond our powers to comprehend.

Even more spectacularly inexplicable are the 300 million tonnes of magnetized basalt that went into the construction of an artificial island built in the water atop a coral reef off the shores of Pohnpei, an obscure island in the Carolinas, north of New Guinea. The islanders call it Nan Madol, the 'Places in Between', a reference to ninety-two man-made islands enclosed within 29 square kilometres. All are interconnected by an extensive network of what appear to be canals, each 10 metres across and more than 1 metre deep at high tide. The entire site was originally encompassed by an immense wall, only portions of which have survived millennia of jungle growth and wave erosion. The site's tallest tower, referred to by the Micronesian natives as Nan Dowas, rose perhaps 13 metres high. Although archaeologists cannot guess who was responsible for such a mind-boggling achievement, or when, the islanders speak of twin sorcerers who arrived at Pohnpei in the dim past from a sunken kingdom. Aided by a 'flying dragon', they were said to have built the incomparable city of Nan Madol.

In the aggregate, these and numerous other ruins spread throughout the remote islands of the Pacific comprise the surviving if broken relics of an extensive civilization that long ago dominated half the globe before it was overwhelmed by a natural catastrophe, echoed in the folk traditions of native peoples from Australia to Alaska, from Japan to Chile. Referred to variously as Horai, Haiviki, Mu or Lemuria, it was humankind's seminal culture emerging from millennia of myth into something more than mere fable. The exciting process of transformation began during the 19th century, when a German archaeologist, Heinrich Schliemann, demystified the lost city of Troy by excavating its walls above the Turkish plains of Hissarlik. Today, researchers such as Dr Greg Little are doing the same for Atlantis that Schliemann did for Troy in the late 19th century.

OTHER LOST CIVILIZATIONS

Atlantis and Lemuria are not the only enigmas of their kind materializing from the mists of legend. The paradise of Shangri-La; the arctic Thule and Hyperborea; sinful Sodom and Gomorrah; the elusive El Dorado; Antilia; Hy-Braeasail; the Seven Cities of Gold; St Brendan's Isle; and many other shadowy realms that once figured so prominently in the consciousness of man, now find their rightful place in the mythological and archaeological landscapes of the early 21st century.

Ongoing advances in technology are inexorably dispelling all doubts that once concerned these lost realms. The latest breakthroughs in oceanography, climatology, geology, genetics and related fields are revealing an unprecedented panorama of humankind's unexpectedly deep past, wherein these realms played a more formative role than previously imagined. Civilizations formerly deemed entirely legendary are emerging as cultural Meccas and imperial capitals of powerful empires that dominated the world long ago, leaving their irrevocable stamp on enduring myth. These scientific revelations have been so rapid, numerous and far-reaching in their effects that even otherwise well-informed readers are unaware of their impact on our changing perspective of human origins.

Throughout the following pages are presented some of their most dramatic and recent discoveries which, for the first time, remove places such as Atlantis, Lemuria and the rest from the domain of fable, bringing them back to life after centuries of neglect or misunderstanding. In their stories we glimpse not only our human origins as a civilizing race, but also the startling recognition of parallels and patterns with present-day crises. As they stand revealed in the light of our investigation, the Lemurians and, particularly, the Atlanteans are surprisingly modern, and not only because of the technological sophistication they enjoyed. Like us, they faced fundamental alternatives between security or liberty, materialistic self-indulgence or selfless idealism. We can sympathize with them because, in the choices they made and the consequences that confronted them, they are so much like ourselves.

The past, no matter how ancient, does not die; it was lived by our fellow men and women, separated from us only by time. The outcome of their actions and energies formed and continues to form our world and its future. As the long-lost drama of their splendid, surprisingly advanced societies is again played out in our imagination, something of their awful greatness and violent fate stirs the imagination and incites us to higher degrees of curiosity. Atlantis, Lemuria and the rest – they certainly live in us, their descendants.

CHAPTER 1

VISUALIZING ATLANTIS AND LEMURIA

'IN THE IMMEASURABLE
SPACE OF THE MIND'S EYE,
ALL THINGS MAY BE GLIMPSED.'
IGNATIUS DONNELLY, 1878

The island of Atlas was mountainous and broadly forested. South of its towering dormant volcano was a plain 55 kilometres long by 37 kilometres wide. It was irrigated by a network of canals carrying water to the crops flourishing in the richly fertile volcanic soil and under the temperate sun. South of this agricultural complex was the city of Atlantis, capital of an oceanic empire that stretched from Italy in the east to Yucatán in the west. The metropolis was not unlike a gigantic landscaped target of concentric rings, alternating circles of land and water, interconnected by bridged canals accommodating both ship and foot traffic. Each of these artificial islands was surrounded by high walls interspersed with mighty watchtowers manned by soldiers. The smallest, central island bore the imperial residence and the magnificent Temple of Poseidon.

THE CAPITAL CITY

Plato's *Kritias* clearly defines Atlantis – at least in its ultimate stage – as having belonged to the Heroic Age, confirming a 13th-century BC time frame for the events surrounding the Atlantean empire in its last days. A visitor at that time would have been awed by the city's walls, not only for their prodigious dimensions, but also for the sheets of orichalcum (high-grade copper) and mosaics of semi-precious minerals gleaming in the sunlight. Plato writes:

Some of their buildings were simple, but in others they put together different stones, which they intermingled for the sake of ornament, to be a natural source of delight. The entire circuit of the wall which went around the outermost one they covered with a coating of brass, and the circuit of the next wall they coated with tin, and the third, which encompassed the citadel, flashed with the red light of orichalcum.

The horserace track occupying the city's outermost land ring, and the monumental canals with their tunnels large enough to allow passage of a warship are described in the *Kritias*.

As its civilization spanned the age of the megalith-builders to the Bronze Age, Atlantis may have made a somewhat odd picture in its ultimate manifestation, perhaps resembling the cyclopean walls of South America's Sacsahuamán (near the former capital of the Inca empire, Cuzco), surmounted by an Etruscan temple. The Etruscans were themselves nothing more than late Atlanteans who colonized western

Italy, so their surviving material culture offers us a glimpse of Atlantis at its cultural height.

An Etruscan terra cotta at the Tarquinia Museum in Italy portrays the winged horses Plato said pulled Poseidon's chariot in his colossal statue at the temple of Atlantis; it is the only such likeness from antiquity. Atlantean and Etruscan columns, often painted Tuscan red, were unfluted and tapered slightly from top to base, thereby magnifying the monumental perspective.

Overlapping Atlantean roofs were high-gabled, sometimes red-tiled, with an entablature featuring sculpted images of the gods. Volcanic rock, being in the greatest abundance, provided the leading building material, and resulted in the black (lava), white (pumice) and red (tufa) colours Plato said characterized Atlantean architecture. Supplemented as they were by decorative sheets of orichalcum, and arranged in an attractive natural setting of reflective water and lush vegetation, public and private structures in Atlantis comprised the appealing vision of a unique and powerful state.

THE ROYAL PALACE

The interior of the imperial residence was not described in Plato's dialogues. Fortunately, its details survive in

Homer's description of Scheria, yet another name by which the island of Atlantis was known, in the *Odyssey*. The palace sat at the centre of a large orchard thick with trees bearing apples, pomegranates, pears, figs and olives. In the same enclosure was a prosperous vineyard, where grapes were drying on large wooden racks in the sun. Vegetable beds of various kinds were neatly laid out nearby. The garden featured two springs. One irrigated all parts of the enclosure, while the other provided a watering place for the townspeople, then coursed under the courtyard towards the mansion. The enclosure itself comprised a hedgerow interspersed with gates, as another courtyard separated the palace from the surrounding gardens, vineyard and orchard.

The royal residence was likewise in keeping with the Atlantean style of monumental opulence. Stone walls inset with coppery sheets of orichalcum topped by decorative bands of blue enamel tiles entirely encircled the courtyard. The palace featured a massive pair of gilt doors swinging on silver posts. On either side of the threshold stood the sculptures of two dogs – one of gold; the other, silver. Inside, the banquet hall featured an enormous central table of heavy, dark, ornately sculpted wood surrounded by high-backed throne-like chairs adorned with colourful woven hangings. Life-size statues of golden youths bearing torches provided illumination for night-time revels.

THE PEOPLE OF ATLANTIS

What did the Atlantean people look like? A masterpiece of portrait sculpture has survived to answer that question. The 'Lady of Elche' is the life-size terra cotta portrait bust of a woman excavated in Andalusia, Spain. The realistic sculpture was executed with a high degree of skill and dates to some pre-Roman epoch. The facial characteristics of the woman and her singular attire belong to a sophisticated, affluent people, utterly unknown to archaeology, but strongly suggestive of her Atlantean provenance. Discovery of the masterpiece in an area of Iberia that had been mentioned by Plato as the Atlantean kingdom of Gadeiros, and the slight slant of the subject's eyes (supposedly an Atlantean racial characteristic) imply that the artwork portrays a lady from Atlantis residing in its Spanish dominion.

Several other portraits from life of Atlantean soldiers are still well preserved, incised on the walls of Pharaoh Ramses III's Victory Temple, at Medinet Habu, in the Valley of the Kings, Upper Egypt. They show a tall, slender, broad-shouldered man with somewhat aquiline facial profile, firm mouth, and almond-shaped eyes.

Redheads were supposedly common among the Atlanteans, as were blondes. The men (particularly civilians and the emperors) were sometimes bearded, but all military personnel, including commanders, were clean-shaven with close-cropped hair. Ancestral traditions throughout Mesoamerican and Andean civilizations consistently represent their Atlantean founding fathers as tall, bearded, light-skinned and red- or yellow-haired. Appropriately, the Egyptians, who fought two life-and-death wars with the Atlanteans, regarded red hair very unfavourably. The Guanche natives of the Canary Islands were among the last surviving population group from Atlantis, until their extermination by the Spaniards in the 16th century. Their physical characteristics were a strange mix of Cro-Magnon and Indo-European features – above-average stature, ectomorphic (a slender physical type), dolichocephalic (long-skulled), with occasional blondism and light eyes, suggesting that the Atlanteans may have been a race unto themselves. While the Guanches were unquestionably Caucasian, their speech was a mixture of Indo-European, Egyptian, Basque and mostly unknown words. Quite possibly, a distinct Atlantean genotype, from which they descended, may have developed in isolation on its own island home.

According to Plato, the emperors dressed in magnificent azure robes, and the Roman historian Aelian recorded that royalty wore headbands made from the fillets of 'sea-rams' (perhaps frigate birds, which are known to dive into, or 'ram', the sea for fish). Judging from the Lady of Elche's raiment, prosperous Atlantean women did not shrink from elaborate headgear. Two apparently cloth discs were fastened vertically at either temple, and she was adorned with jewelled pectorals. The early 12th-century-BC military uniforms of Atlantean marines are vividly portrayed in representations of the 'Sea Peoples' at Medinet Habu. Their chin-strapped helmets were bronze, topped by a short, stiff horsehair rayed crown, dyed dark red. Bronze breast- and backplates were sewn into an X-pattern on a leather jerkin, belted at the waist.

ARMY, POPULATION AND EMPIRE

At its zenith, Atlantis boasted immense armed forces to protect its far-flung empire. According to Plato, the Atlanteans fielded no fewer than 79,600 men-at-arms. These included 7,200 hoplites – heavily armed foot soldiers – and as many archers and slingers, supported by an additional 33,600 slingers and javelin-throwers. They were joined by 10,000 chariots, each one manned by a driver and warrior bearing a light shield. Atlantis was a sea power. Her 14,400 naval personnel – marines, sailors, shipwrights, and dock hands – serviced 1,200 ships, by far the most potent thallasocracy of the ancient world.

These figures suggest that the Atlantean population stood at c.1,034,800 persons at the peak of its imperial power. This rough figure is deduced from the supposition that there were five workers (including farmers, sailors, artisans and merchants), three women, three children and two elder persons for every warrior. It does not, however, include the populations of its confederated kingdoms, nor of the millions of colonials under Atlantean sway. The empire of Atlantis stretched from the North American copper mines of Michigan's Upper Peninsula and the shores of Mexico and Colombia to Iberia and Italy, across North Africa to the Egyptian border, encompassing more territories and peoples than Roman imperialism, and unmatched until the rise of the British Empire.

The Atlantean empire was governed by ten kings, all directly descended from the sea-god founder of their civilization. They enjoyed absolute command over their own cities and regions, but the exercise of power was strictly applied within the laws of Poseidon. These demanded that each monarch submit himself to the judgement of the other rulers on any complaint made against him. The laws also constrained the kings from making war on each other, and required the unified action of all if one or more were attacked.

The head of the House of Atlas acted as Emperor, whose decisions took precedent and were final. The laws of Poseidon enjoined the regents to rule with wisdom and forbearance 'on a soil of common goodwill' (*Kritias*, 5). Any who deviated from the laws were liable to charges of holy perjury and oath-breaking, capital offences subject to harsh punishments. Thus, the Atlantean system of government, while authoritarian, was not totalitarian.

THE DISPERSAL OF THE PEOPLE OF MU

More is known about the physical appearance of Atlantis and the Atlanteans than of Mu – or Lemuria – and its inhabitants. Colonel James Churchward, the early 20th-century authority on this Pacific civilization, concluded that white, brown and black races were spread over the lands of Mu. These were former archipelagos stretching from the Peruvian shores of South America to the South China Sea.

Mu was not a kingdom, but a culture spread out over a series of islands and landmasses before most of these territories were swallowed by the ocean. Some were destroyed in violent cataclysms of seismic and volcanic upheaval; others sank gradually beneath rising sea levels or were eroded beyond habitation. With the forced abandonment of Mu, its peoples dispersed to east and west. Most of the black population settled in Melanesia to become the Negritos, but a few travelled to Mexico, where some of them were memorialized in monumental stone heads sculpted by the Olmecs, Mesoamerica's first known civilizers, at La Venta in Mexico.

The brown-skinned survivors mostly took root throughout Polynesia and migrated to South America. The white Lemurians went everywhere. Their arrivals were sung in myth, from the Incas' Con-Tiki-Viracocha folk and the Hawaiians' Menehune, to the people of Horai in Japanese myth and Burma's Naacals. These Lemurians were not Nordic Indo-Europeans, but a different white race related, instead, to the original, Caucasian inhabitants of Japan (today's mixed Ainu), the Pacific Northwest Haida Indians (with their Caucasoid physical traits) of British Columbia, and reflected in the so-called 'Kennewick Man'. This is a popular name given to the skeletal remains of a man who belonged to a previously unknown Caucasian population residing in North America 11,000 years ago, discovered in 1991 on the banks of Washington State's Kennewick River.

LEMURIAN CIVILIZATION

Mu preceded but was also contemporaneous with Atlantis, but no two civilizations could have been more different. The Atlanteans were a technologically advanced, materially sophisticated, imperialist people, the builders of cities and impressive monuments, interested in wealth, power, culture and outward expansion, similar to the much later Romans.

Few of these values had any appeal for the Lemurians. About the only thing they shared with Atlantis was maritime skill. But their seafaring served different ends. The Atlanteans operated great oceangoing cargo ships, transporting millions of tons of copper to barter with their clients in Europe and the Near East. And they manned powerful warships to conquer their enemies. The Lemurians' chief purpose in sailing to other parts of the world, on the other hand, was to spread the tenets of their spiritual beliefs throughout the world. They had no navy, no standing armies, no military of any kind. They built ceremonial centres, but no cities. Agriculture developed, spurred on by the natural fecundity of the volcanic soil and tropical climate of these islands. Botany flourished, and herbalists attained heights of achievement never equalled since.

The Lemurians constructed impressive roads (like those which may still be visited at Micronesia's Tonga and Malden

Island) and raised monumental edifices and sculpture, as attested by the colossi of Easter Island and the magnetized crystal city at Nan Madol, in the Caroline Islands. In contrast to Atlantean architecture, which was predominantly curved and circular, Lemurian building styles were largely right-angled and rectangular. Atlantean influences were not, however, missing altogether from the Pacific Motherland.

'Domes or curved roofs were quite frequent in connection with these larger structures,' wrote the Rosicrucian researcher W.S. Cerve, 'and whenever a building was constructed for religious purposes the main entrance was a portal with the two crescent curves at the top symbolic of the sacred curve which was the basis of their religious-scientific doctrines.' Remarkably, just the style of architecture he described first in 1931 appears illustrated on an inscribed stone found nearly sixty years later, and associated by the renowned Japanese geologist Professor Masaaki Kimura (University of the Rykyus) with the lost civilization of Mu. The tablet is today in the possession of the Okinawa Prefecture Museum.

Their lands were productive, but also overgrown with tenacious jungles, against which human settlements had to struggle for living space. The Lemurians lived in small villages of modest wood-and-grass homes, clustered around their great stone ceremonial centres, located almost without exception either by the sea or a river. The focal points of society, these meeting places comprised plazas surrounded by massively broad staircases leading up to spacious platforms, surmounted by smaller temples made of perishable materials. Religious pageantry, rituals, sporting events – all took place at the ceremonial centres.

The Lemurians were a musically skilled people, excelling in the performance of a cappella choirs, yet another legacy preserved among the Polynesians. They were skilled in creating coloured sand-paintings, an art that spread with their migrations to the American south-west, among the Navaho Indians, and, in the opposite direction, to Tibet. The same melding took place in Mu, as demonstrated in the Lemurian word for 'art', *ord*, which, according to Cerve 'was used only in reference to the Deity'.

The Lemurians developed their own written language, and carried it with them as they travelled east and west, where it became, respectively, the Indus Valley script at Mohenjo Daro, India's first civilization, and the rongo-rongo of Easter Island's 'talking boards'. A Lemurian link alone explains the commonality of these two distantly separated, otherwise unconnected syllabaries. The Lemurians invented mathematical computation and accounting in the form of coloured knotted cords, a method left behind in both Polynesia and Bolivia.

LEMURIAN SPIRITUAL LIFE

The Lemurians were not much interested in internal trade or external commerce or material riches of any kind. What most concerned the people of Mu were questions of healing and spiritual development. They formed an extended religious community under a single spiritual leader believed to be the perpetually reincarnating soul of a saint, much like the Japanese concept of the Amida Buddha (the Buddha of Compassion), or the Dalai Lama. This theocratic personage, regarded with awe by the whole population as a living god, deferred to a hierarchy of priestly initiates, who gently exercised political power as infrequently as possible. There was no state structure in Mu, which was ruled less by law than through a national ethic.

Crime was virtually unheard of, and there were no prisons, capital punishment or police. A very small detachment of part-time guards answered only to the spiritual leader and his priestly colleagues, who acted as judges when occasion demanded. Misdemeanour criminals, such as thieves, liars and braggarts, were submitted to extra religious training as a kind of spiritual behaviour modification. More serious cases, including repeat offenders, physically violent troublemakers or murderers, were for ever banished to distant, barbarous lands. Human sacrifice was unknown in both Atlantis and Mu, but slaves may have been common in the former culture during its final, imperial period. The pervasive influence of their national religion prevented the Lemurians from engaging in slavery.

Cerve points out that in Mu, 'the graves were always in lines running east and west and the head of the deceased was always placed toward the east'. An underwater structure near the Japanese island of Yonaguni and associated with Lemurian sacred architecture is likewise oriented on an east–west axis. While this antediluvian motherland was variously known as 'Lemuria' and 'Mu', both names appear interchangeably throughout world mythic traditions.

The Lemurians were apparently self-indulgent sexual activists, whose family ties were loose and not clearly defined. Such attitudes were part of the legacy passed down to their mixed descendants, the Polynesians, whose sexual behaviour was later branded 'licentious' by Christian missionaries. Freed from the necessity of overwork to survive because of the super-abundance of food, and inhabiting a very hot climate where anything more than semi-nudity was impractical, the Mu (as they are still remembered by the Hawaiians and

Tibetans) developed a sensible, guiltless sexuality that was regarded merely as an aspect of physical life.

It was in the spiritual arts that the Mu most excelled, surpassing even the skilled adepts of Atlantis. The soul-practitioners of Mu engaged in mass-meditation sessions, involving hundreds or even thousands of participants. The psychic power generated from these single-minded assemblies was beyond anything comparable before or since. Levitation of otherwise immovable objects, psychokinesis, communal telepathy, remote viewing, metaphysical healing, the shifting of space and time, prophecy, interspecies communication, interdimensional travel – the whole gamut of known psychic phenomena were being developed and practised in Mu. Cerve wrote of the Lemurians:

> *To them the spiritual part of the world was the most important, because it was the only real aspect and only dependable and safe side of life. Thousands of years of accumulated knowledge had taught them that the very foundation upon which they stood, composed as it was of earthly materials, and subject to the mighty changes that had taken place and would take place, was a most unreliable and unreal part of life.*

CONTACT BETWEEN ATLANTIS AND MU

Although lacking aggression, the Lemurians did not generally welcome foreigners, who were met with deportation. Select individuals were allowed temporary stay in Mu for religious training, diplomatic reasons or other sanctioned business only. If the Atlanteans foreshadowed the Caesars, the Lemurians most resembled today's Tibetan Buddhists.

The Lemurians and Atlanteans were aware of each other; limited contacts had always taken place. But perhaps the Lemurians' reserved cordiality towards visitors from Atlantis stemmed from a nervous mix of disdain and fear. According to Cerve, the Atlanteans referred to them as the 'Holy Lemurians' for their popular spiritual disciplines, or 'the blind race', because of the many people who suffered eye disorders in sunny Mu. As Atlantis grew increasingly decadent, however, materialistic Atlanteans began to deprecate them as a superstitious, backward people.

The Lemurians allegedly foresaw the demise of their lands, but either could do nothing to avoid it or chose not to, believing in the fundamental transience of existence and a universe that continuously creates, destroys and re-creates.

CHAPTER 2
THEY SAW ATLANTIS

'HE WAS WISE. HE SAW MYSTERIES
AND KNEW SECRET THINGS. HE BROUGHT US
A TALE OF THE DAYS BEFORE THE FLOOD.'
PROLOGUE, SUMERIAN *EPIC OF GILGAMESH*, C.2800

The earliest known person to describe Atlantis is also one of European civilization's leading figures. Together with Socrates and Aristotle, Plato is still considered one of the most influential thinkers in the history of the Western world. Declared the prominent 20th-century metaphysician A.N. Whitehead, 'The safest general characterization of the European philosophical tradition is that it consists of a series of footnotes to Plato.' It is impossible to imagine a more credible source for Atlantis as fact.

THE DIALOGUES OF PLATO

Plato's narrative concerning Atlantis is contained in two dialogues. The earlier *Timaeus* is presented as a colloquy between Socrates, Hermocrates, Timaeus and Kritias, whose own dialogue immediately follows. In the *Timaeus*, Solon, the influential Greek legislator, visits the Temple of Neith (a pre-dynastic war goddess), in Sais, at the Nile Delta. There, the high priest tells him that long ago the Athenians saved the Peloponnesus and Egypt from invading Atlantean forces. He learned that the kingdom of Atlantis, located on a large island 'beyond the Pillars of Heracles' (the Straits of Gibraltar), was greater than Libya and Asia Minor combined, exercising dominion over all neighbouring islands and the 'opposite continent'. In other words, the Atlantean sphere of influence stretched eastwards as far as Italy and the Libyan border with Egypt. But in the midst of its war against the Mediterranean world, the island of Atlantis sank 'in a single day and night' of earthquakes and floods.

Plato's second dialogue, the *Kritias*, was left unfinished a few years before his death in 348BC. The text is in the form of a conversation (largely a monologue) between Plato's teacher and predecessor, Socrates, and Kritias, an important fifth-century BC statesman. He begins by saying that the events described took place more than 9,000 years previously, when a far-flung war between the Atlantean empire and 'all those who lived inside the Pillars of Heracles' (the Mediterranean) ended with geological violence.

Prior to these events, Zeus, king of all the gods, assigned various regions of the world to his fellow deities. As part of his portion, Poseidon was given the ocean, including a large island 'beyond the Pillars of Heracles'. Its climate was fair and the soil rich, and animals, even elephants, were in abundance. There were deep forests, freshwater springs of hot and cold water (suggestive of a volcanic environment), and an impressive mountain range that went right around in a complete circle. The island was already inhabited, and Poseidon wed a native woman. As the sea god's wedding gift to his bride Kleito, he prepared a place for her by laying the foundations of a magnificent, unusual city.

He created three artificial islands separated by concentric moats, but interconnected by bridged canals. At the centre of the smallest, central island stood his wife's original dwelling place on a hill, and it was here that the Temple of Poseidon was later erected, together with the imperial palace nearby. They had five sets of twin sons, and named the island after their firstborn, Atlas. These children and their descendants formed the ruling family for many generations thereafter, and built the island into a powerful state, primarily through the mining of precious minerals, with which they decorated their capital and bartered with other kingdoms. The resulting city is described in some detail, with emphasis on the empire's political and military structures.

Although their dominions kept expanding in all directions, the Atlanteans were a virtuous people ruled by a beneficent, law-conscious confederation of monarchs. In time, however, they were corrupted by their huge wealth and lusted for greater power. The Atlanteans built a mighty military machine that stormed into the Mediterranean world, conquering Italy and marching across North Africa up to the Egyptian frontier, but were soundly defeated by Greek forces and driven back to Atlantis. The *Kritias* breaks off abruptly when Zeus, observing the action from Mt Olympus, convenes a meeting of the gods to determine some terrible judgement befitting the Atlanteans.

This remarkable account was originally brought to Athens by Solon, sometime in the late fifth century BC. The most important legal reformer in Greek history, he toured Egypt around 470BC, while his sweeping proposals back home were being debated by fellow legislators. In the course of his travels, Solon visited the new capital, Sais, at the Nile Delta. There he entered the Temple of the goddess Neith, and heard the story of Atlantis translated from a hieroglyphic report inscribed on memorial pillars. Returning to Greece, Solon finished a detailed draft of everything he had learned about the lost island in preparation for a major epic he planned to compose. In addition to his role as great lawgiver, Solon was known as the 'first poet' of early Classical civilization. He died, however, before this project could be completed. Fortunately, his notes were preserved and passed on to Plato, who based his own dialogues on them.

PLATO'S HISTORICAL ACCURACY

The information presented by the *Timaeus* is entirely credible, with many details verified and supported by geology and the traditions of dozens of disparate cultures in the circum-Atlantic region. The only (and consistent) exceptions concern the numerical values applied to Atlantis: they seem unmanageably excessive. Atlantis is supposed to have flourished 12,000 years ago; it was larger than Libya and Asia Minor combined; its canals were 30 metres deep; and so on. The difficulty is clearly one of translation. Psonchis, the Egyptian high priest who narrated the story for Solon, spoke in terms of lunar years to the Greeks, who knew only of solar years. The discrepancy perpetuated itself whenever numerical values were mentioned. Given the common error in translation, the hitherto unmanageable date for Atlantis comes into clearer focus, placing it at the end of the Late Bronze Age, around 1200BC.

The actual extent of the Atlantean island must subsequently downsize into reality, as well, but by how much it is difficult to know because the true extent of the Libya and Asia Minor of Solon's or Plato's day is not known. During the fourth century BC, 'Libya' was a loosely defined stretch of narrow territory skirting the Mediterranean shores of North Africa, from Tunis to the Egyptian border.

Asia Minor could not have comprised all of Anatolia, but probably included considerably less than half of what is now Turkey, concentrated mostly along the coast, including interior regions formerly dominated by the Hittite empire. These combined territories of ancient Libya and Asia Minor would result in an island smaller in area than Portugal – something large, but still far short of a 'continent'. That Plato undoubtedly had something far less extensive than modern-day notions of Libya and Asia in mind is borne out by the physical dimensions he provides for the island of Atlantis – 588 kilometres from west to east by 365 kilometres north to south. Geologists find it difficult to imagine that a landmass of that size could have perished 'in a single day and night'. But when we consider the magnitude of the geologic violence that concentrated in the eastern Atlantic Ocean during the final Atlantean period (see Chapter 13), the empire's sudden demise becomes more credible.

One of the most revealing details of the *Timaeus* is its mention of the 'opposite continent', the first written reference to America. Its inclusion strongly suggests that the ancient Greeks knew what lay on the other side of the Atlantic Ocean 2,000 years before Columbus rediscovered it, thereby underscoring the veracity of Plato's Atlantis account.

Many historians believe Plato travelled to Sais himself, perhaps specifically to verify the Egyptian account he had inherited from Solon. The existence of this temple record was documented by two other highly influential thinkers. The last major Greek philosopher, Proclus, wrote 800 years after Plato, but his *In Platonis theologiam* (Platonic Theology) he cited the credibility of Atlantis by pointing out that Egyptian columns inscribed with the story were visited and identically translated more than half a century after Plato's death. They were examined by yet another influential thinker, Krantor, who went to Sais as part of his research for a biography of Plato. Proclus writes that Krantor found the Atlantis story preserved exactly as described in Plato's dialogues.

There may be no other report from ancient times supported by men of such stellar credentials. Modern skeptics, particularly archaeologists, are convinced that Atlantis was only a legend. They fail to consider that, beyond his position as the seminal philosopher of Western civilization, Plato based his entire body of thought on an uncompromising pursuit of truth. The *Timaeus* and *Kritias* cannot comprise a fictional allegory for his notion of the ideal state, as some critics insist, because the Atlantis he portrays is far from his utopian conception as developed in *The Republic*. It seems likely, however, that Plato, had he completed the second dialogue, would have used the rise and fall of Atlantis as a historical example illustrating the fatal consequences of civil degeneracy. In the *Kritias*, he did not inexplicably change from philosopher to historian. Instead, his intended citation of corrupted Atlantis to provide a factual basis for the dialogues appears more probable.

THE FIRST MAP OF ATLANTIS

That the oldest surviving version of the Atlantis story should have been told by the Western world's most influential philosopher says much for its credibility. Had Plato's dialogues failed to survive the collapse of Classical civilization and the long Dark Ages which followed, Atlantis would be known today only through the enduring myths of the various peoples affected by it. With the fall of Classical civilization, Plato's story of Atlantis was condemned as pagan fiction until reconsidered by the German polymath Athanasius Kircher (1602–80). This Jesuit priest was a pioneering mathematician, physicist, chemist, linguist and archaeologist; the first to study phosphorescence; and inventor, among numerous, futuristic innovations, of the slide projector and a prototype of the microscope. The founding father of scientific Egyptology, his was the first serious investigation of temple hieroglyphs.

Kircher was also the first scholar to seriously investigate the Atlantis legend. Initially sceptical, he cautiously began reconsidering its credibility while assembling the mythic traditions of numerous cultures in various parts of the world about a great flood. Recalling is exploration of these various European traditions of Atlantis-like kingdoms he wrote:

> *I confess for a long time I had regarded all this as pure fables to the day when, better instructed in Oriental languages, I judged that all these legends must be, after all, only the development of a great truth.*

His research led him to the immense collection of source materials at the Vatican Library, where, as he was an eminent scholar, its formidable resources were put at his disposal. It was here that he discovered a single piece of evidence that proved to him that the legend was actually fact. Among the relatively few surviving documents from Imperial Rome, Kircher found a well-preserved treated-leather map purporting to show the configuration and location of Atlantis. The map was not Roman, but brought in the first century AD to Italy from Egypt, where it had been made long before. It survived the demise of the Classical period, and found its way into the Vatican Library. Kircher copied it precisely, adding only a visual reference to the New World, and published it in his book *Mundus Subterraneus* (The Subterranean World), in 1665.

His caption describes it as 'a map of the island of Atlantis originally made in Egypt after Plato's description', which suggests it was created sometime after the fourth century BC, perhaps by a Greek mapmaker attached to the Ptolemies – Greeks descended from Alexander the Great and rulers of the Nile Valley from 300 to 30BC. More probably, the map's first home was the Great Library of Alexandria, where numerous books and references to Atlantis were lost, along with another million-plus volumes, when the institution was burned by religious fanatics in AD392 on the orders of Christian Emperor Theodosius I. With its relocation to Rome, the map escaped that destruction.

Similar to modern conclusions forced by the current understanding of the geology of the Mid-Atlantic Ridge, Kircher's map depicts Atlantis, not as a continent, but as a large island. It indicates a high, centrally located volcano, most likely meant to represent Mount Atlas, possibly the same Mount Ampere discovered in the mid-20th century by a National Geographic team, together with six major rivers.

The *Kritias* also describes important rivers on the island of Atlantis. That Kircher's map shows six of them recalls the sacred number of Atlantis – six – an apparent piece of internal evidence for his find's authenticity. Although it vanished after Kircher's death in 1680, the Vatican map was the only known representation of Atlantis to have survived the demise of Classical civilization. Thanks to his research and book, it survives today in a close copy. Kircher was the first to publish a map of Atlantis, probably the most accurate of its kind to date.

Curiously, the map is depicted upside down, contrary to maps in both Kircher's day and ours. Yet, this apparent anomaly is evidence of the map's genuine origins because Egyptian cartographers, even as late as Ptolemaic times, designed their maps with the Upper Nile Valley located in the south ('Upper' refers to its higher elevation), at the top because the river's headwaters are located in the Sudan.

Kircher's fascination with the subject was sparked by another great thinker, Sir Francis Bacon (1561–1626). In *The New Atlantis* (1623), Bacon envisioned a modern meritocracy based on the virtues of Atlantean civilization during its golden age. The novel was itself engendered by contemporaneous reports from travellers to the New World, where the indigenous Indians recounted a Great Flood long ago, when a great island kingdom was engulfed by the sea. Europeans were struck by the close similarity of these native accounts with Plato's version of Atlantis, as was Bacon, whose work of fiction was based on these parallels. He set his story during the early 17th century, off the coast of the Americas on an imaginary island populated by descendants from lost Atlantis.

THE SWEDISH CONNECTION

A Swedish contemporary of Kircher was Olaus Rudbeck (1630–1702), Professor of Medicine at Uppsala, discoverer of the lymphatic system at just 22 years of age, inventor of the anatomical theatre dome, designer of the first university gardens, astronomer, architect, shipyard builder, musician, historian of early Sweden, and so on. He also established Latin as the lingua franca of the international scientific community.

Rudbeck's ambition to create a life-size woodcut of every plant known to botany resulted in more than 7,000 carved images. He financed and personally led the first professional expedition beyond the Arctic Circle to bring back numerous plant and animal specimens previously unknown to science. A brilliant scholar fluent in Latin, Greek and Hebrew, Rudbeck possessed a grasp of Classical literature that was nothing less than encyclopedic.

Combining his vast knowledge of the ancient world with personal archaeological research in his own country, he concluded during a long period of investigation (1651–1698) that Atlantis was fact, not fiction – and the greatest civilization in prehistory. From 1679 until shortly before his death twenty-three years later, he composed *Atlantica*, published in a bilingual Latin–Swedish edition. According to this four-volume work, Norse myths and some physical evidence among his country's megalithic ruins show how a relatively few Atlantean survivors may have come to Sweden, contributing to its cultural development, and laid the foundations – particularly in ship construction – for what would much later become the 'Viking Age' from the 9th to 12th centuries AD.

Although Atlantologists have since dismissed Rudbeck's chauvinist belief that Sweden and Atlantis were synonymous, the main thesis of *Atlantica* – that Scandinavia was among the first lands occupied by Atlantean survivors – continues to persuade through the vast amount of still-valid cultural evidence Rudbeck marshalled to support his argument. He identified some Atlanteans with the biblical tribe of Magog, whose members migrated from their antediluvian homeland after the Deluge far across the

Black Sea, following Russian rivers to the Kimi districts in northern Finland, moving on to the plain around Uppsala in the middle of what would much later become Sweden.

Rudbeck's tracing of Atlantean influences appeared to have been verified more than 250 years later, when during the early 1960s Swedish archaeologists identified Scandinavia's earliest known Bronze Age site in digs at Uppsala, Sweden. Radiocarbon testing revealed a habitation date c.2200BC. The Swedish savant had stated that the Atlanteans arrived at Uppsala around 2400BC. This time parameter is particularly significant because it has been identified with the Second Atlantean Flood, brought about by the near miss of a debris-laden comet in 2193BC, as shall be described in Chapter 13.

AN ATLANTEAN BESTSELLER

Rudbeck's Atlanto-Nordic researches were taken up by another 18th-century scholar, the French astronomer Jean Sylvain Bailly (1736–93), who concluded that Spitzbergen, in the Arctic Ocean, was all that remained of Atlantis. Before he could pursue his investigations further, however, Bailly fell victim to the French Revolution. His contemporary during that turbulent time was William Blake, the far-famed British poet and engraver, who wrote of:

*Those vast, shady hills between America and Albion's shore
Now barr'd out by the Atlantic Ocean, call'd Atlantean hills.
Because from their bright summits you may pass to the
golden world
An ancient palace, archetype of mighty Emperies,
Rears its immortal pinnacles...*

These lines from his epic verse, *America: A Prophesy,* found a kindred spirit in Edgar Allan Poe's poem *The City in the Sea*:

*Death has reared himself a throne in a strange city lying
alone far down within the dim West. There, shrines and
palaces and towers ... resemble nothing that is ours. No rays
from the holy heaven come down on the long night-time
of that town.*

Although Poe did not specifically mention Atlantis in *The City in the Sea*, its implication is clear enough.

The very word 'Atlantis' was practically unknown, save among romantic poets and scholarly antiquarians, until the end of the 19th century. Suddenly, in 1882, the all-but-forgotten civilization became a household name, when *Atlantis, the Antediluvian World* was published by Harper Brothers.

It was a unique book that seized upon the public imagination, because it subjected the old legend for the first time to scrutiny under the scientific method, but in so engaging a fashion that it still reads more like a mystery novel than an obtuse academic tome. Yet, for all its wonderful clarity, its arguments for the former existence of the drowned civilization are enduringly persuasive. Here was the key to the book's immediate, long-lasting success. A few years after its release, *Atlantis* sold out twenty-three American editions, and an additional twenty-six overseas editions, a runaway bestseller, even by today's standards. The book is still published in more than a dozen languages, and has been regarded by Atlantologists around the world as the chief textbook in their research for more than 125 years.

The author of this remarkable work was Ignatius Donnelly, the 'Sage of Ninninger', as he was known to his fellow late 19th-century Americans for the town he founded outside Saint Paul, Minnesota. After serving as the state's lieutenant-governor, he became a congressman with ideas far in advance of his time. He was the first to advocate (and obtain) federal protection of the natural environment from uncontrolled industrial development. He was a proponent of women's suffrage long before it became a national issue.

A radical, fist-pounding orator, in the 1890s, Donnelly was the populist People's Party's nominee for President of the United States.

His advocacy of the United States as a world power, equal education, workers' compensation, his opposition to corporate monopolies – all were out of step with turn-of-the-20th-century America. Even his Atlantis book was eventually savaged by professional critics for sometimes political if not always scientific motives. Due to their unremitting, often caustic ridicule, he died convinced his life had been a failure. In the early morning of 1 January 1901, he passed away at a friend's home, as the bells of Saint Paul were ringing in a New Year and a new century.

STEINER'S COSMIC EPOCHS

An Old World genius who found something beyond the merely mythical in Atlantis was Rudolf Steiner (1861–1925). Born in Kraljevic, Austria, on 27 February 1861, Steiner was a scientist, artist and editor who founded a gnostic movement known as anthroposophy based on comprehension of the spiritual world through pure thought and the highest faculties of mental knowledge. Steiner's views on Atlantis and Lemuria are important if only because the educational Waldorf (or Steiner) movement he founded still operates about 100 schools attended by tens of thousands of students in Europe, the United States and elsewhere.

In his 1904 book *Cosmic Memory: Prehistory of Earth and Man*, he maintained that, before Atlantis was destroyed, its earliest inhabitants formed one of humankind's 'root races', a people who did not require speech, but communicated telepathically in images, not words, as part of their immediate experience with God. According to Steiner, the story of Atlantis was dramatically revealed in Germanic myth, wherein fiery Muspelheim corresponded to the southern volcanic area of the Atlantic land, while frosty Nifelheim was located in the north. Steiner wrote that the Atlanteans first developed the concept of good versus evil, and laid the groundwork for all ethical and legal systems. Their leaders were spiritual initiates able to manipulate the forces of nature through 'control of the life-force' and development of 'etheric technology'. He identified seven 'epochs' that comprise a Post-Atlantis Period, of which ours, the Euro-American Epoch, will end in AD3573.

Cosmic Memory went on to describe the earlier and contemporaneous Pacific civilization of Lemuria, with stress on the highly evolved clairvoyant powers of its people. But Steiner defined Atlantis as the turning point in an ongoing struggle between the human search for community and our experience of individuality. The former, with its growing emphasis on materialism, dragged down the spiritual needs of the latter, culminating eventually in the Atlantean cataclysm. Steiner died on 30 March 1925 in Dornach, Switzerland, where his 'school of spiritual science' had been founded 12 years earlier.

A COMPANY OF ILLUSTRIOUS SCHOLARS

The American successor to Ignatius Donnelly was Charles Berlitz (1913–2003). He was the grandson of Maximilian Berlitz, who founded the Berlitz language schools; he himself spoke thirty-two languages. He authored *The Mystery of Atlantis* (1974) and *Atlantis, the Eighth Continent* (1984), which revived popular interest in the subject after more than forty years of general neglect. As the innovative president of an internationally famous language-training school in France, his expertise in various tongues, ancient and modern, led him to conclude that many derived from a single, prehistoric source. Beginning in the Bahamas, Berlitz followed his line of research back to the lost civilization of Atlantis. His renowned credentials as a professional linguist, combined with twenty-six years' service as an intelligence officer in the US Army, helped to restore credibility to Atlantean studies, which continue to this day.

Among the most intellectually brilliant champions of Atlantis as fact was Otto Heinrich Muck (born 30 January 1883). An Austrian physicist at the University of Innsbruck, he invented the snorkel, a device that enabled German U-boats to travel underwater without surfacing to recharge their batteries, thereby escaping Allied detection in the Second World War's Battle of the Atlantic. He later helped to develop German rocketry on the research island of Peenemunde in the Baltic Sea. Published at the time of his death in 1965, *The Secret of Atlantis* was internationally acclaimed for its scientific evaluation of Plato's account of Atlantis. It helped to revive popular interest in the lost civilization, and remains one of the most important books on the subject.

Among the many other prominent scholars who undertook the quest for Atlantis were early Rome's great geographer of the first century BC, Diodorus Siculus; the first-century theologian Philo Judaeus; the second-century Greek naturalist Elianus; the third-century Roman biologist Aelian; Rome's fourth-century historian Ammianus Marcellinus; Krantor of Soluntum, the fourth-century neo-Platonist philosopher who confirmed Plato's account by personally travelling to the Nile Delta, where he found the same Temple of the Goddess Neith, its pillar inscribed with identical information presented in the dialogues; Christoph Cellarius (1638–1707), a prominent French geographer; Alexander von Humboldt (1769–1859), the founder of ecology and after whom the Humboldt Current was named; the pioneering French chemist L.C. Cadet de Gisancourt (1802–91); the revered German palaeobiologist Oswald Heer (1809–83); the pioneering Mayanist Teobert Maler (1842–1917); Wilhelm Geiger (1856–1943), the doyen of Middle Eastern archaeology; the renowned novelist Sir Arthur Conan Doyle (1859–1930); one of the early 20th century's leading physicists, Hanns Hoerbiger (1860–1931); Leo Frobenius (1873–1938), founder of modern African studies; Lewis Spence (1874–1955), the early 20th century's leading authority on world myth; the British poet laureate John Masefield (1878–1967); Ellen Whishaw (1868–1932), the widely respected director of Spain's prestigious Anglo-Spanish-American School of Archaeology after the First World War; the leading 20th-century naturalist C.P. Chatwin (1873–1964); J.R.R. Tolkien (1892–1973), whose drowned civilization of Numenor and city of Gondor were clearly based on Atlantis; and the United States's Pulitzer prize-winning poet Conrad Aiken (1889–1973), whose

1929 work, *Serlin*, celebrated Atlantis. To name but a few …

It says something for the credibility of Atlantis as fact that many of the most eminent thinkers in the history of Western civilization – from Solon and Plato to Kircher and Rudbeck, and into our own time with names such as Berlitz and Hoerbiger – have been among its most prominent advocates.

CHAPTER 3
ATLANTO-LEMURIAN TECHNOLOGY: FACT OR FANTASY?

'AT ONE TIME THE EARTH HAD AN
INCALCULABLY ANCIENT CIVILIZATION
WHICH WAS, IN MANY RESPECTS, SUPERIOR
TO OUR OWN, AND FAR IN ADVANCE OF US
IN SOME IMPORTANT ESSENTIALS WHICH THE
MODERN WORLD IS JUST BEGINNING TO HAVE
COGNIZANCE OF. WHAT IS, HAS BEEN. ALL THAT
WE LEARN AND DISCOVER HAS EXISTED BEFORE;
OUR INVENTIONS AND DISCOVERIES ARE BUT
RE-INVENTIONS AND RE-DISCOVERIES.'

COLONEL JAMES CHURCHWARD, *BOOKS OF THE GOLDEN AGE*

Writers of both fiction and non-fiction have made extraordinary claims for technological sophistication in Atlantis and Lemuria. In novels such as H.G. Wells' *Men Like Gods* (1923), or popular films such as Walt Disney Production's *2001 Atlantis, The Lost Empire*, antediluvian science has embraced everything from genetic modification and electric lifts to aircraft and submarines. Unfortunately for the Atlanteans, they operated neither an air force nor an undersea fleet when they were defeated by defending Egyptian forces in the early 12th century BC. If they ever did possess such advanced military capabilities, their scientific advances may have belonged to some previous era, which, during the course of geological upheavals that sank much of the land, were forgotten, just as the science of the Classical world was lost with the onset of the European Dark Ages. In any case, the question of so advanced a technology in ancient times is the most difficult argument for many sceptics and even Atlantologists to accept. There are nonetheless tantalizing indications that a kind of superscience – or, at any rate, a science in many respects on a par with that of the modern world – did exist in deep antiquity.

That any society in the Ancient World could have attained such a high level of material progress seems incomprehensible and beyond belief to mainstream scholars. Even so, other anient civilizations currently better understood than Atlantis reached surprisingly high levels of technological proficiency, accomplishments which were forgotten when their societies collpased, for whatever reason, only to be rediscovered, often millennia later. Among the Maya, for example, advances in celestial mechanics were not matched until the late 20th century. Although abandoned with the Spanish Conquest, Inca agricultural techniques yielded three times as much produce than farming methods employed in Peru today.

When the story of Atlantis was being written by Plato in the fourth century BC, some fellow Greeks were sailing in the Alexandris, a colossal ship more than 120 metres in length, the dimensions of which would not be seen again for another 2,000 years. A pregnancy test performed by 18th-Dynasty Egyptians was not rediscovered until the 1920s. Doubtless, far more was lost with the recurrent fall of past civilizations than has yet been rediscovered. Arrogance assumes that our own times have a monopoly on human beings of great genius and inventiveness. But that men were able to develop complex technologies in other eras and cultures long since forgotten should not overtax our credibility. Perhaps one of those lost epochs belonged to a place known as Atlantis.

THE BAGHDAD BATTERY

That lost land's alleged mastery of electrical power was implied in 1938, when Dr Wilhelm Koenig was taking inventory of artefacts at the Iraq State Museum in Baghdad. The German archaeologist noticed what seemed to be the impossible resemblance of a collection of 2,000-year-old clay jars to a series of dry-cell storage batteries. He had been intrigued by the singular internal details of the jars, each of which contained a copper cylinder capped at the bottom by a copper disk and sealed with asphalt. After the Second World War, an American technician at the General Electric High Voltage Laboratory, in Pittsfield, Massachusetts, built an exact reproduction of the Baghdad jars that Dr Koenig believed might be electrical batteries. Willard Gray found that, when filled with citric acid, an iron rod inserted into the copper tube generated 1.5 to 2.75 volts of electricity. It was not much, but sufficient to, say, electroplate an object with gold. His experiment demonstrated that practical electricity could have been applied to metalworking by ancient craftsmen after all. The 'Baghdad Battery', as it came to be known, was surely not the first of its kind, but must have represented a hitherto unsuspected technology that preceded it by possibly thousands of years – a technology that perhaps included far more impressive feats of electrical engineering long since lost.

ANCIENT AVIATORS

While conventional scholars may find suggestions of ancient aeronautics even more incredible than 2,000-year-old electrical devices, tantalizing evidence does nevertheless exist to at least suggest that manned flight may indeed have taken place in the ancient world. The first substantiated voyages aloft took place even before Plato was born, when a fifth-century BC scientist, Archytas of Tarentum, invented a leather kite large enough to carry a young boy. In the earliest known example of aerial reconnaissance, the high-flying young man actually served as an observer for Greek armies on campaign.

More amazing was the discovery made in the Upper Nile Valley near the close of the 19th century. According to the US author and explorer David Hatcher Childress:

> In 1898, a model was found in an Egyptian tomb near
> Sakkara. It was labelled a 'bird' and catalogued Object
> 6347 at the Egyptian Museum, in Cairo. Then, in 1969,
> Dr Khalil Massiha was startled to see that the 'bird' had
> not only straight wings, but also an upright tailfin. To Dr
> Massiha, the object appeared to be that of a model airplane.
> It is made of wood, weighs 39.12 grams and remains in good
> condition. The wingspan is 18 centimetres, the aircraft's
> nose is 3.2 centimetres long, and the overall length is 18
> centimetres. The extremities of the aircraft and the wingtips
> are aerodynamically shaped. Apart from a symbolic eye and
> two short lines under the wings, it has no decorations nor has
> it any landing legs. Experts have tested the model and
> found it airworthy.

In all, 14 similar flying models have been recovered from ancient digs in Egypt, dating from the Roman era back to the early Old Kingdom of the first part of the third millennium BC. The Sakkara specimen, for example, was retrieved from an archaeological zone identified with the earliest dynastic periods, at the very beginning of Pharaonic civilization. The context of its find suggests that the aircraft was not a later development, but belonged to the first years of civilization in the Nile Valley. Were the Egyptians' anomalous artefacts actually flying 'models' of the real thing operated by their Atlantean forefathers?

Sceptics tend to categorize these out-of-place items as weathercocks, not aircraft, and point to the discernibly avian features painted on the untypical grave goods, though they are at a loss to explain why anyone would have been buried with something as mundane and commonplace as a weather vane. Were these objects instead the emblematic artefacts of the mummified aviators they were meant to identify and accompany to the next world? At the very least, the Cairo Museum's wooden model of a working glider implies the ancient Egyptians grasped the fundamental principles of heavier-than-air man-made flight. Perhaps such knowledge was the only legacy to survive from some former era, when those principles were applied on a broader scale than Egyptologists have been so been unwilling to imagine.

Childress's book *Vimana Aircraft of Ancient India and Atlantis* is the most complete examination of the subject of Atlantean aviation. In it, he was able to assemble surprising evidence from the earliest Hindu traditions of aircraft supposedly flown in ancient times. Then known as Vimanas, they appear in the famous *Ramayana and Mahabharata*, and the less well-known but earliest of the Indian epics, the *Drona Parva*. Aircraft were discussed in surprisingly technical detail throughout several manuscripts of ancient India.

The *Vimaanika Shastra, Manusa* and *Samarangana Sutradhara*, all classic sources, additionally describe 'aerial cars', which were allegedly operating from deeply prehistoric times. Each of these epics deals with a former age hinting at the last bellicose cataclysmic years of Atlantis. Childress's collection of impressive source materials dates back to the dawn of Hindu literature. It is important to understand, however, that these Vimanas had virtually nothing in common with modern aviation because their motive power was supposedly unlike combustion or jet engines, and had little to do with aeronautics, as we have come to understand this science.

If stories of Atlantean aircraft were limited to Hindu sources, we might be inclined to dismiss the discussion as an Indian subcontinental fantasy. The authors of the best known Indian epics, such as the *Mahabharata, Bhagavatam,* or *Ramayana,* were chiefly interested in the past as a metaphor for spiritual concepts. Hence, separating religious allegory from historical reality in these sources is difficult. But Vimanas, or something very much like them, were also known in pre-Columbian America. Hopi Indians of the North American Southwest told of *pauwvotas* – airborne vehicles flown over immense distances by an ancestral people before their beautiful island perished during a Great Deluge.

In one of several stories describing Con-tiki-Viracocha's departure, this Andean flood-hero – after accomplishing his civilizing mission among the Incas' ancestors – allegedly rose high into the air aboard a 'temple' known as an Orichana, then vanished toward the setting sun (towards Lemuria?). Interestingly, in Quechua, the Inca language, the word 'Orichana' refers to something metallic and polished to a high sheen, so as to appear fiery. *Orichana* echoes Plato's *orichalcum*, the Atlanteans' high-grade copper which they used to brightly adorn the walls of their capital city. Perhaps fading folk memories of the Hindu Vimanas, Hopi *pauwvotas*, and Inca Orichana are all that remain of a lost supertechnology that once, millennia before our Industrial Age, manufactured some kind of aircraft for the inhabitants of Atlantis.

SUBMARINES AND PYRAMIDS

No less surprising are the submarines known to the early fifth-century BC Greek historian Herodotus and the first-century AD Roman naturalist Pliny the Elder. Even Aristotle wrote about submarines in the fourth century BC. His most famous pupil, Alexander the Great, was said to have been on board a glass-covered underwater vessel during an extended shakedown cruise beneath the eastern Mediterranean Sea, around 330BC.

While these submersibles may have gone back 23 centuries or so, Atlantis had already vanished about 1,000 years earlier. Even so, if such inventions took place in Classical times, they might just as well have operated during the Bronze Age, which was, in technological terms, not that different.

No suggestion of aircraft or submarines appears, however, in Plato's account of Atlantis. If the Atlanteans were able to create such a technologically advanced society, they would only have been able to do so because their civilization was very old. Their cultural evolution would have needed to have been graced with millennia of growth in which to develop and perfect the scientific arts. We may rightly infer that they did indeed possess – if not exactly aircraft and submarines – mastery of the monumental building arts that have never been surpassed. The Great Pyramid of Egypt is the most obvious specimen illustrating such a conclusion. Egyptologists know it had no precursor from within Egypt

(Sakkara's Step Pyramid was once deemed a prototype, but late 20th-century testing dated its construction to after the Great Pyramid), while the ancient Egyptians themselves recorded that Thaut, survivor of the Flood that brought his fellow 'Followers of Horus' to the Nile Delta at the advent of Dynastic civilization, was the Great Pyramid's chief architect.

VEINS OF BRONZE

Additional inferential information from the other side of the world likewise suggests an Atlantean technology thousands of years ahead of its time. The Menomonie Indians of North America's Upper Great Lakes region still tell of the 'Marine Men' – white-skinned aliens from across the Atlantic Ocean, who blasphemed against Mother Earth by digging out her shiny bones. This was how Native Americans referred to the copper miners who excavated more than half-a-billion tons of the raw metal from 3100BC to 1200BC. The pale-faced foreigners were able to determine the precise location of subterranean veins by dropping 'magical stones' – known to the Menomonie as *Yuwipi* – which made the copper-bearing rock 'ring, as brass does'.

Remarkably, this indigenous account conforms to, or at least suggests, a prospecting technique actually practised by ancient Old World miners more than 3,000 years ago. Bronze with a high tin content – from one part in four to one in six or seven – emits a full, resonant sound when struck with a stone. Such bronze is today known as 'bell metal' for the ringing tone it produces. To the Menomonies' ancestors, the local copper and manufactured bronze, of which they knew nothing, must have seemed one and the same. When they saw the bronze being struck with a stone to test its quality by the chiming sound it made, they assumed the copper had been magically transformed by the *Yuwipi*.

LEMURIA'S 'WONDER OF THE WORLD'

The Pacific motherland's technological accomplishments were of an altogether different kind because the entire thrust of Lemurian society was radically different from the materialistic needs and imperialist agendas of Bronze Age Atlantis. But the magnitude of Mu's achievements was no less spectacular. Among the grandest was the largest food factory ever constructed, still humankind's largest engineering feat, although mostly unrecognized by the outside world.

What modern-day visitors describe as the 'Eighth Wonder of the World' still exists at Luzon in the Philippines, 250 kilometres north of Manila, some 1,220 metres above sea level. A tremendous stairway rises continuously and unbroken to 915 metres above the valley floor of Ifugao province, forming a series of artificial plateaus. Their vertical distance from bottom to top exceeds the height of the world's tallest skyscraper, the United Arab Emirates' Dubai Tower, at 818 metres. The Banaue rice terraces, as they are known, cover more than 10,360 square kilometres of the Cordillera mountain range. If laid end to end, their paddies would form a line stretching halfway around the earth. Even so, less than 50 per cent of the original agricultural network survives. When they were functioning at their maximum capacity more than 2,000 years ago, the Banaue rice terraces yielded prodigious crops, due not entirely to their vast scale, but in large measure because of their ingeniously efficient irrigation systems. Unfortunately, present neglect and abuse caused by unsanitary shantytowns has prompted UNESCO officials to downgrade Ifugao's ancient paddies from the United Nations' World Heritage List to its List of World Heritage in Danger.

Banaue's original 40,470 hectares of rice-producing paddies yielded enough food to feed several million people at a time when conventional archaeologists believe humans throughout the whole of the Pacific numbered fewer than 100,000. In spite of mainstream reluctance to recognize the implications of Luzon's ancient agricultural capacity, its mere existence not only affirms the existence of massive populations during prehistory, but also testifies to the advanced technology and immense organizational power of some as yet unknown civilization.

COLOSSAL ENGINEERING

Some 2,820 kilometres east of the Banaue food factories, 1,610 kilometres north of New Guinea and 3,703 kilometres south of Japan, lies the small, obscure island of Pohnpei. Off its northern shore stands, in the words of David Childress, a project 'of such huge scale that it easily compares with the building of the Great Wall of China and the Great Pyramid of Egypt in sheer amounts of stone and labor used, and the gigantic scope of the site'. The comparison Childress made with Egypt's Great Pyramid is no exaggeration, as some of the hewn or splintered prisms that support Nan Madol are larger and heavier than the two million-plus blocks of Khufu's Pyramid.

Built on a coral reef only 1.6 metres above sea level, Nan Madol is a series of 92 rectangular man-made islands and colossal towers enclosed within the central area's 2.6 square kilometres. The artificial islands are interconnected by a spreading network of canals, each one 9 metres across and more than 1.3 metres deep at high tide. Most incredibly, this strange city was built from 250 million tons of prismatic basalt spread over 70 hectares.

The native Micronesian inhabitants of Pohnpei make no ancestral claim to such a colossal work, which was, they say, created by a pair of overseas sorcerers, Olisihpa and Olsohpa, who floated the huge quantities of stone through the air, a skill they learned in their homeland, Kanamwayso, before it was overwhelmed by a terrible catastrophe. Between four and five million stone columns went into the construction of this Caroline Island's prehistoric metropolis. These prismatic columns usually range in length from 3 to 3.7 metres, although many reach 8 metres, with an average weight of 5 tons each, though heavier specimens weigh 20 or 25 tons apiece. Nan Madol was originally surrounded by a 5-metre-high wall 857 metres long, and some existing ramparts are more than 4 metres thick. A tall, square hollow windowless tower known as Nan Dowas is composed of 5-metre-long, hexagonal black basalt pillars laid horizontally between courses of crudely cut boulders and smaller stones. The southeastern side of this tower contains the city's largest block, a single cornerstone weighing no less than 60 tons. Despite the stone's impressive tonnage, it had been raised, then set on a buried stone platform by the ancient builders.

It is estimated that 20,000 to 50,000 construction workers were needed to build Nan Madol, a figure in sharp contrast with the native population of little Pohnpei, with its modern population of 2,000 souls. Its 5–25-ton pillars of magnetized basalt lifted to heights beyond 13 metres, and the immense blocks fitted with astronomical perfection at Stonehenge were all allegedly levitated into position by ancient 'sorcerers' – Olishpa at the former and Merlin at the latter. Both sites represent some spiritually powerful kingdom overseas, according to Micronesian and Celtic traditions, respectively. Myths extolling the power of gifted individuals to levitate massive stones occur around our planet. In building the Greek city of Thebes, for example, Amphion lifted colossal blocks and fitted them into place through the music of his lyre. Likwise, North America's Ho Chunk Indian tradition recounts that the pyramidal mounds at the bottom of Wisconsin's Rock Lake were constructed through the power of communal song.

Other surviving Lemurian construction, such as Easter Island's 100-ton *moai* statues, Tonga's 105-ton coral gate or Waimea Canyon's 7-metre-high Menehune Ditch in the Hawaiian island of Kauai, all bespeak peoples highly skilled in the cutting and placement of often massive stone to high architectural and aesthetic standards.

In each case, such extraordinary masterpieces were explained in native oral traditions as the achievement of 'sorcerers', gods or flood heroes from some formerly powerful, eventually engulfed island of great beauty and magic.

QUESTIONS REQUIRING ANSWERS

By the mid-1990s, scientific evidence had established some credibility for these worldwide stories. Christopher Dunn is a British master craftsman now living and working in the United States. Among his most remarkable finds were the unmistakable impressions made by ultrasonic drills in surviving building cores at several ancient Egyptian construction sites in Aswan and Giza. Dunn found that Egypt's Great Pyramid was built as a monumental "power plant" designed to transform the Earth's tectonic energy into electrical discharge. Constructed by those same Atlantean culture-bearers responsble for the rest of Dynastic Civilization, similarly advanced technologies appeared in the Pacific. The Rosicrucian researcher W.S. Cerve explained:

> ...that the Lemurians achieved a great scientific
> comprehension of natural laws and at the same time

*developed inwardly certain human abilities to a degree much
greater and higher than we have attained today, with all of
our boasted advancement in civilization.*

A remnant of these Lemurian methods survives in a
Hawaiian magical practice, the Pohaku Olelo Huna. This
occult 'language of the talking stones' takes place when
the human mind properly focuses on a crystal to spark
subconscious knowledge (past life memories, innate mental
powers, etc.) otherwise hidden from consciousness. The
extraordinarily high crystalline content of basaltic columns
used for the construction of Nan Madol – regarded as Mu's
important ceremonial centre by Churchward – implies that
they were deliberately chosen for their psychic-enhancing
properties.

The material accomplishments of antediluvian civilization were not limited to monumental architecture. The
Lemurians excelled in herbology. According to a well-
travelled Lemurian scholar during the early 1990s, Mark R.
Williams, they developed comfrey to stimulate telepathy,
snapdragon for improved speech, and the lotus for helping
to open the pineal gland, or 'crown chakra', associated in
Hindu mysticism with spiritual attainment, while lavender
and lemon were scents used in ritual activity. Squash and

watermelon were thought to aid fertility and sexual potency, while pomegranate was a female love potion.

Abundant archaeological evidence supports worldwide indigenous accounts of a superscience possessed by the inhabitants of Mu and Atlantis in the deep past. While we might prefer to think of ourselves, today, as the most technologically sophisticated generation human history has ever known, our civilization has been preceded by others which matched and surpassed in some important particulars our material achievements. More important than the conveniences or luxuries afforded by inventiveness, then or now, is the social cohesion and communal sense of destiny a people experience. In this, our Industrial Age is woefully behind the Atlanto-Lemurian Bronze Age, from which we still have much to learn.

CHAPTER 4
THE RELIGION OF ATLANTIS

'THE HEROES ONCE WORSHIPPED IN ATLANTIS
BECAME THE GODS LATER WORSHIPPED IN EGYPT
AND GREECE.'

IGNATIUS DONNELLY, *ATLANTIS, THE ANTEDILUVIAN WORLD*

It was not for nothing that Plato described Atlantis as 'that sacred island'. Its inhabitants built 'many temples for different gods' on each of the capital's land rings. The identity and significance of all these immortals have been lost, but a close reading of Plato's dialogues, plus an examination of those Egyptian and Greek deities with discernibly antediluvian pedigrees, should restore some of the Atlanteans' spiritual worldview.

The earliest and most hallowed ground, located at the very centre of Atlantis, and from which the city grew outwards, was a low hill where a native woman, Kleito, who married the Greek god Poseidon, conceived the empire's royal lineage. This holy-of-holies was enclosed by a circular wall of gold, accessible only to a high priest and the Atlantean emperor himself on rare, ceremonial occasions. What the sacred precinct of Atlantis might have concealed, other than the place where Kleito lay with Poseidon, was never disclosed. On the other side of the world, the Incas, who claimed direct descent from Atlantean-like flood-heroes, raised the Coricancha, or 'Enclosure of Gold', around their holiest ground at the centre of the imperial capital in Cuzco, pre-Hispanic Peru's own 'Navel of the World'.

Sharing the same artificial island with Kleito's mysterious shrine was a grandiose edifice dedicated to the divine father of her sons. At 185 metres long, 92 metres wide and 30 metres high, Poseidon's temple was the foremost structure in Atlantis, the architectural epitome of Atlantean culture. In describing a pediment containing sculpted figures for the structure, Plato helps us to imagine that it was proto-Greek in appearance; that is to say, not unlike Etruscan sacred buildings, with their smooth unfluted 'Tuscan columns', an impression fortified by his statement that the Temple seemed 'somewhat outlandish in appearance'. His was a typically Greek reaction to anything more detailed – especially something foreign – than the sparse aesthetics and clean symmetry of Classical form. So, too, Etruscan designs featured greater attention to varieties of materials and ornamentation.

Plato's *Kritias* goes on to report that the temple's exterior was entirely adorned in sheets of silver, which contrasted with the pediment's golden statuary. The choice of these precious metals was in keeping with the Atlantean esoteric principle of honouring opposites, thereby achieving spiritual equilibrium – in this case, the sun (gold) and moon (silver), the ultimate manifestations of male (i.e. solar) and female (lunar) energies.

SACRED NUMBERS

The same concept appears in the Atlantean sacred numerals – five and six – which signified the gender antipodes, representing male and female energies, respectively. Atlantean mystics venerated a pair of the sacred numerals, five and six, 'showing equal respect to both odd and even numbers', as Plato makes clear in his second dialogue. The seventh-century BC philosopher, Pythagoras, had taught that numbers correspond to certain aspects of existence and, by properly incorporating them in a culture, they endowed it with their particular qualities. American numerologist Patricia Rose Upczak wrote in 2001:

Pythagoras taught that numbers represented spiritual qualities and processes. The meanings of figures are exoteric, or easily understood, and that numbers are esoteric, with hidden meanings.

Peter Tompkins (1919–2007), in his exhaustive study of Egyptian mathematics applied to sacred architecture, concluded that 'numbers are but names applied to the functions and principles upon which the universe is maintained. The interplay of numbers causes the phenomena of the physical world'. Five represented male energy (five fingers of a hand); full consciousness (the five senses); material achievement; acquisition; the sun, light and enlightenment; Father Sky; civilization; society; conquest; justice; honour; duty; 'hard facts'; self-control; discernment; the outward-going. Sometimes the sacred centre was symbolized by a circle enclosing a cross or a single point at the centre, where the imperceptible is perceived (i.e. manifests).

Six stood for woman and the moon; female energy; intuition; Mother Earth; nature; nurturing; the inward-going; artistry; emotion; acceptance; tolerance; liberty (always represented by a woman); instinct; premonition; darkness and mystery; creativity; fairness; acceptance; forgiveness; fecundity, as signified by the *hexalpha* – a hexagram formed by the intersecting of two triangles for fire and water, respectively. The earliest known *hexalpha* was used by the Sumerians in Mesopotamia's Fertile Crescent between the Tigris and Euphrates rivers, where wooden or straw six-pointed stars were planted among their crops to promote fertility.

James Churchward wrote that the *hexalpha* was originally

a Lemurian emblem brought to Mesopotamia by culture-bearers from Mu, long before it became more known as the Jews' magan David (better known to non-Jews as the so-called 'Star of David'). The renowned mythologist Mircea Eliade (1907–86) wrote that six:

> ... is the number of mother-love
> ... It is an even number,
> which means it is female and passive
> ... the number of marriage from the
> female point of view
> ... Six is essentially the number of the wife and mother.

These metaphysical implications reappear in the hexagram because it exemplifies the *hieros gamos*, the 'sacred marriage' between Father Sky and Mother Earth – the holy union of fertilizing force from above with innate potentiality below operating in the principle of 'As above, so below'. Stated at the beginning of an ancient Egyptian magical text, *The Emerald Tablet*, it implies the interconnectedness of all phenomena, seen and unseen, such as the relationship between man and God. The hexagram combines the spiritual with the material, or, as A.E. Abbot has it in his *Encyclopedia of Numbers*, 'the external and the transitory'.

THE TEMPLE OF POSEIDON

To appreciate the mystical significance of five and six is to grasp the Atlantean soul, and to understand why they were incorporated into the architecture and spiritual life of Atlantis; namely, to create a balance between the fundamental forces represented by these sacred numerals, thereby maintaining a spiritual accord between gods and men. The very layout of the city itself was an expression of this principle, built as it was of two rings of land and three of water; including the central islet with its imperial palace, Temple of Poseidon, holy-of-holies, comprising a sixth part. This innermost area was itself five stades (925 metres) across. The royal house comprised five pairs of twins.

There were significant variations of five and six: 'Each allotment (of land) was ten square stades (1,900 square metres), and there were in all 60,000 allotments' (*Kritias* 4). The Atlantean navy operated 1,200 ships. Military leaders were 'bound to provide a sixth part of the equipment of a war chariot, up to a total complement of 10,000.' In the Temple of Poseidon, his colossus was surrounded by 100 Nereids (statues of boys riding dolphins), and his chariot was pulled by six winged horses, a reference to the First Lady of Atlantis, Leukippe; her name, 'White Mare', signified the sea god's foaming wave. The island of Atlantis was made up of ten provinces. Plato's *Kritias* informs us that 'beyond the three, outer harbours there was a wall, beginning at the sea, and running right round in a circle, at a uniform distance of 50 stades (9 kilometres).' Even the Atlantean kings 'assembled alternately every fifth and sixth year'.

The interior of the Temple of Poseidon comprised a single, immense hall. According to Plato's *Kritias*, visitors entering through the 2-metre-tall doors would gaze upwards to see that the full length of its ceiling was entirely carved ivory 'picked out with gold, silver and orichalcum'. That high-grade copper, responsible for much of the Late Bronze Age wealth that coursed through Atlantis, likewise covered pillars, floor and walls, against which were regularly spaced the golden statues of all the Atlantean kings with their wives (yet again venerating male and female energies), together with 'many others dedicated by kings and private persons belonging to the city and its dominions'. These assembled representations of Atlantean royalty stared unblinking at an immense, finely crafted altar that stood in the middle of the hall.

The building was without windows, so light was allowed to enter a high celestory at the far end of the otherwise gloomy interior. Noontime particularly illuminated a gold colossus of the sea god so gigantic that his head brushed the ceiling. He was portrayed standing in a chariot drawn by six winged horses, the base of the statuary surrounded by one hundred Nereids. These were dolphins ridden by very young men. The Greeks' famous 'Boy on a Dolphin' was the emblem of an Atlantean mystery school, which initiated male youth into personal, spiritual development through an intimate rapport with dolphins, what today would be understood as a kind of interspecies communication. Like their avatar – the dolphin – the Nereids were notable for their devoted protection of shipwrecked humans. They were also said to be oracular, a suggestion of their cultic function.

THE ORIGINS OF POSEIDON

The name of the foremost oracle of the ancient Old World, Delphi, was Greek for 'dolphin', an indication that its mysteries were descended from Atlantean adepts. Indeed, the Delphic oracle was governed by a *hoisioi*, or 'college' of priests required to trace their family lineage to Deucalion before taking office, because he was believed to have brought the principles of divination to Delphi from a former Golden Age overwhelmed by the Deluge. Deucalion was the Greek flood hero, who escaped with his wife, Phyrra, in an 'ark' from a cataclysm that engulfed their homeland. Mount Parnassus, site of the oracle, was itself consecrated to Poseidon.

Poseidon's name (Enesidaone) – like the word 'bronze' (*broncea*)– is among the few, identifiable examples of the long-dead Atlantean language because his name stands out among his fellow Olympian deities as decidedly non-Indo-European. 'Poseidon' derives from a contraction of the un-Greek Posis Das, 'Husband of the Earth', and Enosichthon, or 'Earthshaker', together with the very Greek Hippios, 'He of the Horses'. This synthesis implies that Poseidon did indeed come from outside Greece, where he was eventually adopted as one of the supreme divinities. With no linguistic or mythic parallels among eastern cultures, he arrived, according to Herodotus, from the western direction of Atlantis: 'Alone of all nations, the Libyans have had among them the name Poseidon from the first, and they have ever honoured this god.'

Poseidon's role in the story of Atlantis continues to puzzle investigators. They wonder if he represented the arrival of some culture-bearing maritime people at the island, which was originally inhabited by a relatively primitive, perhaps Paleolithic race. As Plato wrote, Poseidon created the canals and natural springs, and 'caused the Earth to grow abundant produce of every kind'. He was not responsible for the palaces, temples, encircling walls, harbours and other monumental structures, however, which were built by the Atlanteans, his descendants, who were named after his first son on the island, Atlas. 'There were still no ships or sailing in those days,' according to the *Kritias*, referring to the island before Poseidon and his entourage first landed there.

These arriving 'Poseidians', with their superior building and organizational skills and more advanced material culture, transformed the indigenous inhabitants into a civilized and civilizing people, probably because of their island's strategic position vis-à-vis the copper trade between mined supplies of the mineral in North America's Upper Great Lakes Region, and royal customers in Europe and the Near East.

But who might these pre-Atlantean 'Poseidians' have been? From where could they have come? Some investigators, such as William Donato, believe the Bahamian island of Bimini, with its underwater 'road', holds most of the answers. The credibility of this feature has been substantially enhanced in recent years by supplementary discoveries of colossal square columns found at the same depth along Moselle Shoals, some 5 kilometres northeast of Bimini; an upright stone pillar at the southwestern end of the island; sunken structures resembling hexagons and the letter 'e'; side-scan sonar images of apparent staircases with rectangular foundations under water; and white-sand effigy mounds in the configuration of a 155-metre-long shark, a cat and other, less identifiable figures at East Bimini.

Hydrologists have determined that the submerged sites would have been above sea level around 1,000 years prior to the known beginnings of civilization in the Near East, c.3500BC Bimini was a far larger island then, because the ocean was some 8 metres feet lower than it is today, and vast tracts of presently inundated territories would have stood above the surface as dry land. Did its inhabitants, the Poseidians, after developing civilization there, leave about 5,500 years ago because of the rising waters that covered their homeland? Did they reach the opposite Atlantic island, later to become Atlantis, sometime before 3500BC?

POSEIDON'S SYMBOLISM

The emblematic weapon Poseidon holds symbolizes the triune nature of his godhood: creativity. Three is associated with god-power through his phallic trident for the male genitalia, and wielded as a sceptre over all creation. It is not unlike the three-pronged wand held by the Hindu 'Master of Creation', Shiva, simultaneously signifying his omniscient third eye, which reappears in the triangular pyramid with its eye of god at the apex. The Hindu trinity of Brahma, Vishnu and Shiva personifies, respectively, *sat*, or Being; *cit*, Consciousness, and *ananda*, Love – the components of godhood which cyclically create, maintain and destroy the universe. Among the Greeks, the Fates, Furies and Graces also came in threes.

Like every such conception, Poseidon had his exoteric and esoteric sides. To most Atlanteans, he was simply the sea god, and therefore a deity befitting their thallasocratic civilization. For the initiated, however, he personified the sacred duality of life's contrary forces – odd and even numbers, male and female, etc. – that made up the perpetual exchange of polarities in an ever-shifting balancing act. As the spirit of the ocean, Poseidon at once embodied its reflecting surface and enigmatic depths. In this, he differentiated the world of appearances from the underworld, the conscious from the subconscious mind, this life from the afterlife, while showing they were component parts of the same reality. The Nereids who served him (as students of his mystery cult) epitomized this fusion of opposites in the androgynous boy riding the non-human dolphin, aimed at attaining an empowering spiritual union.

RITUAL IN THE TEMPLE OF POSEIDON

Although Plato described the Temple of Poseidon in some detail, he told of only one ritual activity that took place there with ceremonial regularity. In the *Kritias* we learn how the ten Atlantean rulers, representing various regions within their imperial network, convened together in the Temple of Poseidon alternately every fifth and sixth year – again, the sacred numerals – during the late afternoon of a holy day. Alone and without the assistance of priests or advisers, they 'consulted on matters of mutual interest' – the diplomatic, commercial and military concerns of the empire.

In their decisions they were guided by Poseidon's ancient laws engraved on an orichalcum pillar at the centre of his temple. These injunctions were accompanied by 'an oath invoking horrible curses on anyone who disobeyed it'. But before any judgements could be passed, a special sacrifice was required to sanctify them. The ten monarchs began by forming a circle around the column, raising their hands in prayer to the sea god that he might bless the offering they were about to make him.

They then repaired to an outside corral, where sacred bulls were allowed to roam freely, subduing one of them with staves and nooses, only because custom forbade the use of any metal utensils. Dragging their prey into the temple, they used a sharp flint or obsidian blade to slit the beast's throat atop the orichalcum pillar, allowing the blood to flow over its inscription. Into a bowl of wine one clot of blood was dropped for each of the kings, who disposed of the carcass, lighted an altar fire, washed the pillar, and bathed themselves. Thus refreshed, they dipped golden cups into the bowl, poured a libation over the fire, and swore by Poseidon's oath to give judgement according to his laws, and neither give nor obey any order contrary to them. They then drank from the cups to signify their pledge, each man dedicating his golden cup to the Temple.

The kings' ceremony appearing in Plato's dialogue has a ring of authenticity beyond his power to invent, if only because it was mostly unlike the religious practices of his own times. In fact, two of the golden cups – or something very much like them – were discovered in a beehive tomb for royalty known as a *tholos* at Vapheio, a region near Sparta in what is today southern Greece. Both date from the Late Bronze Age (the 16th to 13th centuries BC), and depict a shared scene: a man attacking a bull with staff and rope. Whether these cups were carried by survivors of the Atlantean catastrophe or colonizers from Atlantis in the Aegean is not known. The cups nonetheless portray the same hunt described by the *Kritias*, but nowhere else in Classical antiquity.

THE AGE OF TAURUS

Moreover, the manner in which the Atlantean hunt was conducted seems to have derived from a remote, pre-civilized era prior to the introduction of metallurgy. This is in sharp contrast to Plato's Atlantis, which he characterized as a copper-, bronze-, silver- and gold-rich economy. The ritualistic use of staves and nooses harkens back to a very early time – Neolithic, Paleolithic, perhaps even 16,000 years ago to the cave painters at places such as Lascaux and Trois Freres in France – when Poseidon's laws, which the ceremonial hunt was meant to commemorate, were first propounded.

Bull sacrifice implies astrological significance; specifically, the end of the Age of Taurus. It ended, according to Max Heindel (1865– 1919), the famous Danish authority on the Zodiac, in 1658BC. His calculation is remarkable because it is virtually coincidental with the penultimate destruction of Atlantis. Geologists have determined that, in 1628BC, a series of major natural catastrophes beset the Earth, from a historically unprecedented eruption at the volcanic island of Thera-Santorini in the Aegean to its nuclear-like equivalent on the other side of the world in New Zealand.

The late 17th-century BC cataclysm drew a line in history, separating the Old from the Middle Bronze Age. It was precisely within this period lasting until the end of the Late Bronze Age around 1200BC that Plato set his account of Atlantis. He could not have known that the Age of Taurus almost perfectly coincided with the global upheavals of 1628BC.

Yet it uniquely fits the Atlantean kings' sacrifice because, to them, the victim was an astral bull whose slaughter meant the end of the Age of Taurus. In numerous other cultures – Minoan, Mycenaean, Hittite, Trojan, Assyrian, etc. – bull sacrifice was regarded as a prelude to renewal in the rhythm of growth. Taurus himself signified rejuvenation and revival.

In much later Mithraism, Taurus assisted in the creation of life by having his own throat cut, thereby enabling plants and animals to spring from his blood. His myth was re-enacted in a rite called the *taurobolium* to commemorate the death and resurrection of the hero, Mithras, who impersonates the next age and baptized initiates into his cult.

Drinking wine clotted with bull's blood also occurred among other peoples. As late as the 15th century AD, Turkish soldiers, following an ancient tradition, drank red wine mixed with bull's blood before battle to imbibe strength and resistance to injury.

Clearly, the Atlantean kings celebrated a tauroctony, in which bull sacrifice not only marked the close of the Age of Taurus, but was also their appeal to Poseidon against the recurrence of such an awful catastrophe that blasted the world in 1628BC. Plato's description of this ritual demonstrates the authenticity of his account, which finds its extraordinary close parallels in ages of the zodiac, and comparative cultures. The 30-year discrepancy between the close of the Age of Taurus and its contemporaneous global catastrophe means only that the calculations of either the geologists or Max Heindel, or both, are off by an insignificantly minute degree.

If, as it would appear, the Age of Taurus was synonymous with the Age of Atlantis – at least until the end of the Middle Bronze Age – then we may infer that Taurus and Atlantis began at the same moment. Heindel gave the start of the Age of Taurus at 3814BC. Here, too, his date is a remarkable fit because it coincides with the likely founding of Atlantis. The Atlanteans would have needed centuries of cultural development to make their impact on the outside world before the end of the fourth millennium BC.

PARALLELS WITH PARADISE
Poseidon's first son by Kleito – Atlas, the king after whom the island and the entire ocean surrounding it were

named – appears in a non-Platonic version of his myth (in Hesiod's *Theogony*, 700BC). It describes the Garden of the Hesperides and the seven daughters of Atlas (and, hence, Atlantises), who guarded the Tree of Life, the golden apples of which granted immortality to anyone fortunate enough to eat them. They were assisted in their stewardship by Ladon, a powerful serpent entwined about the bough. The seven Hesperides correspond to the seven major chakras, or metaphysical energy centres that, collectively, comprise the human personality. So, too, the Tree of Life symbolizes the spinal column along which the chakras are arranged. The Hesperides' mystery cult promised immortality for successful initiates, as signified by the Tree of Life with its snake – a symbol of regeneration because of the animal's ability to slough off its old, dead skin and emerge with a new one.

Comparisons with the Garden of Eden in Genesis are unavoidable, and doubtless represent an Old Testament corruption of the Atlantean original. As such, kundalini yoga originated in Atlantis, from which it spread around the world. In Norse myth, for example, the goddess Iduna likewise tended a tree bearing apples filled with immortality, while the Celtic otherworld, Avalon, derived from the Old Welsh Ynys Avallach, or Avallenau, the 'Isle of Apple Trees'. The lost Druidic *Books of Pheryllt* and *Writings of Pridian*, both described by generations of scholars, including Sir James Fraser of *Golden Bough* fame, as 'more ancient than the Flood', celebrated the return of King Arthur from Ynys Avallach, 'where all the rest of mankind had been overwhelmed'. Avalon, with its life-bestowing apples and watery destruction, was clearly the British version of Atlantis.

INFLUENCE ON ANCIENT EGYPT

Religious traditions of the Nile Valley were no less deeply influenced by Atlantean metaphysics, as made particularly evident in the Egyptian god of wisdom, Thaut. To the Greeks, he was Hermes, grandson of Atlas by the Atlantis (daughter of Atlas), Maia. The Theban Recension of the Egyptian *Book of the Dead* quotes Thaut as having said that the Great Deluge destroyed a former world-class civilization:

> *I am going to blot out everything which I have made. The Earth shall enter into the waters of the abyss of Nun (the sea god) by means of a raging flood, and will become even as it was in the primeval time.*

His narration of the catastrophe is related to the Edfu Texts, hieroglyphic inscriptions from the Temple of Horus at Edfu in Upper Egypt, which locate the 'Homeland of the Primeval Ones' on a great island that sank with most of its inhabitants during the Tep Zepi, or 'First Time'. Only the gods, led by Thaut, escaped with seven favoured sages, who settled at the Nile Delta, where they created Egyptian civilization from a synthesis of Atlantean and native influences.

Metaphysical symbolism represented Thaut in temple art as a man with the head of an ibis. This is a bird that walks along river banks with the singular talent of plucking out crustaceans hidden deep in the mud with its long beak. The ibis, therefore, represented the process of wisdom, which finds something valuable from the unapparent.

Another Egyptian deity with a distinctly Atlantean pedigree was Anpu, better remembered by his Greek name, Anubis. Prayed to as the 'Westerner', Anubis was said to have 'written annals from before the flood' which destroyed his island home in the distant West, whence he arrived to re-establish his worship in Egypt. He was also known as the 'Great Five', one of the two sacred numerals of Atlantis. The funeral rites associated with his divinity became Egyptian mortuary practices after their importation from the sunken civilization. Although most Egyptologists describe him as jackal-headed, his title, the 'Great Dog', demonstrates he was canine-cephalic. And, like the seeing-eye dog, Anubis loyally guided the recently deceased through the darkness of death. He was, in modern-day parlance, a spirit guide, who comforted the *ba*, or soul, leading it to the otherworld.

The clues offered by Plato's dialogues combine with Greek and Egyptian religious ideas to provide at least an outline of the belief system in the even more ancient Atlantis. The chief agenda of Atlantean mysticism appears to have been to bring civilization into accord with the cosmic harmony that pervades all existence by recognizing the ebb and flow of pairs of opposites. Therein lay the way to social order and public peace. On a more personal, esoteric level, this same striving after spiritual balance aimed at developing one's psychic potential by awakening the seven energy centres personified by the Hesperides with their promise of golden immortality.

CHAPTER 5
THE CRYSTALS OF ATLANTIS

'PERHAPS THESE BRIEF INSIGHTS INTO THE USE
OF THE CRYSTAL IN ATLANTIS GIVE SOME IDEA
OF THE AWESOME SCOPE OF THE POTENTIAL OF
CRYSTAL POWER.'
DR JUDITH LARKIN, 'COUNSELING WITH CRYSTALS'

O f all the mysteries of that most mysterious place, none is more intriguing than the crystals of Atlantis. Were they mystic symbols of spiritual and political power? Or mineral storage batteries for arcane technological and psychic influences? Do they still lie under unknown fathoms of ocean amid the broken ruins of that drowned metropolis? Or were they carried by survivors of the catastrophe into new lands?

EDGAR CAYCE – A PSYCHIC CONNECTION

In attempting to answer these questions, it is impossible to avoid at least a passing encounter with Edgar Cayce, the early 20th-century American psychic still remembered as the 'Sleeping Prophet'. Since his birth in Kentucky in 1877, he had been mostly known for medical cures uttered during a deep trance. But, after his 45th year, he reported flashbacks of life in Atlantis. These 'life readings', as he called them, were recorded by a stenographer attending every session, and are still regarded by some modern Atlantologists as valuable glimpses of the lost civilization.

His extraordinarily prescient remarks are worthy of consideration. Outstanding among them was his statement in 1930 that the Nile river flowed across the Sahara desert to empty into the Atlantic Ocean during early Atlantean times. Scientists of his day and for decades thereafter scoffed at such an apparently outlandish possibility. Yet, in 1994, nearly half a century after Cayce's death, a satellite survey of North Africa discovered the bed of a former tributary that flowed westwards from the Nile all the way across the Sahara Desert, connecting Egypt with the Atlantic Ocean at Morocco in prehistory.

With his death in 1945, Edgar Cayce left behind 14,256 stenographic records documenting his clairvoyant pronouncements for some 8,000 different clients over a 43-year period. Most of his readings were concerned with diagnosing spiritual and physical health concerns, with no references to vanished civilizations. His uncanny accuracy in personal analysis impressed not only thousands of sufferers who benefited from his curative insights, but the medical establishment as well. As early as 1910, the Sleeping Prophet's psychic procedures were substantiated in a report to Boston's Clinical Research Society by Dr Wesley Ketchem. Accordingly, some researchers argue that using Cayce's 'life readings' to learn about Atlantis is no different from the increasing employment of psychics by police departments to help solve crimes.

The United States' Federal Bureau of Investigation not only employs psychic detectives for some of its most difficult cases, but also actually recommends particularly prescient individuals to police departments throughout the United States. The success rate of some of these unorthodox investigators is so high that their visions have been admitted as sworn testimony in regular court proceedings. If judges and law-enforcement officers rely on such modern-day seers for important assistance, archaeologists might stand to gain no less by taking advantage of psychic colleagues. It would be counterproductive, therefore, to forgo unconventional assistance simply because of current prejudice against such apparently gifted persons.

THE ATLANTEAN FIRE STONE

For Edgar Cayce, crystal technology played as central a role in Atlantis, for good or ill, as California's 'Silicon Valley' plays in the modern world. 'There were those destructive forces,' he explained, 'brought through the creating of the high influences of the radial activity from the rays of the sun, that were turned upon the crystals into the pits that made for the connections with the internal influences of the earth'. And later he mentioned 'the principles of the stone upon the spheres ... these brought destructive forces'. 'Both constructive and destructive forces were generated by the activity of the stone.'

This was the Tuaoi, or 'Fire Stone'. It represented the zenith of Atlantean crystal technology, and possessed the power to harness geophysical energies for material and spiritual purposes. According to Cayce:

'It was in the form of a six-sided figure in which the light appeared as the means of communication between infinity and finite; or the means whereby there were the communications with those forces from the outside (outer space?). Later, this came to mean that from which the energies radiated, as of the center from which there were the radial activities guiding the various forms of transition or travel through those periods of activity of the Atlanteans.'

A special structure housed the Tuaoi:

The building above the stone was oval, or a dome, wherein there could be or was the rolling back, so that the activity of

the stone was received from the sun's rays or from the stars;
the concentrating of the energies that emanate from bodies
that are on fire themselves – with the elements that are found
in the earth's atmosphere. The concentration through the
prisms or glass, as would be called in the present, was in such
a manner that it acted upon the instruments that
were connected with various modes of travel, through
induction methods – that made much the character of
control through radio vibrations or directions would be in
the present day; through the manner of the force that was
impelled from the stone acted upon the motivating forces in
the crafts themselves.

There was the preparation so that when the dome was rolled
back there might be little or no hindrance in the application
directly to the various crafts that were to be impelled through
space, whether in the radius of the visioning of the one eye, as
it might be called, or whether directed underwater or under
other elements or through other elements. The preparation of
this stone was in the hands only of the initiates at the time.

Long before their destruction, the Atlanteans learned that
the proper use of crystal technology amplified and focused
spiritual energies, as well as physical forces. Cayce spoke

of 'a crystal room' in Atlantis, where 'the tenets and the truths or the lessons that were proclaimed by those that had descended to give the messages as from on High' were received by the initiates of a mystery cult. They 'interpreted the messages that were received through the crystals'. Atlantean adepts achieved levels of proficiency in all the transformational arts and mastery of humankind's innate psychic powers through their understanding and use of crystals, a lost science of the paranormal only just beginning to be reclaimed in our times, almost instinctually, it would seem, through growing popular interest in the spiritual qualities of quartz crystal.

HISTORICAL 'FIRE STONES'

Researchers who first encountered Edgar Cayce's story of Atlantean crystal technology reacted with disbelief, until they began finding traces of similar or confirming evidence among other ancient civilizations. They were particularly surprised to learn that the name he gave to this most important power crystal, the Tuaoi, appeared in the languages of several peoples directly influenced by Atlantis. For example, the Nile Delta's Giza Plateau, site of the Great Pyramid, its pyramidal companions and Great Sphinx, were known to the ancient Egyptians as the 'Valley of Tuaoi'. It was here that Thaut's Emerald Tablet had been enshrined. Thaut (also known as Thoth – the Greek Hermes; the Roman Mercury) was remembered as a flood survivor who carried away the Emerald Tablet from Sekhret-Aaru, or the 'Field of Reeds', before the island kingdom in the distant west slipped for ever beneath the waves. The Emerald Tablet was also referred to as the Ben-Ben, or 'fire stone' for the energy it radiated.

No less remarkably, the Quiche-Maya wrote of the Giron-Gagal, a 'power-crystal', in their *Popol Vuh*, or Council Book. The anonymous author of this cosmological work relates that Nacxit, the 'Great Father' of Patulan-Pa-Civan – the Maya version of Atlantis – envisioned a cataclysmic deluge in the crystal. To save the precious object, he handed it over to Prince Balaam-Qitze, leader of the wise U Mamae, the 'Old Men', who escaped the destruction of Patulan-Pa-Civan by sailing with them across the ocean to Yucatan. The *Popol Vuh* describes the Giron-Gagal as a fiery 'symbol of power and majesty to make the peoples fear and respect the Quiches'. Appropriately, the Mayan word *tuuk* means 'fiery'; according to Cayce, Tuaoi was an Atlantean term for 'Fire Stone'. He also said that 'the records (describing the Tuaoi) were carried to what is now Yucatán, in America, where these stones (that they know so little about) are now'.

In pre-Columbian Mexico, the Toltecs' chief deity was Tezcatlipocha. He was also known as Hurakan, from which our word 'hurricane' derives, because he ruled over a period of tremendous natural violence, the Ocelotonatiuh, or 'Jaguar Sun'. This was the first of four 'worlds', or 'ages', annihilated before the present time. Tezcatlipocha's most important possession was a crystal mirror. It showed him past, present and future at his bidding. He was, in fact, named after this centrally important object, as 'Tezcatlipocha' means 'Smoking Mirror'; smoke is still regarded as the mystical bond between the mundane and spiritual worlds by Native Americans everywhere. The Toltec god's Atlantean origins are evident from his sovereignty over a world catastrophe to his omniscient crystal mirror, recalling the remote-viewing crystals, according to Cayce, that belonged to the paranormal sciences in Atlantis. As mentioned above, the Sleeping Prophet specifically cited Mexico and Yucatán in context with the Tuaoi crystals, which were brought there by flood survivors.

In South America, a legendary Inca prince was also said to possess a power crystal, in which he envisioned his future greatness as emperor. His name was Pachacutec, or 'Transformer of the Earth', and he claimed that the sacred object was a family heirloom handed down over the generations from Con-Tiki-Viracocha, or 'Sea Foam', the red-haired culture-bearer from a terrific flood who appeared at Lake Titicaca, where he established Andean civilization. Pachacutec's prognosticating crystal has long since vanished, but its former existence is suggested by a surviving pair of crystals carved in the images of condors (emblems of Inca royalty) and still preserved at Lima's Museo Arqueologico in Peru.

On the other side of the world, the Sumerian counterpart to the Mayas' seafaring Prince Balaam Quiche was Utnashpitim, another deluge hero who rode out the watery destruction of a former age in an ark with selected animals on board. He belongs to the oldest Mesopotamian mythic traditions, which also include a mysterious sacred object called the 'Stone that Burns', the 'Fire Stone' – precisely the same term used by Cayce. Remarkably, its original Sumerian word is *Napa-Tu*, from the Persian version of which the English word 'naphtha' derives.

Roughly midway between the Mayas of America and the Sumerians of Mesopotamia lie the Canary Islands off the coast of North Africa. Until their extermination by the Spaniards beginning in the 15th century, indigenous inhabitants who called themselves the Guanches likewise told of a catastrophic flood; well they might, situated as they were in the immediate vicinity of lost Atlantis. The Guanche word for 'fire' was *tava*; through phonetic evolution, a standard linguistic process, *tava* may be traced back to the sound value from which it originally sprang: *tua* or *tuoh*.

Nor is such a stone missing from the Old Testament story of the Deluge. In Genesis 6:16, the *tsohar* is described as 'a light which has its origins in a shining crystal' used by Noah to illuminate the interior of his ark for the duration of the Great Flood. In Hebrew, *tsohar* means 'a brightness, brilliance, the light of the noon-day sun', signifying something that 'glistens, glitters, or shines', adjectives commonly used in reference to precious gems.

All of these widely disparate peoples, separated by vast distances and many centuries, never knew each other. Yet, they shared common accounts of a flood associated with a 'fire stone' described, despite the otherwise complete dissimilarity of their languages, by the same word value: *tuuk, napa-tu, tava, tua, tuoh, tsohar* – cultural-linguistic variants of Edgar Cayce's Tuaoi.

Such provocative cognates were not the only pieces of evidence his investigators began to find. Turning to the folk heritage of other cultures possibly influenced by Atlantean survivors, they were astonished to learn that power crystals often figured as story elements in ancient though enduring traditions of a great flood. Among the Plains Indians of North America, the Pima tell how the heroic progenitor of their tribe, South Doctor, 'held magic crystals in his left hand', as he guided the survivors of a cataclysmic deluge to safety in the new land. Interestingly, the left hand is generally regarded by practitioners today as the receptive position, which worked well for South Doctor, as he prayed to the Great Spirit for salvation from the waters of destruction.

LEMURIAN CRYSTALS

The crystal theme is not excluded from the traditions of that other sunken civilization, Lemuria. It was memorialized in the 'Land of Mystery', also known as the 'Land of Perfection', as recalled throughout indigenous Australia, which fell within the Lemurian sphere of influence. As envisioned in Australoid myth, this was a huge city surrounded by four walls, their exterior covered entirely in white quartz. The Land of Mystery was described as mountainous, volcanic and luxuriant in plant growth, among which stood great buildings of domes and spires – this from a people to whom architecture was unknown until modern times. Interestingly, the 'domes and spires' of the Land of Perfection are the same features described by Colonel James Churchward in his book, *The Lost Civilization of Mu*, and featured on an inscribed stone tablet at Okinawa believed to illustrate several Lemurian structures.

Entrance to the city was flanked by a pair of cone-shaped crystals 60 metres high and 200 metres in diameter at the base. A great serpent coiled round each crystal, another caduceus-like theme that Churchward independently identified as Lemurian. (In the myths of Sumer, Egypt, Greece and many other cultures, the caduceus was a staff entwined by a pair of snakes, the ancient emblem of regeneration still recognized as symbolic of medical healing around the world.) But one day a great storm 'raised the water of the ocean with tremendous force, and drove it through the wall of the Land of Perfection'.

In 1999 scuba divers discovered four stone towers standing on the bottom of the Pacific Ocean near the Japanese island of Okinoshima, facing the Korean Straits. The exterior of one of the structures is entwined with a spiral staircase winding its way from bottom to top like an immense serpent.

The Tuaoi stone, or, at any rate, a similar crystal technology, may have been shared in Mu as well. Cerve, in his classic study of Lemuria, seems almost to parallel Cayce's description of the Atlantean 'fire stone', when he writes:

... there seems to have been another stone having some sort of magnetic repulsion, radiating an energy from it that was used to turn wheels that had large pieces of iron or some similar metal attached to their surfaces. Light was also produced in homes or enclosures by means of some stone or mineral that was like the radioactive ones discovered today, but which gave a very brilliant light continuously.

Cayce's Tuaoi may have been related to Ta-oo, the Lemurian word, according to Churchward, for a constellation, the Southern Cross – the 'stars which bring the water'. If so, then Tuaoi, or Ta-oo, may have been a title both civilizations shared through a common crystal technology.

CELTIC CRYSTAL TRADITIONS

On the other side of the Atlantic Ocean, ancient Irish tradition tells the story of Ethlinn, a goddess, who was confined in a 'crystal cave' by Balor, king of the giant Formorach, the earliest inhabitants of Ireland. With her imprisonment, the world grew ever dark, cold and barren. She and the earth languished for just one day short of a year, until she was freed by Lugh, leader of the Tuatha da Danann, 'Followers of the Goddess Danu'. The gods rewarded Lugh's heroism with the secret of eternal life. On every anniversary of his rescue, the longest night of the year, he returned to the crystal cave, where he transformed himself into a coiled snake. When dawn light entered, Lugh unwound himself and rose up a young man again.

This pre-Celtic legend of the crystal cave apparently describes the megalithic mound at New Grange, remembered in Gaelic as Am umagh Greine, the 'Temple of the Sun'. Thousands of white quartz stones comprise the structure's facade. Situated atop a hill overlooking the Boyne Valley, 28 kilometres north-west of Dublin, New Grange is a 5,200-year-old sacred observatory. A 'roof box' over its entrance was aligned to admit a shaft of light 20 metres into its innermost chamber, where a triple spiral has been etched into the far wall. It is illuminated only once each year, during the sunrise of the winter solstice.

The Persephone-like imprisonment of Ethlinn, with wintery consequences for the world, and her deliverance by Lugh (whose name, appropriately, means 'light') are the poetic rendering of actual events as they still transpire in New Grange every winter solstice. Even the hero's serpentine rebirth each year materializes in the carved spiral design illumined every sunrise after the year's longest night.

If nothing else, the validation of this ancient tradition is confirmation of myth's unsuspected power to preserve high truths in metaphor, even to Ethlinn's crystal cave, a reference to the mound's quartz facade. Its builders were supposed to have been the Formorach, who arrived in Ireland from a distant island known as Lochlann. Similarity between the Irish Lochlann and the Greek Atlantis is more than philological, as both were said to have vanished beneath the sea. And Atlas, the Greek figure from whom the island of Atlantis derived its name, was, like the Formorach king Balor, a titan. The early date for New Grange, its circular construction, sophisticated solar orientation and mythic tradition all point to Atlantean origins.

The crystal link to Atlantis through Irish legend is carried further by another pre-Celtic hero, Maildune. His account of an island city in the mid-Atlantic is similar to Plato's description, including the circular layout of the capital in concentric ramparts. But the smallest inner wall surrounding the temple dedicated to Poseidon, the sea god, was decorated with crystal.

In a Welsh epic poem suggesting Bronze Age origins, *Preddeu Annwn*, the 'Spoils of Annwn', King Arthur and his men escape from a rapidly sinking island in the mid-Atlantic. Its capital was the magnificent Caer Wydyr, the 'Glass Fortress'. Nennius, a 12th-century chronicler, wrote in his *Historium Brittanum* of a splendid city, the capital of an ancient seaborne empire, swallowed up long ago by the ocean for the evil practices of its unrepentant inhabitants. He called the city Turris Vitrea, the 'Tower of Glass', recalling Edgar Cayce's description of the special building in which the Tuaoi crystal was kept.

More than a thousand years before Nennius, Druid priests told Julius Caesar that the Gauls believed their ancestors came to the European continent from the Isle of Glass Towers, long drowned in the Atlantic Ocean, far from Iberian shores. The survivors' legendary landfall was made at Oporto, which the Romans subsequently referred to as the 'Port of the Gauls', or Portus Galle, from which Portugal took her name. Throughout his life readings, Cayce referred to crystals as 'cut glass', 'white stone', 'faceted glass', etc. Similarly, Celtic descriptions of 'glass' structures were poetic renderings for crystal.

In the early second century AD, Lucian of Samosata was a famous Roman writer whose *Historia Vera,* the 'True History', described a large, highly civilized island that sank into the ocean 'ages before our own'. Before it disappeared, one of its outstanding features was a 'crystal building'.

The common theme of an Atlantean disaster associated with powerful crystals appears in widely scattered mythic traditions from North and South America to the British Isles, Portugal and Rome. They comprise provocative evidence to support Edgar Cayce's vision of the Atlanteans, whose material and spiritual greatness was achieved through their mastery of crystal technology. Abused, it was also the means of their destruction.

CHAPTER 6
THE FACE OF THE CRYSTAL SKULL

'THE BAFFLING STORY OF THE SKULL OF DOOM,
AS IT HAS BECOME KNOWN, IS ALMOST AS
STRANGE AS THE OBJECT ITSELF.'
BRIAN HOUGHTON, *HIDDEN HISTORY*

'IF WE CARE TO SPECULATE, COULD THIS HAVE
BEEN THE MISSING LINK CONNECTING THE
HISTORY OF A PREVIOUS ATLANTEAN-TYPE
CIVILIZATION WITH COSMIC EVENTS THAT
CAUSED ITS DESTRUCTION?'
LEHMAN HISEY, *CRYSTALS AND THE KEYS OF ENOCH*

The Atlantean crystals described in the folk memories of world myth were not magical objects in themselves. They acted instead as mighty amplifiers powerfully magnifying, concentrating and directing the electrical, bio-electrical, solar and other forms of energy focused in them. Their effectiveness was entirely dependent upon the input they received from an elite group of highly trained and deeply motivated caretakers. Frank Dorland, the United States' leading crystallographer until his death in 1997, demonstrated that:

> ... *the crystal is an advantageous electronic device,*
> *the world's first solid-state tool, but it is the human*
> *mind that controls the crystal. The mind is the power*

*supply, the crystal is the reflecting amplifier. It [the
human intellect] is the most beautiful power there is;
yet, when gone wrong, it is the most loathsome and
fearful monster in existence.*

A POWER FOR GOOD OR ILL

Therein lies the real power of the crystals – their capacity to
magnify the force human beings put into them, for good or
ill. IBM's Second Quarter Stockholders' Report (for 1989)
echoes Dorland's cautionary statement: 'A crystal "memory
chip" has recently been invented by a German firm that
contains more than four million bits of information.'

The laser is a modern outcome of crystal technology,
as explained by *Physical Review* magazine in almost
Atlantean terms:

*The amplification is achieved by storing up energy in a small
insulating crystal of special magnetic properties. The release
of energy is triggered off by an incident signal, so that the
crystal passes on more energy than it receives.*

The crystals of Atlantis were themselves amoral. In the
hands of responsible initiates, they were repositories
for important information, survival tools for healing,

transducers of destructive forces into productive energies. So, too, in modern times, the laser can figure at the centre of life-and-death situations. In the hands of a dedicated surgeon, it represented a wonderful curative instrument. But to the military man, it was once a laser cannon in the US government's so-called 'Star Wars' programme.

DISCOVERY OF THE CRYSTAL SKULL

Certainly, the most extraordinary mineral of its kind is the famous Crystal Skull, discovered under circumstances still deemed controversial.

On an unbearably hot morning in 1926, Anna Mitchell-Hedges poked through the jungle ruins of a lost temple. She was visiting British Honduras (today's Belize) with her adopted father. Adventurer, explorer and tourist guide, F.A. 'Mike' Mitchell-Hedges was involved in excavating Lubuaantun, 'Place of the Fallen Stones', as it was known to the Lacadonian Indians serving as his labourers at the site. About 1,200 years ago, this late Classic ceremonial centre of untypical pyramids and palaces made of brick-shaped stones supported a large Maya population with a flourishing regional market system.

Mike had enrolled Anna in an exclusive New York high school and, during a semester break coinciding with her 17th birthday, sent her ocean-liner tickets with an invitation to join him at Lubuaantun. It was there that she suddenly glimpsed something glinting deep among the ancient blocks of what appeared to be an altar toppled by more than ten centuries of forest growth and earthquake activity. She ran back to her father, who was having breakfast at a makeshift table in front of their expedition tents with Dr Thomas Gann, an archaeologist in charge of the digs.

'Daddy, there's treasure in the ruins! I saw it shining!' Mike smiled. Whatever it was could wait until after they finished eating Eventually, the two Englishmen stirred themselves, then followed the impatient teenager back to the jungle city with some native workers.

'There!' she pointed excitedly, and the Indians began cautiously removing piles of collapsed stonework. They had hardly begun to clear the debris when Anna dashed in ahead of them, reached under some overturned blocks, and pulled out a large, gleaming jewel. Slowly approaching her father and Dr Gann with the ponderous gem in her tender care, she was surprised to see the wide-eyed Indian helpers surrounding her abruptly fall to the ground and cover their heads with their arms. A few paces more and she stood before her stepfather with the startlingly lifelike reproduction of a human skull in clear quartz crystal. Only the lower jaw was missing.

As she related decades later, 'I came upon the skull buried beneath the altar, but it was some three months later before the jaw was found which was about 25 feet (8 metres) away.'

But did Anna really find the skull, as she said she did? While supposedly first brought to public attention in British Honduras, it appears doubtful that the Crystal Skull originated there. Nothing at Lubuaantun connects the city's late Classical culture with cranial or lunar imagery. No skull themes appear at the site, nor does the ceremonial centre feature any symbolism referring to the deity it represents, the moon goddess, Ixchel. Mike Mitchell-Hedges may have discovered the Crystal Skull himself on either Isola Mujeres or Cozumel, two islands off the extreme eastern tip of Mexico's Yucatán peninsula.

A MORE LIKELY SITE

Spanish conquistadors in the 16th century named the uninhabited Isola Mujeres ('Isle of Women') after its numerous freestanding statues, all portraying the same woman. At the south end of the island they found a small stone shrine to Ixchel. The larger island of Cozumel featured many temples to this prohesying moon goddess, and was venerated by the Mayas as the chief sacred refuge of her cult.

But in the 1920s, Yucatán was involved in a shooting war for independence from Mexico, and the British authorities warned Mitchell-Hedges to stay out of the area. If he went to Yucatán, any artefacts he might find there would be confiscated, his passport seized, and he would be deported to England. But as a citizen of the Crown, whatever he found in colonial Honduras would be his to keep.

Notwithstanding these official admonishments, Mitchell-Hedges secretly risked sailing to Isola Mujeres and Cozumel after hearing native tales of the islands' 'golden treasures'. It is unlikely he found any gold there, but he may have come back to Honduras with the Crystal Skull in his possession. Returning to Lubuaantun, he hid it in an accessible spot among the ruins for his daughter to find as a surprise on her birthday. The artefact now belonged to him, having been conveniently 'found' on British territory. Mike himself suggested this possible scenario for the actual discovery of the Crystal Skull when he wrote, 'How it came into my possession I have reason for not revealing.'

That 'reason' continued to resurface from time to time with 'requests' from foreign authorities for the return of the pilfered artefact. At least as late as the mid-1990s, government agents from Mexico and Belize actually showed up at Anna Mitchell-Hedges' Canadian home, demanding its return. The feisty old lady always slammed the door in their faces without comment. By the time she passed away at 100 years of age in March 2007, few investigators believed her version of the artefact's discovery.

A DUBIOUS PROVENANCE

An outstanding anomalist, Mark Chorvinsky, researched the Crystal Skull for more than ten years to conclude that Anna Mitchell-Hedges' version of events was entirely fallacious. After his death in 2005, the Wikipedia website described him as:

> ... *a skeptic in the true sense of the word – open-minded, determined to defend neither a belief system that said a phenomenon must be true, nor one that said it must be false – and that his only interest was to get to the bottom of the mysteries he investigated – one of the leading investigators of strange phenomena, and often marshalled the resources of a network of friends and associates all over the world.*

His investigations, Chorvinsky stated, showed that the earliest reference to the Crystal Skull was in a 1933 letter from the owner of a London art gallery, Sidney Burney, to the curator of the American Museum of Natural History. 'The rock-crystal skull was for several years in the possession of the collector from whom I bought it,' Burney explained, 'and he in his turn had it from an Englishman in whose collection it had also been for several years, but beyond that I have not been able to go.' He does not mention Mitchell-Hedges or British Honduras. In 1944, Burney put the Crystal Skull up for auction at Sotheby's, where representatives from the British Museum were outbid by the £400 offer of Mike Mitchell-Hedges, who appeared for the first time in the object's history.

Whatever the real story of its discovery, Mitchell-Hedges believed that the Crystal Skull could only have been made by a technologically sophisticated society far in advance of anything known throughout Mesoamerica. In view of the Mayas' own traditions of Itzamna – the bearded 'White Man' arriving as a culture-bearer in Yucatán from some natural disaster in the Atlantic Ocean – he concluded that the sculpted masterpiece was created in Middle America by Atlantean refugees from the cataclysm that destroyed their oceanic homeland. Or it may have been crafted in Atlantis itself, then carried to safety in Mexico as a sacred heirloom.

His colleagues, however, were less convinced of its

authenticity, Atlantean or otherwise. They chose mostly to ignore the Crystal Skull, and no university-trained professional dared to comment on the alleged artefact in print, unless to denigrate it. They dismissed it as 'too well made' for anything a pre-Columbian people were capable of producing, while hypothetical origins in Atlantis were deemed unworthy of serious discussion. More likely, they believed, the Crystal Skull had been obtained during the chaotic days of post-First World War Germany or Austria, where local craftsmen were long known for their skill in crystal carving, and where such an object might be obtained for relatively little money, given the extreme hardship of the times.

SCIENTIFIC EXAMINATION

With Mitchell-Hedges' death in 1959, the Crystal Skull passed to his adopted daughter, Anna, its supposed discoverer. In 1964, she entrusted it to Frank Dorland, then a leading art conservator in Los Ossos, California, for an extended period of study. Through his auspices, the Crystal Skull was studied by investigators at Hewlett Packard Laboratories, in Santa Clara, California, in November 1970. First, they submerged it in a tank of benzyl alcohol for viewing with polarized light in the hopes of revealing something about its crystalline properties. But what the researchers saw was more startling than they expected: the separate jaw was originally part of and connected to the rest of the object. Yet it had been cut away with such infinite precision that no known tool could have replicated the job. On the Moh's scale of mineral hardness, crystal rates an 8 against the perfect 10 of a diamond. Dorland expressed the amazement of his colleagues when he wrote, 'To cut the jawbone loose from the skull and carve it to shape would be many times more difficult than merely carving a separate jawbone from another chunk of crystal.'

The Hewlett Packard examiners concluded that, given its size and the incomparably skilled level of its execution, nothing of relative quality could be created today. In other words, some lost, superior technology was responsible for the sculpted work. F.A. Mitchell-Hedges' belief that it originated in Atlantis began to seem less fantastic after all.

In the 1970s, the Crystal Skull gained international fame through a series of television documentaries, which, in turn, generated popular interest that has grown ever since. Whole generations of amateur investigators raised questions as intriguing as they seemed unanswerable. How was it made? How long was the work in progress? How old is it? Was it really the product of some ancient civilization?

Did the Mayas actually carve it? If not, who? Dorland thought he knew how it was made:

> *I believe that the Crystal Skull was hand-chipped from a single massive chunk of left-hand quartz crystal that originally weighed more than 9.072 kilograms [against its present weight of 5 kilograms, 198.45 grams].*

Indeed, microscopic investigation of the cranium reveals faint scoop marks almost entirely polished away with a sandy solution applied by the artist. But these marks are confined to the upper portions of the skull only. They do not appear below the eye–ear line. Also, the jaw is so translucently clear, any such marks would be apparent. This jaw, in fact, is the real highlight of the masterpiece because of its anatomical realism. How its creator could render such fluid realism in so hard and brittle a medium has not been satisfactorily explained.

Melting crystals in a cast moulded with the inverse features of the skull would not have worked because crystal becomes opaque if melted. Transferring liquefied or molten crystal from a volcanic source directly into such a cast, however, might have succeeded.

Dorland's determination that the crystal came from California's Calaveras County seems confirmed. Deposits there contain vermicular procholorite inclusions identical to those observed in the Mitchell-Hedges' skull. But just how the artwork was fashioned remains unknown. Nor may we learn the age of the skull. While the formation of the crystal itself may be dated, its carving cannot.

Scientific evaluation of the Crystal Skull shows that it measures 23.76–75.28 centimetres in width, 33.02–40.64 centimetres in height, and 18.38–20.32 centimetres in length. These realistic measurements particularly suggested the skull had been modelled after a human original. Since its discovery, sceptics have argued that the Crystal Skull is the modern creation of Middle European or even Southeast Asian gem-cutters, despite Hewlett Packard's conclusion that it could not be reproduced today.

A FACIAL RECONSTRUCTION

Perhaps its authenticity might be supported if forensic experts could determine that the object was not merely some general artistic rendering of human anatomy, but deliberately modelled after the cranial remains of a real man or woman. If that could be ascertained, they might be able to re-create the individual's face that originally covered the skull and after which the crystal sculpture had been fashioned. By the early 1980s, expertise in forensic reconstruction had reached high levels of accuracy. So much so, it is presently an accepted, important part in criminal investigations among police departments everywhere.

Thus intrigued by the possibilities of applying such methodology to determining the archaeological authenticity of the Crystal Skull, American investigators inquired at the Anthropology Department at Chicago's Field Museum, where they were referred to Dr Clyde C. Snow. Mentioned in *American Men and Women of Science* since the early 1960s, Dr Snow's association with the Forensic Science Foundation and the American Academy of Forensic Science has been illustrious. In spring 1986, Frank Dorland submitted a plaster cast he made of the Crystal Skull, and it was his accurate reproduction that was brought to the Cook County Medical Examiner's Office, in Chicago, where Dr Snow and the City's Chief Coroner Dr Irwin Kirschner were able to examine it for the first time in March 1983.

Impressed by the general accuracy of its anatomical details, they were able to determine that the sculpted work was not some artistic convention, but the superbly (even incredibly) realistic rendering of an actual individual human skull. It had once belonged, they concurred, to a young woman in her late teens or early twenties; short in stature, with possibly Amerindian features. The age range –

that of a 17- to 23-year-old – was determined by the degree of wear (even this had been faithfully transferred to the artwork!) indicated on the last molars. The sculpted crystal was not a composite of various skulls; its cranial elements were too closely related to each other.

Examining the dentition, Dr Snow was amazed to observe that the molars, pre-molars, canines and incisors were properly reproduced, even to the shovel-like obverse of the incisors, a detail not easily noticed, yet incredibly rendered in hard crystal In the occlusal surface on the left side of the mandible the first molar showed an X on the surface; on a human being, it is marked with a plus (+) sign. Strangely, sutures located atop the dome were absent. But most of its anatomical details proved astonishingly correct. For example, its eye sockets are not identical and are slightly off set, as occur in the eye-sockets of a real human skull. As the Crystal Skull investigator Alice Bryant remarked, 'It has the character of an anatomical study done in a scientific age.' It did indeed exhibit an overall medical authenticity. That so many unnecessary, almost imperceptible details should have even been included in a mere 'piece of art' is extraordinary.

With Dr Snow's evaluation in hand, the investigators contacted Peggy C. Caldwell, a consulting forensic anthropologist for the Office of the Chief Medical Examiner, in New York City. A collaborator at the Department of Anthropology in the Smithsonian Museum of Natural History, Dr Caldwell was among the United States' leading researchers in human osteology. She worked with detective Frank J. Domingo (Composite Artist Unit, Latent Print Command, New York City Police Department), whose pencil sketch was the painstaking result of her forensic data. His portrait of the object was determined by the anatomical details Snow and Caldwell supplied.

Domingo attempted to re-create the lost face just as he would the visage of any murder victim. His vivid illustration (see plate section) revealed the face of a Native American woman, although traces of some unknown alien elements are apparent. She suggests mixed ancestry, with dominant Amerindian traits. More significantly, the forensic reconstruction established that the sculpted crystal was, in fact, very closely modelled after the single human skull of a (predominantly) Amerindian female. This would make its identification with the Maya moon goddess, Ixchel, all the more logical. That the Crystal Skull was made in Mesoamerica during pre-Columbian times to represent this lunar deity of prophesy and psychic power seems likely. After unguessed centuries since its creation, the face of the Crystal Skull reappeared.

OTHER CRYSTAL SKULLS

The Mitchell-Hedges' artefact is not alone. At least four other crystal skulls, all allegedly ancient, are known. London's world-renowned Museum of Mankind obtained a crudely executed version of a crystal skull in 1898. Not quite 100 years later, examiners found that it showed unmistakable evidence of modern tool marks. From these, experts determined that the British Museum skull was carved around the time it was sold in the late 19th century.

In the no less prestigious Musée de l'Homme, at the Palais de Chaillot in Paris, a smaller crystal skull is on display. Measuring approximately 13 centimetres in height, it weighs 1.866 kilograms and 240.970 grams. A printed card beneath the French crystal skull reads, 'Aztec civilization, probably 15th century. Death's head in polished quartz probably representing the god of death.' Its relatively poor workmanship closely matches that of the British Museum of Mankind fake, but appears, at least, to be an authentically Mesoamerican artefact.

A small, privately owned, far more expertly made crystal skull in Mexico City, likewise believed to be pre-Columbian, was shown by British Museum authorities in Spanish colonial culture to date from the early 18th or late 17th centuries. Perhaps the most crudely executed crystal skull is one sometimes displayed at New Age get-togethers around the United States, and referred to by its Texas' owners as 'Max'. Although it appears to be the most modern example of its kind, test results obtained in the early 1990s by investigators at the British Museum were never released. What did they find out about 'Max' they were unwilling to share with the public?

IS THE CRYSTAL SKULL PRE-COLUMBIAN?

Of all the known crystal skulls, however, the Mitchell-Hedges specimen alone appears genuinely pre-Columbian. But if so, what is it? And why did some artist go to all the trouble of rendering unbelievably accurate, intricate, apparently unnecessary cranial details in a mineral so notoriously difficult to work? Something of both the Crystal Skull's authenticity and intended purpose may be discerned from its only unrealistic features.

Among the few exceptions to its anatomical correctness are small, inconspicuous holes: a pair found on the underside of its jaw, and two more drilled on either side near the ear cavities, precisely at the object's centre of gravity. If rods were inserted into these holes, the artwork could be made to nod back and forth, while the hinged jawbone moved up and down, as if speaking. In 1993, William Wild, a

Mesoamericanist and professional gemologist, determined that the holes evidenced no modern tool marks, but were created by fire-hardened wooden dowels, a technique known to have been used by Maya and even earlier Olmec jewellers working with precious stones, mostly jade.

The conclusions of Wild's expert observation supports a pre-Columbian provenance for the Crystal Skull. Its deliberately drilled holes strongly suggest that it was used as a religious device, most likely as an oracle for the deity it was meant to represent. Sequestered in the dark interior of its shrine, illuminated only by a single candle flame at Isola Mujeres or Cozumel, a priest's black-gloved hand could easily and surreptitiously manipulate this religious *deus ex machina* pivoting on its rods, its jaw moving up and down like a ventriloquist's dummy so that it appeared to be uttering the prognostications of a disembodied voice emanating from a hidden assistant.

But what of the real skull after which the prehistoric artist's rendition was so meticulously rendered? It may have belonged to some uniquely important follower of Ixchel, perhaps her high priestess, or even the founder of the cult. Or she may have been a particularly significant sacrifice. In any case, her skull was probably removed after death and venerated until it began to deteriorate. To preserve this holy relic for all time, its details were somehow sculpted in crystal.

The process of 'sympathetic magic' – wherein the spiritual power of an originally charged relic is transferred to a simulated object – is universally ancient. It even manifests in Christianity, where crucifixes blessed by a priest are thought to be imbued with some of the spiritual essence or potency of the actual cross upon which Jesus died. The same principle may have arisen between the Crystal Skull and its human original. But what of the evocative reconstructed portrait? Who was this lady? How can we explain what some observers see as her racially mixed cast of facial features? If genuinely pre-Columbian, then who could have been responsible for such an admixture?

Despite decades of testing and research, the Crystal Skull continues to generate more questions than answers.

A SYMBOL OF PSYCHIC POWER

The Crystal Skull may, in fact, be a symbol for the thing it physically represents – the psychic power of the mind. It is important to understand in this context that the religion and science of Atlantis were what today would be termed 'occult', although of such a refined and sophisticated degree as to make our 'New Age' seem crude and rudimentary by comparison. Atlas, the titan who gave his name to the city of Atlantis, was, after all, the mythic founder of astrology, the Supporter of the Heavens. As the leading cultic figure in Atlantis, he personified all the otherworldly powers inherent in human potential.

The intellectual classes of Atlantean society were dedicated to cultivating these powers over many generations as a religious duty. Such long-term dedication to the spiritual disciplines resulted in an abundance of knowledge about the soul and mind that we are only just beginning to appreciate today. Doubtless, these psychically proficient Atlanteans were in possession of powers, technological or otherwise, that would seem truly 'magical' in our time.

Is the Crystal Skull, as F.A. Mitchell-Hedges believed, one of those power stones from lost Atlantis? It would at least appear to symbolize in itself its own purpose; namely, the mind's amplified capacity to achieve power limited only by human imagination. And nowhere else did the mind attain such wide dimensions of power as in Atlantis. All that the Atlanteans knew and did may be locked inside the crystalline memory banks of the Crystal Skull, like the four million bits of information stored in IBM's crystalline 'memory chip'.

The Crystal Skull's Atlantean identity is suggested by more than Mitchell-Hedges' archaeological speculations.

As a cultic symbol, the human skull was widely used by all Middle American civilizations. In artistic representations of the Mesoamerican ball-court, a decapitated skull was portrayed at the centre. As Burr Cartwright Brundage, the American historian of pre-Columbian Mexico, established, *tlachtli*, the Aztecs' sacred ball game, was a re-enactment of the movements of the heavenly bodies, and a ritualistic re-creation of the mystic battle between day and night; heaven and hell; good and evil; and life and death – the sun (as symbolized by the rubber ball) and the moon (the skull).

THE MOON GODDESS

The skull was the particular emblem of the moon goddess: the Aztecs' Coyolxauqui; Ixchel to the earlier Mayas. Her myth, with suggestions of Atlantean origins and Cayce's 'mighty, terrible crystal', sheds considerable light on the Crystal Skull, especially on what it may have meant to the people who created and venerated it.

Coyolxauqui's name means 'She who is decorated with tinkling bells', referring to the stars that she, as the moon, seemed to lead across the night sky. In her previous guise as the Mayas' Ixchel, she was the 'White Lady', also reflecting her lunar identity. In an antediluvian age, so ran her myth, she was involved in a terrible fight with the Hummingbird

Warrior, Huitzilipochtli. He decapitated her, then placed her severed head atop a sacred mountain on an island in the Sunrise Sea (the Atlantic Ocean). There she foretold coming events for men and gods alike. The Aztec builders of their imperial capital, Tenochtitlan, enshrined her story in the Hummingbird Warrior's mountainous pyramid, which represented the original summit occupied by her prognosticating head. Atop its monumental terraced stairway was a stone head executed in pale granite of Coyolxauqui, her eyes closed in death, and attended by astrologer-priests who, through the auspices of the lunar goddess, foretold the future. As C.W. Cooper, an authority on the meaning of symbolism, affirms, 'All moon goddesses are controllers of destiny.'

We recall the Crystal Skull's holes drilled at its centre of gravity as part of the object's probable oracular function. In underscoring its identification with Coyolxauqui–Ixchel, F.W. Armstrong, author of *Man, Myth and Magic*, points out that 'the moon is also associated with rock crystal, which stimulates the faculty for clairvoyance'. In this context it becomes clear that the Crystal Skull was the materialization of the moon, the lunar goddess's decapitated head, regarded as a sublime fortune-telling device, and therefore the most sacred single artefact of Mesoamerican civilization.

QUEENS OF HEAVEN AND DECAPITATED DEITIES

Frank Dorland believed that the Crystal Skull belonged to the 'Queen of Heaven', a conclusion apparently borne out by Aztec and Mayan traditions. Curiously, these same mythological associations may also be found on the other side of the Atlantic Ocean. In the Roman world, Juno (the Greek Hera) was entitled the 'Queen of Heaven', and the stone identified with her was rock crystal. Earlier still, the Egyptian Eset (better remembered by her Greek name, Isis) was similarly venerated by the Romans as 'Regina Coeli'. At the great sanctuary of Tithorea, her festival was held every spring and autumnal equinox, suggesting the same death–rebirth dichotomy the Crystal Skull signified for the Mayas and Aztecs. They identified it with the moon, which seemed to die as its shadow increased each night, until the process reversed and it became full again. This waxing and waning of lunar cycles was applied to life cycles on Earth, reaffirming the old metaphysical concept of 'as above, so below'.

These cultural correspondences hint at a very ancient lineage for the Crystal Skull, implying some key role it may once have played in an esoteric mystery cult that long ago touched both the Old and New worlds in antediluvian times. In any case, it is remarkable that Juno–Isis in Europe and

Coyolxauqui–Ixchel in Middle America – all female deities to whom crystal was particularly sacred – should find themselves thematically linked with an artefact fashioned in the likeness of a crystal skull. Some researchers have even pointed to the philological resemblance between the Egyptian 'Isis' and the Maya 'Ixchel'. This toponymic comparison appears substantiated by the amazing similarity of their myths regarding the sacred skull.

The Egyptians told how Isis was decapitated by her son Horus because she interfered in his battle with the demons of the night. Horus was a sun god symbolized by the falcon, and the story of his confrontation with Isis was known from the beginning of dynastic civilization in the Nile valley. So, too, the legend of the Hummingbird Warrior was associated with the first day of Aztec civilization, as he founded the empire's original capital, Tenochitlan, the site of today's Mexico City. He, too, was a solar deity whose nagual, or animal manifestation, was the eagle, similar to the falcon of Horus. Although Coyolxauqui was his sister (not his mother), he decapitated her, just as Horus did Isis, during a battle with the Centzanhuitzaua, the starry demons of the night sky.

If a detailed correspondence between these Egyptian and Aztec myths cannot be dismissed as mere cultural coincidence, what can their similarity imply? The Aztec state did not come into being until the early 14th century AD, more than 1,000 years after the last Egyptian closed the door on pharaonic civilization. But the Aztecs were the ultimate extension of Mesoamerican culture, with roots contemporaneous to Egypt in the middle of its power, c.1500BC, when the Olmecs – Middle America's first known civilization – flourished in Mexico. Perhaps some other, outside source separately impacted both the Nile Valley and Mexico, carrying the same lunar concept to both peoples. The close parallels between these two myths suggest as much.

A WIDESPREAD SYMBOL

Nor do those parallels end here. Throughout the Old World, from the subcontinent's Indus valley to the Asia Minor of modern-day Turkey and the Greek Peloponnesus, beyond to Germania and west through Gaul to Iberia and the British Isles, the *sauvastika*, or right-handed hooked cross, was universally symbolic of the moon. A good example of its lunar identity may be found in the Milan National Museum, where a statue of Artemis, the Greek moon goddess, wears a long gown decorated with tiny *sauvastikas*. There are numerous other artefacts demonstrating the lunar symbolism of the *sauvastika* from a dozen other European cultures.

Interestingly, a large stone altar piece unearthed during excavations in the 1950s at Mexico City features a relief sculpture of Coyolxauqui with her arms and legs broken and bent to form a right-handed hooked cross. The stone is circular and pale white, like the moon, and her head is shown decapitated, suggesting the disembodied Crystal Skull (which, in fact, appears separately on the same stone disc). That the Sauvastika as the symbol of a moon goddess should appear on both sides of the world at a time when, conventional historians tell us, men did not cross the oceans, is as remarkable as it is mystifying.

UNIVERSAL SKULL MYTHS

Both Isis and Ixchel were, moreover, goddesses of healing. Coincidentally, the ancient Western occult practice (still in use) of burning a white candle in the form of a human female skull was said to assist in curing the sick. More cogently, Ixchel was additionally the goddess of prophesy and psychic power, underscoring her identification with the Crystal Skull, which generations of psychics insist is the single most potent paranormal artefact in the world.

In any case, the Crystal Skull of the moon represents a

high religious concept shared by the peoples of at least two continents from prehistoric times. Whatever the origins of the Mitchell-Hedges' find, a discernibly Atlantean theme in skull myth may be traced on both sides of the ocean. Ymir, the giant of Norse legend, had his skull transformed into the vault of heaven with its stars of destiny, as his blood deluged the world. His story could be a poetic metaphor for the end of the last Ice Age, earmarked as it was by the sudden rise in sea level, with the subsequent inundation of islands and coastal areas in the North Atlantic, a world-class geological event caused by massive glacial melt.

An important French researcher (Andre Foex) concludes from this event that Atlantis did not actually sink, but was instead overwhelmed by the final tides generated by earth's most recent Ice Age, about 12,000 years ago. As an ice giant, Ymir's death might be synonymous for the end of the Ice Age he personified, its floodwaters being his 'blood' covering the world. And his skull, like Ixchel's, became a celestial object.

The Greek Kronos had for his emblem the skull, a particularly cogent detail in view of his identification with the Atlantic: the Romans referred to the Ocean as Chronis Mare, the Sea of Kronos. Hesiod, the Greek mythographer, located Kronos in the Blessed Isles of the Hesperides, beyond the Pillars of Heracles (the Straits of Gibraltar), a Hellenistic reference to Atlantis. Kronos was the father (in the non-Platonic version) of Atlas. After relinquishing leadership of the Gigantomachy (the war against the Olympia gods) to Atlas, Kronos fled into the realm of Albion (the brother of Atlas, and the ancient name for Britain), where he still dreams of the future in a golden cave, thus echoing the skull-divination theme.

But it is with the Mayas' Ixchel that the overtly Atlantean implications of the Crystal Skull become apparent. Her name, as mentioned above, means the 'White Lady', an apt description of her identity with the pale moon. But it may have another parallel meaning. Her husband was Itzamna, the 'White Man', and the Mayan Itzas, who built Yucatán's magnificent ceremonial city of Chichen Itza, traced their name and descent directly back to him. Regarded as the founders of Mesoamerican civilization, the couple arrived at Yucatán after a great natural disaster far out at sea.

From their distant homeland they brought knowledge of the stars, the secrets of writing, pyramid building, a system of justice, a new pantheon of gods, the principles of kingship, irrigation, city planning, agriculture, irrigation, medicine, mathematics, weaving – all the features of an advanced society left behind in the ocean. According to their myth, the cataclysm from which Ixchel and Itzamna fled was a terrible flood caused by the White Lady herself, through the power of her sky serpent. Enraged by the ingratitude and greed of men, she punished them with a world-shattering deluge that brought the cycle of life in a former epoch to a dramatic end. With Ixchel, the Atlantean aspects of the Crystal Skull are apparent. Even her 'sky serpent' conforms to those theories concerning the demise of Atlantis that describe the catastrophe as the result of Earth's close brush with a comet. Its meteoric material bombarded the surface of our planet, triggering geologic consequences for the ultimate destruction of Plato's island. She – the 'White Lady' – and her husband – the 'White Man' – were after all, culture-bearers from a drowned civilization.

The Crystal Skull, the emblem of Ixchel, may represent the most important relic of lost Atlantis. Certainly, no other known object more resembles that civilization's Tuaoi stone, the 'mighty, terrible crystal' described by Edgar Cayce as the chief instrument of Atlantean catastrophe (see chapter 12).

WHERE IS THE SKULL TODAY?
After the Crystal Skull came to light, speculation spread that it was perhaps nothing less than the Holy Grail itself. Such an attribution was not as far-fetched as it may have seemed to persons unacquainted with the Grail literature.

Medieval accounts of this supremely sacred object often described it as a precious, clear gemstone, sometimes an 'emerald', a designation more symbolically descriptive than literal. It also assumed the likeness of a woman's skull, as depicted by Wolfram von Eschenbach in his epic, *Parzifal* (c.AD1212). The Grail was neither his invention nor a Christian convention of the European Middle Ages, but long predated that period. The term from which the name derived, *gral*, was an ancient Celtic or Gaulic word for 'power'; ie, 'ultimate power'.

One hundred years after Eschenbach's death, the Templars (whom he identified as 'Grail Knights') were accused of worshipping a human skull or its replica known as Baphomet. After the French king Philip IV, 'the Fair', criminalized them on behalf of this and other idolatries, his minions thoroughly ransacked the Templars' Paris headquarters in search of the abominated skull, which, together with the Templar treasure, was never found.

Legend had it that both had been spirited away from Paris in advance of the royal authorities, and placed aboard a vessel of the Templars' fleet. Their ships, renowned for sailing throughout the known world, were certainly capable of venturing beyond, should emergency demand. In view of this undoubted maritime advantage, the Knights Templar treasure and crystal Baphomet could have escaped to the other side of the world, far from the grasp of Philip the Fair, perhaps to an island off the Atlantic coast of Mexico. It was here, so speculation goes, that the Crystal Skull's Holy Grail was enshrined at either Cozumel or Isla Mujeres, where its appearance complemented the Neo-Mayas' long-established worship of Ixchel, the 'White Lady', already symbolized by a human skull.

The Templars made the best of their exile, until their lineage was absorbed through inter-marriage with native Indians, whose mythic accounts of fair-skinned culture-bearers arriving over the sea generations before the Spaniards appeared were garbled recollections of Templar refugees in early 14th-century Mexico.

With the collapse of Mesoamerican civilization somewhat more than 100 years later, the Crystal Skull was concealed, along with all other pre-Christian religious items anathematized by Christian priests and missionaries, until either its fortuitous rediscovery during 1924 by a teenage Anna Mitchell-Hedges in British Honduras, or, more likely, its sale by some unknown native for a fraction of its worth to a London artefact broker in the mid-1930s. Ten years later, the object was purchased by F.A. Mitchell-Hedges, who introduced it to the world.

With the death of his daughter, its sole proprietor, the whereabouts and future of the Crystal Skull are in doubt. During the first half of the 1940s, it had been dropped into a desk drawer at a London auction house, where it was forgotten until Anna's adoptive father bought the neglected artefact near the close of the Second World War. Throughout her long life, whenever asked what, if any, provisions had been made for its safekeeping after her death, Anna Mitchell-Hedges would invariably respond that the 'Crystal Skull always takes care of itself.' Now that she is gone, time will tell.

CHAPTER 7
EGYPTIAN CIVILIZATION — AN ATLANTEAN HYBRID

'I HAVE GONE ROUND
ABOUT THE STREAMS IN
SEKHRET-AARU.'
FROM *THE EGYPTIAN BOOK OF THE DEAD*, CHAPTER LXII

The Nile valley was originally inhabited by a low-density population of scattered hunter-gatherers and fishermen living in small, disconnected groups along the river banks, where they dwelt in tiny clusters of one-room, stick-built huts. Their primitive way of life continued unchanged, evidencing little in terms of social or any other kind of development for tens of thousands of years.

Then, in 3,100BC, their sleepy lives were transformed by the sudden introduction of monumental temple building, geometry, surveying, organized labour, standardized units of weight and measurement, a written language, astronomy, massive irrigation and canal works, a codified religion, metallurgy, stratified government, foreign relations, shipbuilding, institutionalized education, agriculture, a variety of complex musical instruments, tool manufacture, medicine, sculpture, painting, linen weaving, a dye and cosmetics industry – everything famously associated with the high civilization of ancient Egypt.

CROSSING THE SAHARA

Perhaps the most remarkable feature of this historical phenomenon was its apparent creation out of nothing, its abrupt appearance against the backdrop of a cultural vacuum. For some 200 years, scholars attempted in vain to understand what had transformed a few backward communities huddling along the River Nile into the land of the pyramids. During the mid-20th century, archaeologists began looking beyond Egypt for answers. By 1955, their first extensive subsurface testing in the Sahara retrieved core samples that proved the desert had been fertile enough to support herds of cattle as recently as 3,000BC. Only in the decades following did North Africa begin to lose its battle with the inexorable sands.

Almost simultaneous with these geological revelations, researchers discovered the first evidence of a nomadic people who inhabited the Sahara, and shared numerous points in common with the Dynastic culture of Egypt. These civilized desert dwellers or travellers appear to have been the pharaonic Egyptians' own immediate ancestors migrating eastwards into the Nile valley from the seismic chaos of their Atlantean homeland. No pyramids have yet been discovered in the Sahara, nor are any likely to be found there, because the wandering refugees from the late fourth millennium BC cataclysm that beset Atlantis probably recognized that the gradually desiccating conditions were increasingly unsuited to permanent habitation. During the late fourth millennium BC, the desert was winning its struggle over the retreating fertile plains, with a consequent decline in the herds of bison and cattle that once roamed its grasses.

But the passing Atlanteans left their mark here, too. Illustrations at Jabbaren and Aouanrhet, painted with the same red ochre the Egyptians used in their temple wall murals, show women wearing wreaths and headdresses identical to their Nile counterparts. The girls pictured with Egyptian facial features and blonde hair at Tassili-n-Ajjer, in the Oran Province of Libya, wear Egyptian robes, including Wadjet tiaras. Wadjet was a cobra goddess, protectoress of the Lower Nile. The figures are poised with worshipful gestures (their hands with raised palms in the Egyptian manner) before animal-headed deities commonly represented throughout the Nile valley.

Those portrayed most often are the lion, falcon and cow, which sports a lunar disc between her horns. In Egyptian religion, these beasts were Sekhmet, the goddess of fiery destruction associated by XXth-Dynasty Egyptians with the Atlantean disaster; Heru (or Horus), the god of kingship, personifying Pharaoh's royal soul; and Mehurt. This trio comprised a most ancient set in the Egyptian pantheon, all of them pre-Dynastic, and said to have arrived 'from the West'. Interestingly, Mehurt's name means, literally, 'the Great Flood.

The Pastoralists, as archaeologists have come to refer to these Atlanteans in transit across the Sahara, practiced deformation of cattle horns, a curious custom shared only with the Egyptians, and employed animal breeding procedures used along the Upper Nile. Dynastic Egypt itself began quite suddenly with the arrival of (as the pioneering British archaeologist, W.B. Emery, defined it) a 'Master Race' from the west. Known as the Semsu-Hr (the Followers of Horus), and the Mesentiu (the Harpooners), they came equipped with all the features of a fully developed civilization. Previous to their momentous arrival, the Nile valley was sparsely populated by Neolithic tribes of indifferent farmers and artless potters who dwelt in mud-thatch huts and eked out a subsistence living on the river banks. Their lands were changed virtually overnight by all the elements of a culture that had already witnessed a long period of development elsewhere.

According to the first-century-BC Greek geographer Diodorus Siculus:

The Egyptians themselves were strangers who in very
remote times settled on the banks of the Nile, bringing with
themselves the civilization of their mother country,
the art of writing and a polished language. They had come
from the direction of the setting sun, and were the most
ancient of men.

THE GREAT PYRAMID

The advanced society that rapidly took root in the sands of Egypt was not merely some transplanted civilization, however. It was instead the outcome of native cultures blending with the genius of the newly arrived Followers of Horus and the Harpooners. The outstanding feature of Egyptian civilization, of course, is the Great Pyramid at Giza, long known in Arab tradition as a 'repository for the wisdom of the world before the Flood'. Thorough investigators of this stupendous 'Mountain of Ra' have competently identified its Atlantean provenance. William Fix convincingly demonstrates that its internal chambers are places for 'rites of passage' and initiation into the mystery religion of the human soul's rebirth after death.

Alexander Braghine, among the best-informed investigators of Atlantis in the mid-20th century, stated very succinctly, 'In the solution of the problem of the origin of the pyramid builders is hidden also the solution of the origin of Egyptian culture and of the Egyptians themselves.' He was seconded by the noted French historian Serge Hutin:

> *Everything seems to indicate that the three pyramids of Giza – for the Great Pyramid is not the only one that should be considered in our inquiry – were left to the initiated Egyptian priests by the first antediluvian civilizers of Egypt, the Atlanteans.*

The Great Pyramid on the Giza Plateau was built as a co-operative effort between Egyptian residents, who formed the labour force, and Atlantean architects, in a successful effort to politically combine immigrants from the west with the native population through a shared public-works project. Hutin is at least fundamentally seconded by the eminent pyramidologist, Kurt Mendelssohn, who concluded that the monument was raised as a state-forming act that called upon the participation of the entire population in the cause of national unification. Placing its construction at the very beginning of Dynastic civilization, Mendelssohn believed its completion coincided with and actually brought about the creation of ancient Egypt.

THE DEITIES OF THE PYRAMID

Arab accounts told of a pre-Flood king, Surid, who was forewarned of the coming cataclysm and commanded to establish the Great Pyramid as a 'place of refuge'. His name is pronounced 'Shu-reed'. Shu, the Egyptian equivalent of Atlas, was likewise portrayed as a man supporting the sphere of the heavens on his shoulders. Perhaps the Arab Surid was actually the Egyptian Shu, the most Atlantean of all the gods. The same Arab writers reported that the Great Pyramid's grand architect was Thaut, the Egyptian god of literature and science, the divine patron of learning, keeper of the ancient wisdom. He was equated by the Greeks and Romans with Hermes and Mercury (sometimes Thoth), respectively, and these names are used interchangeably with Thaut in various traditions, Arabic and Western, describing the Great Pyramid's chief engineer.

Of all the deities associated with the structure, either astronomically or spiritually, the Egyptian Hermes is the most Atlantean. His surviving myth recounts simply that he arrived at the Nile delta before the beginning of Egyptian civilization, carrying with him a body of knowledge preserved on 'emerald tablets' from a flood that overwhelmed his homeland in the primeval sea. Other contemporary writers described Egypt as the "daughter of Poseidon", the sea-god creator of Atlantis.

THE GREAT SPHINX

The most famous anthropomorphic monument on earth, the Great Sphinx's earliest known name was Hu, or 'guardian'. The Greek word, *sphinx,* describes various elements 'bound together', referring to the human head atop its lion's body. Rain erosion appears to fix its creation to c.7,000BC, a conclusion both conventional scholars and Atlantologists find troubling; the former refuse to believe it dates before 2,600BC, while many of the latter are unable to envision an eighth-millennium BC Atlantis – Atlantean investigators find it improbable that they needed 6,400 years to reach Egypt in 3100BC after the destruction of their homeland around 9500BC. Whoever built the Great Sphinx, it was modified on several occasions over time. The head, for example, is clearly Dynastic, and may indeed have been sculpted around the period assigned to it by most Egyptologists. Its face could have belonged to Pharaoh Chephren, or Khafre, as they insist, although evidence suggests he did not build the Great Sphinx, but only restored it in the VIth Dynasty, when it was already centuries old. Who the original head or face depicted could not be determined after Khafre reworked it into a self-portrait.

At its inception, the monument more likely resembled a crouching lion. Although it may or may not have been constructed by Atlanteans, they were probably responsible for at least one of its modifications, if not its conception. As a lion, the Great Sphinx signified the constellation Leo, traditionally associated with heavy rainfall, even floods. As such, it suggests the immigration of Atlanteans after their homeland experienced extensive geological disturbances (see chapter 12) in 3,100BC, when they brought civilization to the Nile delta. Interestingly, the famous Dendera zodiac painted on the ceiling of a New Kingdom temple begins in Leo on the vernal equinox of 9,880BC. While this year is millennia before the suspected beginning of civilization in Egypt, it coincides roughly with the approximate if literal date for the florescence of Atlantis reported by Plato: 9,500BC.

WAR BETWEEN ATLANTIS AND EGYPT

Plato's *Timaeus* and *Kritias* are in large measure concerned with the Atlantean war that embroiled the Egyptians in a fight for their lives. That conflict was no philosophical allegory, but appears to have been personified in an actual historical figure. Ramses III was a XXth-Dynasty pharaoh who defeated the Meshwesh, or 'Sea People''s invasion of the delta in 1,190BC. He subsequently raised a great Victory Temple, Medinet Habu, to commemorate his success in the Lower Nile valley, West Thebes. On its walls he documented his military campaigns in incised illustrations and hieroglyphics. They still exist and document a serious attempt by Atlantean forces to subdue Egypt eight years after the capital of their island empire had been obliterated by a natural catastrophe in 1,198BC.

The wall texts explain that Sekhmet, the goddess of fiery destruction, 'pursued them like a shooting-star' and incinerated their homeland, which immediately thereafter 'vanished beneath the waves'. The Sea People's head city was referred to as Neteru, defining a sacred place; Plato likewise characterized Atlantis as 'sacred'. The Medinet Habu account is accompanied by various scenes from these events, including realistic representations of enemy warships and the Meshwesh themselves in various poses of defeat and captivity. They are the only portraits from life of Atlanteans made soon after their capital was engulfed by the ocean.

Ramses displayed his military genius and personal courage in terrible adversity. The navy of Atlantis had brushed aside Egyptian defences at the mouth of the Nile delta, and its troops of invading marines stormed ashore. They overcame all initial resistance to capture major cities, such as Busiris. Pharaoh withdrew his forces and regrouped, observing how the invaders advanced in common with their ships, which they relied upon for support. At the southernmost end of the Nile delta, he threw virtually all of his surviving naval units against the Sea People. Their vessels not only outclassed the much smaller Egyptian craft, but outnumbered them as well. On the verge of being overwhelmed, Ramses' warships suddenly turned and fled in retreat, with the whole invading fleet in hot pursuit.

SNATCHING VICTORY FROM THE JAWS OF DEFEAT

Ramses had his smaller vessels lure their cumbersome enemies into narrower, shallower areas of the river familiar to the Egyptian captains, but unknown to the Sea People. They suddenly found themselves unable to manoeuvre freely, and began grounding on undetected shoals. The Egyptians now plied the big warships with a barrage of fire-pots, just as thousands of archers suddenly appeared along the shore to launch unremitting flights of arrows at the outmanoeuvred invaders. Cut off from their floating supplies, the Sea People marines were routed up the delta towards its Mediterranean shores, where they disembarked in their remaining ships.

But the war was far from over. The invasion had consisted of a three-pronged attack from the north against the delta, westwards across Libya, and at the Egyptian colony of Syria, in the east. Infantry held the Libyan assault at Fortress Usermare, near the Egyptian frontier, until Ramses was able to bring up his forces, enduring almost annihilating losses in the process of defence, then rolled back the invaders, breaking their massed assault. The Pharaoh never spared a moment for celebration. He moved with great haste. Before they could affect a landing, he met the invaders on the beaches at Amor, where they suffered their final defeat. Ramses personally participated in this last battle, drawing his great bow against the invaders, as described in a passage from the wall texts at Medinet Habu. They make clear that the captive Sea Peoples were bound at the wrists behind their backs or over their heads, together with their allies, including Trojan War veterans from Libya, Etruria, Sicily, Sardinia and other parts of the Mediterranean. They had seen the Atlantean invasion as an opportunity for plunder, and had joined as profiteers. Thousands of these unfortunate prisoners of war were paraded before the victorious Ramses III and his court. After interrogation by his scribes, they were castrated, then sent to work for the remainder of their lives as slave labourers at the Tura limestone pits. Thus ended the imperial ambitions of Atlantis in the Eastern Mediterranean.

THE REEDS OF WISDOM

Atlantean defeat at the Nile delta was tragically ironic because the dynastic Egyptians themselves claimed descent from the 'sacred isle'. But the 2,000 years separating Ramses III from his ancestors who had migrated out of Atlantis across the Sahara had seen Egypt develop its own national identity. At least the priests of his time still knew of Aalu, the 'Isle of Flame', descriptive of a large, volcanic island in the distant west (the Atlantic Ocean). It physically matched Plato's Atlantis virtually detail for detail: monumental canals, luxuriant crops, a palatial city surrounded by great walls decorated with precious metals – all sheltering behind a ring of high mountains. Aalu's earliest known reference appears in *The Destruction of Mankind*, a New Kingdom history (1,299BC) discovered in the tomb of Pharaoh Seti-I, at Abydos. His city was the site of the Osireion, a subterranean monument to the Great Flood that his ancestors had survived by escaping to what would thereafter become Pharaonic Egypt.

On the other side of the world from Egypt, the Apache Indians of the American Southwest claim their ancestors arrived after a world-class deluge destroyed their homeland, still remembered as the 'Isle of Flame' in the Sunrise Sea, evocative of an active volcanic island in the Atlantic Ocean.

An even earlier rendition of Aalu reiterates connec-tions between prehistoric North America and Dynastic Egypt through Atlantis. In the so-called *Book of the Dead* – a collection of ritual funeral texts – Sekhret-Aaru is cited as the original homeland of both men and gods. They lived together in this resplendent kingdom on a 'Primal Mound' in the sea far to the West during the Zep Tepi, or 'First Time', during the ancient past. Sekhret-Aaru means 'field of reeds', a metaphor for widespread literacy, because reeds served throughout the Nile valley as writing instruments; hence, a field of reeds denoted a place of great wisdom. Over time, however, most of Sehkret-Aaru's human inhabitants became insufferably arrogant, considering themselves equals of the gods, who had taught them everything they knew. Unable to endure these mortal ingrates any longer, the divinities departed in the company of a few select men and women navigating a 'solar boat'. As they drifted towards the Eastern Mediterranean, Sekhret-Aaru sank with its flawed humans beneath the ocean. The solar boat eventually landed at the Nile delta, where its elite passengers disembarked to share their cultural advantages with local residents. Thus was born Egyptian civilization, according to the *Book of the Dead*.

Thousands of kilometres and years away, in Mexico, the

Aztecs claimed their ancestors came from a magnificent kingdom on an island across the Sunrise Sea (the Atlantic Ocean) in the distant east. Before Aztlan (Atlantis) was engulfed for ever by the waves, its flood hero, Quetzalcoatl, the renowned 'Feathered Serpent', sailed away with his followers – sorcerers, craftsmen, artisans, and scribes. Arriving at what is today Veracruz, on the coast of Mexico, they enlisted the co-operation of indigenous populations to build society anew, resulting in the establishment of Mesoamerican civilization.

Comparison of these two, seminal myths reveals their remarkably close parallels. Both obviously derived from a single source in the mid-Atlantic Ocean that could only have been Atlantis – a deduction broadly underscored by the phonetically evocative name of Quetzalcoatl's homeland: Aztlan. The connection achieves certainty, however, when we learn that Aztlan, like the Egyptians' Sekhret-Aaru, means 'field of reeds', likewise an Aztec metaphor for a realm of outstanding wisdom, as symbolized by the reed ink pen.

CHAPTER 8
EUROPE'S ATLANTEAN HERITAGE

'THE ANCIENT GREEK STORY OF EUROPA – THE MAIDEN FROM WHOM THE CONTINENT DERIVED ITS NAME – MAY CONCEAL AN ATLANTEAN HERITAGE AFTER ALL, BECAUSE IT TELLS HOW SHE ARRIVED HERE ON THE BACK OF A BULL FROM ACROSS THE SEA. OUR TRADITIONS HAVE IT THAT IRELAND'S EARLIEST KINGS WERE INITIATED IN BULL'S BLOOD, AS WERE THE MONARCHS OF ATLANTIS.'

KEVIN McVEIGH, PROFESSOR OF CLASSICAL LITERATURE, DUBLIN COLLEGE

Soon after Spanish archaeologists began excavating the ruins of an ancient metropolis outside and at least partially covered by Andalusia's modern city of Jaén, they were surprised not only by the prodigious extent of the buried site, but also its configuration, unlike any they had seen before. The pre-Classical urban centre had been laid out in concentric circles of alternating canals separating artificial land rings with a small central island big enough to accommodate a village, but more likely used as a sacred acropolis. The moats were of varying width and depth, larger as they moved out from the ceremonial centre.

Georgeos Díaz-Montexano, who has written extensively about this discovery beneath Jaén, reported that the innermost canal surrounding the central island is approximately 4 metres wide and 3 metres deep, while the next outer moats are, respectively, 13 metres and 22 metres across, and about 3 metres and 7 metres deep. He writes that the ruined bases of towers are spaced at regular intervals around the perimeter, their circular and semicircular designs similar to examples at another Andalusian location, the Neolithic fortress of Los Millares. The Jaén towers must have been particularly lofty affairs, judging from their broad foundations and the abundance of rubble resulting from their collapse. Díaz-Montexano was particularly surprised to observe that the entire archaeological zone displayed advanced construction techniques in the application of mortared stonework extensively combined with adobe brick.

THE SPANISH CITY OF RINGS

While mainstream scholars may be baffled by the subterranean find, its unmistakable resemblance to Plato's description of Atlantis is reinforced by more than the obvious physical comparisons. Carbon-14 testing of human skeletal remains found in the sixth canal helped to place the city's earliest construction between 2,470BC and 2,030BC, with a probable mean date of 2,200BC. As we shall see in chapter 12, this period coincides with the second global cataclysm of 2,193BC, which prompted a wave of immigration from Atlantis to Spain, where the Atlantean ruler cited by Plato, Gadeiros, established his allied kingdom. The Jaén location was badly damaged and entirely abandoned with great suddenness sometime before 1,500BC, about the time a third natural catastrophe swept around the world. Rebuilding began after 1,200BC when a new population took up residence – survivors, it would appear, from the final destruction of Atlantis in 1,198BC.

In its five artificial islands and six moats, the Jaén site incorporated the sacred numerals of Atlantis. Yet, it was not the first of its kind, but imported from outside. 'The plan did not develop gradually,' Florida Atlantologist Kenneth Caroli points out, 'but instead was present from the beginning, as if working from a known model since lost.' He was seconded by Díaz-Montexano, who wrote that:

> ... *the whole city was built with this model*
> *or original design from the first moment,*
> *as if its architects were already familiar*
> *with this circular concentric arrangement –*
> *which is apparent from the relative speed*
> *with which the city was built.*

The Romans knew this strange place as Auringis, from the Greek Ouringis, although neither Romans nor Greeks were its builders, and the meaning of its name is still doubtful. But Díaz-Montexano convincingly speculates that Auringis or Ouringis translates into 'city of the rings', from 'an ancient Indo-European word meaning, precisely, the "Ring".' Whatever its real meaning, the identity of Auringis as an Atlantean colonial centre is affirmed by that other Andalusian find of related significance, the Lady of Elche statue, found just 318 kilometres from the 'City of the Rings', where the portrayed woman may have lived and reigned. Despite the passage of millennia, the race associated with her mysterious city and statue may not have vanished entirely, but live on in a population group straddling the Franco-Spanish border. The American archaeological director Ellen Whishaw uncovered sufficient evidence to convince her that Andalusia was colonized by Atlantean imperialists. In fact, Cádiz has often been associated with Gadeiros, the Atlantean king cited by Plato.

MODERN-DAY DESCENDANTS OF ATLANTIS
The Basque people are the long-time inhabitants of the Pyrenees regions, where they were known to Roman historians as the Vascones. Basque folk tradition still speaks

of the Aintzine-Koak, literally, 'Those Who Came Before', their prehistoric forefathers, remembered as the inhabitants of 'Atlaintika'. They were supposed to have sailed from the sunken 'Green Isle', a powerful maritime nation that sank into the Atlantic Ocean after a terrible cataclysm, and from which a few survivors reached the Bay of Biscay, eventually bringing the holy relics of their mystery religion into the Pyrenees. 'Basque' is actually the English (and French) word used to describe a people who refer to themselves as the Euskotarak. They inhabit the Bay of Biscay in both France and Spain, including the western foothills of the Pyrenees.

Only about 1.25 million Euskotarak, or Basque, people live mostly in Europe, but also in communities in South and North America (particularly the state of Nevada). Stocky, with auburn hair and grey eyes, they are genetically distinct, although only marginally, from the French and Spanish. Racially, the Basque have been associated by some anthropologists with the pre-Indo-European people who occupied the western Mediterranean until the eighth century BC. If so, the Euskotarak may be the last direct descendants of Atlantis, and their atypical language is perhaps that which was heard in that lost world more than 3,000 years ago.

The Basque call their language Euskara. It is a totally

unique tongue, unrelated to any Indo-European speech. Strangely, Euskara shares some affinity with Finno-Urgic Patumnili (spoken in ancient Troy), Etruscan (belonging to the pre-Roman civilizers of western Italy), Guanche (spoken by the highly Atlantean inhabitants of the Canary Islands) and Nahuatl, the language of the Aztecs. These long-dead languages are themselves only very imperfectly understood today. But the fact that Basque Euskara contains legitimate comparisons with the languages of four identifiably Atlantean peoples is not without significance.

THE SACRED MOUNDS OF ATALIA

Perhaps the cognate most revealing in our investigation of Atlantis is 'Atalya'. It is the name of an ancient ceremonial mound in Biarritz, Basque country. 'Atalya' is also a sacred mountain in the valley of Mexico venerated by the Aztecs. 'Atalaia' is a site in southern Portugal featuring Bronze Age tumuli, or domed tombs, dating to the late period of Atlantean florescence, in the 13th century BC. 'Atalya' is also in Gran Canaria, where pyramids built by the Guanches in black, white and red volcanic stone – the same construction materials described for Atlantis by Plato – may still be seen. There is an additional link between the Basque and the ancient Canary Islanders: the Guanches practised a singular goat cult in rituals likewise observed in traditional Basque witchcraft.

The name 'Italy' derives from 'Atalia', when – according to Etruscan tradition surviving in Virgil's *Aeneid* – Atlas ruled there in prehistory. 'Italy' means literally the 'Domain of Atlas', whose daughter was Atlantis. Indeed, this seems to be the meaning of 'Atalia' whenever and wherever it was used, even by such widely diverse and otherwise unrelated peoples as the Basque, Guanches, Aztecs and Etruscans. The implication is obvious; namely, that all of them were impacted earlier in their histories by culture-bearers from Atlantis. It is clear that 'Atalia' carries the same connotation in Euskara, Nahuatl, Iberian and Guanche – the description of a sacred mound, mound-like structure or mountain. Moreover, 'Atalia' would appear derivative of Atlantis itself, where the holy mountain of Atlas was at the centre of the empire's mystery cult.

The 'Atalia' of the Basque, Aztecs, Iberians and Guanches was probably meant to commemorate, in word and image, the original sacred peak, Mount Atlas. No other conceivable connection could have linked such dissimilar and widely separated peoples as the Basque, Aztecs and Guanches, save through the intermediary culture of Atlantis, which stretched so far as to touch them all. To be sure, these peoples fell within the Atlantean sphere of influence.

CONNECTED BY LANGUAGE …

Incredible as it may seem, Euskara's resemblance to Nahuatl and certain North American Indian languages, particularly Algonquin-Lenape, is unmistakable. As the linguist Michel Farrar writes:

> *The fact is indisputable and is eminently noteworthy, that while the affinities of the Basque roots have never been conclusively elucidated, there has never been any doubt that this isolated language, preserving its identity in a western corner of Europe, between two mighty kingdoms, resembles, in its grammatical structure, the aboriginal languages of the vast opposite continent [America].*

Alexander Braghine, an outstanding Atlantologist who travelled the world in the 1930s, wrote:

> *When in Guatemala, I often heard about one Indian tribe living in the Peten district (northern Guatemala): this tribe speaks a language resembling Basque, and I have heard of an occasion when a Basque missionary preached in Peten*

in his own idiom with great success. As to the resemblance
of the Japanese and Basque languages, I once saw a list of
analogous words with the same significance in both tongues,
and I was stupefied by the quantity of such words. The word
iokohama, for instance, signifies in Basque 'a sea-shore city',
and everybody knows the great port of Yokohama, in Japan.

Presumably, some missing culture was the original source of that otherwise unaccountable relationship between the Basque and the native inhabitants of the New World, stretching even farther to Japan, probably through Atlantean contacts with Mu. Donnelly pointed out that one of the few Indo-European words derived from Euskara was *broncea*, or 'bronze':

The copper mines of the Basque were extensively worked at a
very early age of the world, either by the people of Atlantis,
or by the Basque themselves, a colony from Atlantis. The
probabilities are that the name for bronze, as well as the
metal itself, dates back to Plato's island.

... AND BLOOD

The Iberian link to other, often disparate peoples through Euskara is supported by a revealing genetic parallel.

This faithful restoration of a relief mural at the Victory Temple of Ramses III, at Medinet Habu, on the Upper Nile, depicts the attire of Atlantean 'Sea People' captured by Egyptian forces around the turn of the 12th century BC.

Lemuria's population was concentrated not in urban areas, but in ceremonial centres instead. Villages were typically clustered around religious monuments, signifying the spiritual focus of the Pacific Motherland.

Plato did not invent Atlantis as a utopian fantasy. Rather, close scrutiny of his account reveals that he cited Atlantis as an historical example to illustrate cycles in the rise and fall of civilizations.

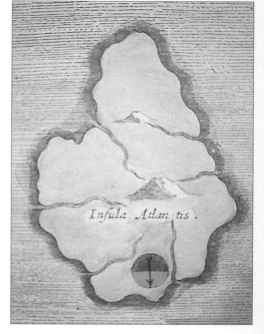

Insula Atlantis.

A copy of the oldest known map of Atlantis, found in the Vatican Library by Athanasius Kircher, 17th-century German genius. The original may have reached Rome from the Library of Alexandria, *c.*AD100.

A model re-creation (at the Oriental Institute, University of Chicago) of the Egyptian pyramid at Sakkara as it appeared c.2700BC. It incorporates variants of the Atlantean sacred numerals in its architectural design.

Edgar Cayce, the famous American psychic, was known as the 'Sleeping Prophet' because he described Atlantis and its crystal technology while in a trance state.

The 15th- to 16th-century mask of Tezcatlipocha, the Aztec-Miztec god of prophecy, made possible by his possession of a 'crystal mirror' that allowed him to glimpse future events.

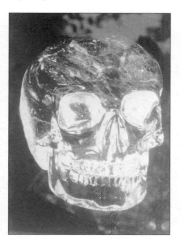

Is the Crystal Skull from Atlantis, where silicon technology was said to have attained levels of development not yet reached by us? To the Maya, it symbolized Ixchel, the culture-bearer of great wisdom from a sunken kingdom.

Detective Frank Domingo, forensic artist with the New York City Police Department, is responsible for this recreation of the original face of the Crystal Skull, based on anatomical data remarkably carved into the object.

This sculpted relief from Chichen Itza's Temple of the Warriors depicts the Maya goddess Ixchel with an upturned vase of descending water signifying the Great Flood that overwhelmed her Atlantean homeland.

El Carocol – the 'Snail', as the Conquistadors called it – was an observatory at Yucatán's ceremonial city, Chichen Itza. Its Maya builders claimed that astronomical science was introduced by a flood hero, Itzamna.

A Maya version of Atlas, the central mythic figure of Atlantis, supporting a glyph for 'heaven', as did his Greek counterpart. Plaster impression made from stone relief at the ceremonial centre of Coba, in Yucatán.

The Aztec Calendar Stone is a complex astrological computer. A quartet of squares at its centre contain symbolic images of four global catastrophes, the most recent one having been the Great Flood that destroyed Aztlan.

The 'Gilded Man', appropriately depicted in gold, escapes over the sea with his companions from the Atlantean destruction of their homeland to Colombia, where the Chibchan Indians honoured him as their founding father.

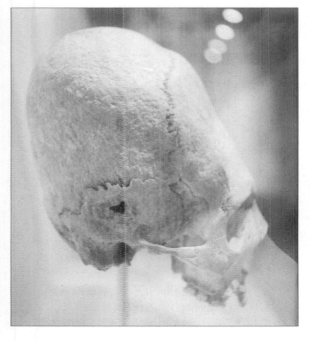

Inca royalty practised skull deformation to distinguish themselves from commoners and identify their descent from the Ayar-chaki, or 'Master Craftsmen', who escaped a natural catastrophe by sailing to South America during the remote past.

A deep-sea submarine equipped with state-of-the-art underwater cameras and side-scan sonar dives in the seas surrounding the Bahamanian island of Bimini, 90 kilometres east of Miami, Florida, in search of Atlantis.

Twenty metres down, a diver examines a boulder set upon its plinth at Isseki Point, near the Japanese island of Yonaguni, and amid other underwater ruins associated with the lost motherland of Mu.

The Basque exhibit a high percentage of O-group blood type, which is found in as much as 75 per cent of the population. Paul Lemesurier, author of *The Secret of the Great Pyramid*, points out that the lands where this blood type predominates include the Atlantic coasts of Western Europe and North Africa, the Canary Islands, and coastal areas within the Mediterranean Basin. This genetically defined area corresponds specifically with the territories Plato said were dominated by Atlantis. Lemesurier observes that the O-type blood group occurs as high as 94 per cent among exhumed mummies in the Canary Islands, where the Guanche language demonstrated an affinity with Euskara.

This extraordinarily high percentage was seconded by Stanley Mercer, an historian specializing in the Canary Islands. These genetic and linguistic ties between the Guanche and the Basque clearly define a closely related if not single people, both of whom preserved folk memories of the Atlantean catastrophe from which their common ancestors escaped: 'There was once a prodigious cataclysm in the course of which fire and water confronted each other,' so goes the Basque story of Atlaintika. 'But the majority of the Basque took refuge in caves and survived.'

THE GUANCHES OF THE CANARY ISLANDS

The Guanches cited above as Atlantean cousins of the Basque people were native inhabitants of the Canary Islands. 'Guanche' is a contraction of Guanchinerfe, or 'Child of Tenerife', largest of the islands. They were discovered by Portuguese explorers in the mid-15th century, but subsequently exterminated by the Spaniards through wars and disease. A few, far from pure-blooded Guanches may still survive, but their lineage is doubtful. Although their estimated population of 200,000 resided in most of the Canary Islands, they were concentrated on Tenerife, Gran Canaria, Fuerteventura, Las Palmas and Lanzarote. Tall, fair-haired and light-eyed, the Guanches were a white race that some modern investigators believe were the last examples of Cro-Magnon man.

The Guanches raised massive, finely crafted step-pyramids not unlike those in Egypt and Mesoamerica, though on a less colossal scale. Many of these structures were built of native volcanic tufa, pumice and lava stone, the same materials Plato described as the construction components of buildings in Atlantis. The Guanches' chief deity was Atlas, known to them as Ater. Variants of the name reflect the attributes by which he was known in Greece: Atamanm (Upholder of the Sky); Atara (Holy

Mountain), etc. Approximately 25 per cent of Guanche personal names began with 'At'.

The Guanches told the Portuguese that their islands were anciently part of a larger homeland engulfed by the sea, a cataclysm their fore-fathers survived by climbing to the top of Mount Teide, Tenerife's great volcano. Guanche oral tradition of this catastrophe concluded with the words, *Janega qyayoch, archimenceu no haya dir hando sahec chungra petut* – 'The powerful Father of the Fatherland died and left the natives orphans.'

As might be expected, the Atlantis story was preserved at the Canary Islands perhaps in far greater detail than even Plato's account before the imposition of Christianity. Perhaps the most revealing of all surviving material connecting the Canary Islanders to Atlantis is found in the *Tois Aethiopikes*, by Marcellus. In AD45, he recorded that:

… the inhabitants of the Atlantic island of Poseidon preserve a tradition handed down to them by their ancestors of the existence of an Atlantic island of immense size of not less than a thousand stadia [about 185 kilometres], which had really existed in those seas, and which, during a long period of time, governed all the islands of the Atlantic Ocean.

Pliny the Elder seconded Marcellus, writing that the Guanches were in fact the direct descendants of the disaster that sank Atlantis. And Proclus reported that they still told the story of Atlantis in his day, c.AD410.

Atlantis in the Canary Islands does not end with these ancient sources. Like the Atlanteans in Plato's account, the Guanches met for prayer by forming a circle around a sacred pillar with arms raised and open palm in the Egyptian manner. The Christians threw down all the pillars they could find, but at least one perfectly preserved specimen survived in the Barranco de Valeron, on Tenerife.

DOG WORSHIPPERS

The Canaries received their name probably sometime in the mid-first century AD from Roman visitors to the islands, who observed the inhabitants' worship of dogs (*canarii*) in association with mummification, two more ritual ties to the Nile valley, where dog-headed Anubis was a mortuary god.

But the islands also appear to have been so characterized five centuries earlier, when the Greek historian Herodotus wrote about the Kyneseii, who dwelt the farthest away of men, in the west, on an island beyond the Mediterranean Sea. 'Kyneseii' means 'dog-worshippers'. Centuries previous to the discovery of the Canary Islands by the Portuguese, there were medieval accounts of the Cynocephali, a dog-headed people living somewhere in the vicinity of northwest Africa.

In the Old Testament story of Japheth's son after the Flood, he:

> ... *abandoned the society of his fellow men and became the progenitor of the Cynocephalii, a body of men who by this name denoted that their intelligence was centered on their admiration for dogs.*

Following this line of thought we note that when men are represented as dog-headed one interpretation is that they are to be regarded as pioneers of human progress through hitherto untrodden ways. Dogs always played significant roles in Egyptian society. Herodotus describes how Egyptian males shaved their heads in mourning after the death of a family dog, just as they did for their fellow humans. In Book II of his *History*, he writes that the consumption of wine or bread, or any other food which happened to be in the house at the time of the animal's death, was not permitted. The wealthy had lavish tombs built specifically for their dogs. An entire sacred city, Cynopolis, was the centre of a canine cult reminiscent of the Canary Islanders, and the location of an immense cemetery for dogs, which were mummified and buried.

But there is no indication that the Pharaonic Egyptians themselves knew the Guanches ever existed. Numerous comparisons between them indicate diffusion from west to east, as Atlantean influences spread from the vicinity of the Canary Islands, across the Mediterranean and to the Nile delta in pre-Dynastic times. The persistence of mummification, dog worship, pyramid building, and so forth, among the Guanches centuries after these practices vanished from Egypt was a remnant from Atlantean epochs. The Canary Islands' 'Egyptian' cultural characteristics can be explained only by their origin in the Atlantic, not in the Nile valley, where they arrived later, c.3100BC. In other words, civilization spread to both the Canary Islands and the Nile delta from Atlantis. And it went much further, to the other, far side of Ancient Europe, on the Aegean shores of Asia Minor.

DARDANUS AND ELECTRA

In Greek myth Dardanus was the offspring of Electra – in other words, a son of Atlantis; his mother was an 'Atlantis' – a daughter of Atlas, his grandfather. As Virgil wrote in the *Aeneid* (Book VIII, 135–138), 'Dardanus, who was first father to our city, Ilium, and made her strong, was, as the Greeks relate, sprung from Electra, the daughter of Atlas.' She warned Dardanus of a coming deluge, and he fled to the northwest coast of Asia Minor. There he became the monarch of a new kingdom, Troy. The straits controlled by the Trojans were named after him, and are still known as the Dardanelles. The Trojans sometimes referred to themselves as 'Dardanians' to emphasize descent from their Atlantean fore-father. He gave them the Palladium, a sacred stone from Atlantis, as the centrepiece of the religion they revered until it was seized by the victorious Greeks in the Trojan War.

The historical myth of Dardanus signifies the arrival in Troy of culture-bearers from Atlantis following a major but not final natural catastrophe 5,000 years ago, which coincides with the earliest date or event horizon archaeologists find at Ilios, the Trojan capital.

The mother of Dardanus bears closer examination. Electra's myth bears commonality with those of her sisters, the Pleiades, in that they were mothers of culture-creators, who restarted civilization after the Great Flood. Interestingly, 'Electra' means 'amber', a medium for ornamentation much prized in the ancient world, but available from only two major sources: the shores of the

Baltic Sea, largely from what is now Lithuania, and the Atlantic islands of the Azores, Madeira and the Canaries. As Atlas has never been associated with the north, Electra's amber name and the Atlantic source for the mineral combine to reaffirm her Atlantean provenance.

Her connection to Asia Minor through Dardanus suggests the easternmost extent of Atlantean influence. The Trojans were nonetheless their own masters, despite ancestral origins in and a military alliance with Atlantis. Like Electra, the other Pleiades corresponded to important locations within the Atlantean empire or its sphere of influence. Her sister Taygete, for example, was actually a confederated Atlantean kingdom in the Canary Islands, as demonstrated by a Guanche province on the big island of Tenerife known as Tegueste. Plato relates that the forces of Atlantis occupied western Italy, where Oenomaus, son of the Pleiade Sterope, founded the Etruscan Pisae, better known today as Pisa. His father was Poseidon, the sea-god creator of Atlantis, who gave Oenomaus a victorious chariot, with which he founded the Olympiad. Thus, even our Olympic Games are steeped in Atlantean ancestry.

So, too, the names of Atlantean rulers listed by Plato were associated with various kingdoms that made up the imperial confederation. As he states in the *Kritias*: 'Each of the ten kings had absolute power in his own region and city.' In Iberia, for example, Elasippos was the original name, still used by the Phoenicians during Classical times, of Portugal's leading city, from which derived today's Lisbon, just as the Spanish Cádiz (known to the Romans as Gades) descended from the second king cited in the *Kritias*, Gadeiros.

In the British Isles, the Euaemon Plato mentions was Ireland's pre-Celtic flood hero, Eremon, while Bronze Age Britain's Atlantean king may have been Mestor because his name – literally, 'counselor' – perhaps referred to that astronomical computer, Stonehenge. The megalithic monument does, in fact, evidence several recognizably Atlantean features. The sacred numerals, five and six, incorporated in Atlantean architecture recur throughout Stonehenge, and the structure itself echoes the concentric city plan of Atlantis itself. Stonehenge was first laid out by 3000BC, began to reach the apex of its construction 1,500 years later, and was suddenly discontinued around 1200BC. Thus, its development, use and abandonment parallel Atlantean immigration at the close of the fourth millennium BC, the zenith of Atlantis as the foremost Bronze Age civilization, and final destruction in 1198BC.

CHAPTER 9

LEMURIANS AND ATLANTEANS IN NORTH AMERICA

'... THESE LEGENDS AND CARVINGS ON THE
TOTEM POLES STRONGLY CONFIRM THE FACT
THAT THE FOREFATHERS OF THOSE INDIANS
CAME FROM MU ...'

COLONEL JAMES CHURCHWARD, *THE LOST CONTINENT OF MU*

Of gigantic proportions, North America's two effigy earthworks were referred to by early pioneers who travelled across the southern part of Wisconsin during the 1830s as the 'Man Mounds'. Both represent a water spirit that led the Wolf Clan ancestors of the Winnebago, or Ho Chunk Indians, to safety in North America after the Great Flood.

GIANTS IN HORNED HELMETS

One of the geoglyphs still exists, although in mutilated form, on the slope of a hill in Greenfield Township, outside Baraboo. Road construction cut off his legs below the knees around the turn of the 20th century, but the figure is otherwise intact. The giant is 65 metres long and 10 metres across at his shoulders. His anthropomorphic image is oriented westwards, as though striding from the east, where the Deluge was supposed to have occurred. His horned helmet identifies him as Wakt'cexi, the flood hero.

The terraglyph is no primitive mound, but beautifully

proportioned and formed. Increase Lapham, a surveyor who measured the earthwork in the mid-19th century, was impressed: 'All the lines of this most singular effigy are curved gracefully, and much care has been bestowed upon its construction.'

A companion of the Greenfield Township hill figure, also in Sauk County, about 50 kilometres to the northwest, was drowned under several fathoms of river by a dam project in the early 20th century. Ironically, the water spirit that led the Ho Chunk ancestors from a cataclysmic flood was itself the victim of another, modern deluge.

The Atlantean identity of Wakt'cexi as materialized in his Wisconsin effigy mounds is repeated in an overseas counterpart. The Wilmington Long Man is likewise the representation of an anthropomorphic figure – at 95 metres, the largest in Europe – cut into the chalk face of a hill in the south of England, about 65 kilometres from Bristol, and is dated to the last centuries of Atlantis, from 2000 to 1200BC. Resemblances to the Wisconsin earthwork grow closer when we learn that the British hill figure was originally portrayed wearing a horned helmet, obliterated in the early 19th century.

A third man terraglyph is located in the Atacama desert of Chile's coastal region. Known as the Cerro Unitas Giant, it is the largest in the world at 120 metres in length. It, too, wears a horned headgear, but more like an elaborate rayed crown.

The Old and New World effigy mounds appear to have been created by a single people representing a common theme; namely, the migration of survivors from the Atlantis catastrophe led by men whose symbol of authority was the horned helmet. Indeed, such an interpretation is underscored by the Atlantean 'Sea People'; invaders of Egypt during the early 12th century BC, when they were depicted in the wall art of Medinet Habu wearing horned helmets.

DESCENDANTS OF MU

The Mesoamerican, Andean and North American Indians were rich with accounts of light-skinned visitors from across the sea, who arrived following a terrible flood, and stayed on to rebuild civilization in co-operation with the native peoples. In what are today Southern California's coastal areas from San Jose to San Diego resided the Chumash Indians. Traditions of the Great Flood from which their ancestors arrived, combined with their surprising Caucasoid characteristics and prodigious seamanship, clearly define them as a people apart on the North American continent.

More specifically, they used several variants of the word 'Mu' in referring to Southern California's offshore islands, such as Santa Barbara, which the Chumash called by the provocative name of 'Limu'. 'Mu' was also used by them to describe things related to the sea and village sites, such as Pismu, today's Pismo Beach.

In southern New Mexico, the Navajo preserve a flood legend with distinctly Lemurian details, such as the gradual but inexorable encroachment of the waters upon the land of a former people whose spirits now reside in a great 'lodge' at the bottom of the sea. Navajo sand paintings esoterically contain descriptions of this event and its migrational consequences. It might seem strange that a people living so far inland from the ocean would perpetuate such information, until we learn that the Navajo are relative newcomers to the southwest, having arrived there only some 300 years ago from their ancestral homeland along the British Columbian shores of the Pacific northwest, facing the direction of lost Lemuria.

MAZE STONES AND SWASTIKAS
An artefact of that post-flood migration is the Hemet Maze Stone, a grey boulder emblazoned with the intricate design of a labyrinthine maze enclosed in a 1.7-metre square. The

petroglyph is located on a mountainside just west of Hemet, California, some 145 kilometres southeast of Los Angeles. Accumulation on its surface of a light patina known locally as 'desert varnish' suggests the incised carving was executed between 3,000 and 4,000 years ago, despite the insistence of mainstream archaeologists, on tenuous physical evidence, that it could be no more than a few centuries old.

About 50 such maze stones have been identified throughout Orange, Riverside, Imperial and San Diego counties, and at least 14 examples of labyrinthine rock art are known in the remote area of Palm Springs. All of them have been found within 240 kilometres of each other, and virtually every one is rectangular, although varying in size from 10 centimetres to 1 metre across. They are invariably located on boulder-strewn mountainsides, and are perhaps the remnants of a pilgrimage route dedicated to commemorating a seminal event in the deep and distant past.

The maze itself is in the form of a swastika, a sacred symbol for numerous Native American tribes across the continent. Among the Hopi Indians, the hooked cross signifies the migration of their tribe from the east following a great flood that overwhelmed early humankind. Although it is not known if Hopi forefathers actually carved the Hemet

Maze Stone, the Atlantean significance of their ancestral myth is suggested by its westward oriented design. These implications are complimented by a late 15th-century example of Mexican featherwork in a similar, swastika-like design (with reversed orientation, however) belonging to a transparently Atlantean figure in Mesoamerican myth, Chalchiuhtlicue: 'Our Lady of the Turquoise Skirt' was the Aztec goddess of death at sea.

Hopi sand paintings, spiritual devices for the removal of illness, are often formed into swastikas, with the patient made to sit at its centre. In the bottom-left corner of the square outline of the Hemet Maze Stone is a simple, much smaller, reversed or right-oriented hooked cross, known in Buddhism as the *sauvastika*. Both swastikas and *sauvastikas* are common images throughout Asia, where they denote Buddha's right and left foot, respectively, and refer to his missionary travels throughout the world. On the Hemet Maze Stone it symbolizes the waxing and waning of lunar change coinciding with the coming and going of tribal migrations and/or sacred proselytizing. As such, the Buddhist *sauvastika* and California petroglyph appear to share a parallel symbolism that both Asians and ancient Americans may have received independently from a common source. James Churchward, the best-known writer on lost Mu, stated that the swastika was the Pacific civilization's pre-eminent emblem. He referred to it as the 'key of universal movement', a characterization complementing both Hopi and Buddhist symbolism.

KHURA KHOTA

Churchward believed that Lemurian colonizers and missionaries sailed east from their Central Pacific homeland, as well as west. They arrived, he said, in what is now the Gobi Desert before its ecological transformation. There, they built an imperial state known as the Uighur empire, which dominated parts of Asia between the mid-eighth and ninth centuries AD, before a natural disaster of some kind destroyed its chief city. Churchward's sources lay entirely within the Hindu monastery libraries he was privy to in the 1870s. Unfortunately, these sources have never been published because of the secrecy imposed on him by the religious authorities.

But material evidence of a sort was uncovered in 1906, when an American archaeologist named Robert McClelland excavated the historically ancient city of Khura Khota in the Gobi Desert, south of Lake Baikal. The bottom level of Khura Khota, McClelland found, was resting on a stratum composed of boulders, gravel and sand between 12 and

15 metres thick. Digging further to determine the full depth of apparently catastrophic debris, he unexpectedly encountered the ruins of another city, which Churchward believed could only have been the Uighur capital, and 'thus geologically confirming the fact that a destructive cataclysm had passed over and buried the capital city. It also confirms the legend that the capital city was destroyed by a flood'.

That a natural catastrophe should have no less thoroughly obliterated the Uighur empire than Mu or Atlantis underscores the violent geology of our planet. If better known examples extinguished the Roman cities of Pompeii and Herculaneum, or the pre-Toltec civilization of Cuicuilco, south of Mexico City, then surely those same geological forces could have similarly overwhelmed older cultural centres in other parts of the world.

That natural cataclysms have triggered mass migra-tions of peoples beyond the geographical limitations imposed on them by mainstream science has long been the argument of largely independent scholars. A burgeoning richness of physical evidence supports these so-called 'diffusionist' researchers, who believe the Americas were impacted by numerous peoples from various parts of the world millennia before Columbus. And accumulating proofs on behalf of cultural diffusion as it pertains to the Americas clearly show

how Atlantean influences predominated in the early or formative periods of pre-Columbian civilizations.

THE EPOCHS OF NORTH AMERICAN PREHISTORY

In fact, archaeologists define four major epochs in North American prehistory, with numerous subdivisions. The earliest, the Copper Culture, belongs to Louisiana's Poverty Point, with its numerous Atlantean features (importation of Michigan copper, concentric layout, incorporation of the sacred numerals, religious use of crystals, etc.), in 1500BC, and its sudden florescence three centuries later. These time parameters coincide perfectly with the imperial period of Atlantis and its final destruction.

The second period is known, for lack of any other name, as the Adena, which began about 3,000 years ago with the erection of great stone mounds. It was followed by the Hopewell about 200BC, when complex earthworks and bizarre effigy mounds appeared throughout the Ohio valley. With the inexplicable disappearance of the Hopewell around AD400, a dark age, during which the civilized achievements of the Adena and Hopewell cultures were neglected, overlaid North America until the tenth century. Then the Mississippi Culture flourished from Wisconsin to the Gulf of Mexico in great cities with colossal temple mounds, but had mostly collapsed 300 years before the arrival of modern European in the 16th century.

ATLANTEAN INFLUENCES IN THE PRE-COLUMBIAN ERA

Plains Indians did not live in individual homes. They dwelt as extended families in communal structures, sometimes known as longhouses, such as those erected by various coastal tribes of the Pacific Northwest, or, more usually, in tepees. However, residents behind the great stockaded walls of Mississippian cities in west-central Illinois (Cahokia) or southern Wisconsin (Aztalan) did indeed occupy individual homes of baked clay (the so-called 'Aztalan brick') and thatch, large enough for one immediate family only. It was, in fact, their agricultural abilities that most fundamentally distinguished them from the outside world of the Plains Indians, who were not farmers but hunters, and traded raw meat for the mound builders' harvested crops. The pre-Columbian cities of Illinois's Cahokia, with Monks Mound greater at its base than Egypt's Great Pyramid, or Wisconsin's Aztalan, a ceremonial centre for astronomer priests, were built by these agriculturalists, whose lineage extended back to Atlantis.

Indeed, virtually every Indian tribe throughout the

Americas has its own account of a great flood from which their forefathers arrived in a new land. Versions told by indigenous peoples who dwelt in the east – the Oneida, Cherokee, Mohawk, etc. – describe a violent catastrophe sometimes associated with a celestial event, such as a comet or meteor, while natives west of the Mississippi River – the Navajo, Tlinget, Haida, etc. – speak of a less sudden but inexorable inundation of ancestral territories. This disparity is appropriate because it accurately reflects two different disasters: Atlantis perished 'in a single day and night', as Plato wrote, when its volcanic mountain collapsed into the sea. But the lands of Mu succumbed over a period of months or years to a more gradual process that even left several Lemurian structures standing intact, off the coast of Okinawa.

Perhaps the most overtly Atlantean influence in North America was found among the Mandans of North and South Dakota, where their *O-kee-pa* ceremony was personally witnessed and documented by the great American portrait painter George Catlin, in the early 19th century. He reported that the *O-Kee-Pa* was an annual commemoration of the Great Flood, in which the Mandans painted their skins white to mimic their ancestors, who arrived from over the Atlantic Ocean in a powerful vessel symbolized in the ceremony by a large, wooden ark positioned at the centre of the village. Moreover, the Mandans were racially dissimilar from neighbouring tribes, sometimes evidencing grey eyes, fairer complexions and brunette hair, particularly among the youth. Catlin concluded they were mixed descendants of Madoc a Welsh prince who supposedly vanished over the sea 1,000 years ago. The Welsh theory does not explain the Mandans' cultural obsession with the Great Flood, however, and all points of comparison originally believed to connect them to Madoc's people have long since been discounted. More likely, the Mandans preserved a ceremonial memory of their Atlantean heritage.

Prehistoric influences reached Californian shores from a Pacific civilization, as well. Historical writer Vada Carlson points out that 'The Kootenay Indians of Washington and British Columbia have a legend stating that their forefathers came to America from "The Land of the Sun". "Land of the Sun" and "Empire of the Sun" were common names of Mu before its submergence.' The Pacific Northwest features a majority of native folk traditions describing ancestral arrivals from the lost motherland.

ANCIENT MYSTERIES PRESERVED

Churchward appears to have correctly interpreted the destruction of Mu from recurring features on several so-called 'totem poles' raised by Canada's Haida Indians of British Columbia. These tall, carved pillars of wood do not actually function as totems because the animals often portrayed are not worshipped. Instead, they are memorial or heraldic devices that preserve and relate in images the mythic-historical past of a particular household or tribe. Sometimes, an eagle attacking a whale is symbolically used as a kind of heraldry to designate the earliest beginnings of a family, whose current members can boast that their ancestors arrived along the Pacific Northwest coast after the flood that destroyed their tribal homeland.

Churchward affirmed that at least some of these 'totem poles' symbolically depict the demise of Mu (the whale) brought about by the judgement of the Great Spirit (the eagle). Their common supposition is strongly suggested by the totem pole's internal evidence. For example, the Haida still speak of the 'Steel-Headed Man', their founding father, who arrived on the shores of Canada after a flood caused when the whale, Namu, was killed by a sky god, the Thunderbird.

North America's 'cliff dwellers' were the Anasazi, or the 'Ancient Enemies', as they were known to the Jicarilla Apaches, Navajo, Southern Paiute and other southwest tribes. Beginning about 100BC, the Anasazi built cities high up in the recessed areas of mountains or in remote valleys, such as Colorado's Mesa Verde. Although their immediate origins are obscure their *kivas* – circular ceremonial structures – embodied numerous features of the Omphalos religion practiced in Atlantis. The Omphalos, or 'Navel of the World', was an egg-shaped stone that served as the central ritual object of a mystery cult focusing on the principle of human immortality via reincarnation. From origins in Atlantis, it spread with the Atlantean diaspora of survivors fleeing the natural catastrophe that shattered the Bronze Age, sending them east as far as Delphi, and west across the Americas. There, this 'Navel of the World' was represented by a natural cave or a subterranean temple signifying the sacred centre of existence. In this sanctified precinct, rituals for the eternal rebirth of the human soul were enacted. Perhaps like no other building of its kind to have survived from prehistory, the *kiva* typifies these esoteric principles first enumerated in Atlantis.

The Anasazi (or, at any rate, their shamans) might have had some Atlantean blood still flowing through their veins, and were able to preserve the old mysteries. Or they may have learned them from an even earlier people who had come into direct contact with adepts from Atlantis. In any case, more than 1,000 years separate Atlantis's final destruction from the moment the Anasazi began building their *kivas* and cliff dwellings.

Plato describes the Atlanteans as great miners and metalsmiths whose national wealth largely depended on the world's highest-grade copper to produce extraordinary bronze; he refers to this superior metal as 'orichalcum'. Little known to the general public is North America's greatest archaeological enigma; namely, the excavation of at least half a billion pounds of copper ore in a stupendous mining enterprise that began suddenly in the Upper Great Lakes Region of the Michigan Peninsula about 5,000 years ago. Although the identity of these prehistoric miners is unknown, Menomonie Indian tradition remembers them as the 'Marine Men', white-skinned bearded foreigners who sailed out of the East.

Coincidental with the Michigan operations, the Old World Bronze Age began; high-grade copper, never in plentiful supply throughout Europe, combined with zinc and tin for the production of bronze. Both the American copper mining and the Old World Bronze Age came to a sudden halt in 1200BC. That is also the date for the final destruction of Atlantis, which lay between both continents.

CHAPTER 10
MIDDLE AMERICA'S ATLANTEAN HERITAGE

'THE WORLD WAS FLOODED AND THE SKY FELL UPON THE EARTH. WHEN THE DESTRUCTION AND ANNIHILATION HAD BEEN ACCOMPLISHED, THE SPIRITS OF THE BACAB BEGAN TO ARRANGE THE PEOPLE OF MAYA.'

THE MAYA *CHILAM BALAM* (CHAPTER V)

THE OLMECS

The Mexican civilizations confronted by modern Europeans in the 16th century were still Bronze Age-like cultures, unchanged for millennia and essentially frozen in time since their inception. The 16th-century Aztecs were culturally no further advanced than the Olmecs, who preceded them by 30 centuries. Like the ‑‑s and Toltecs, their societies were less unique than ‑‑‑‑ ‑n a Mesoamerican theme common to them all.

‑‑gest quality of Mesoamerican civilization ‑‑‑ ‑ its appearance. For at least 20,000 ‑‑‑ ‑‑populated by disjointed tribes ‑‑‑ ‑l level of culture did n‑‑ ‑s and a f‑‑

Olmec, although it is a name of scientific convenience only, as the real identity of these earliest culture-bearers is not known. Where before there had been savagery, the Olmecs introduced literacy, sculpture, monumental architecture, a complex religion, advanced textile production, astronomy, calendrics, commerce, social stratification, systems of weights and measures, divisions of labour, metallurgy, standardization of the crafts, government, and every aspect of a full-blown civilization. It did not develop in place slowly over centuries, but appeared all at once in its entirety, as though suddenly imported from somewhere outside Mexico.

This impression is heavily underscored by the numerous representations of persons from other parts of the world surviving in Olmec sculptural art. These unequivocally portray non-Amerindian faces, including bearded men with Near Eastern features and Asians bearing strong resemblances to modern Cambodians, together with West Africans depicted in colossal stone heads sculpted from black basalt.

Around 1200BC, the Olmecs experienced an abrupt surge in population and reached the height of their influence. Thereafter they entered into a slow decline, eventually merging into the next stage of Mesoamerican civilization.

THE MAYA

The Mayas arose in the Lowland Yucatán about 400BC, and, although clearly derivative of the Olmecs before them, they developed their own distinctive culture of city-states. These were all built on a common general plan, but no two were alike, and styles varied enormously, resulting in a civilization of great colour and originality. Long assumed to have been a people of peaceful astronomer-priests more interested in the heavens than in mundane affairs, recent translation of the Mayan glyphs paints a completely different portrait.

The Maya city-states were entangled in ceaseless warfare with each other, and grabs for power were common. They also engaged in human mutilation and sacrifice, although not on the terrific scale achieved much later by the Aztecs. Despite their relentless battles for ascendancy, the Mayas achieved prodigious feats of astronomy, accurately computing, for example, the precise position of a certain star 1,000,000 years ago. Strangely, it was this advanced astronomy that was their undoing. The Mayas became so enamoured of science that they made it their religion. Although they worshipped a pantheon of various gods, they were all subordinate to the Great God of Time, who ruled the entire universe. Everything and everyone had to obey him, and no sacrifice was too great for his favour. So,

CHAPTER 10
MIDDLE AMERICA'S ATLANTEAN HERITAGE

'THE WORLD WAS FLOODED AND THE SKY FELL
UPON THE EARTH. WHEN THE DESTRUCTION AND
ANNIHILATION HAD BEEN ACCOMPLISHED, THE
SPIRITS OF THE BACAB BEGAN TO ARRANGE THE
PEOPLE OF MAYA.'

THE MAYA *CHILAM BALAM* (CHAPTER V)

THE OLMECS

The Mexican civilizations confronted by modern Europeans in the 16th century were still Bronze Age-like cultures, unchanged for millennia and essentially frozen in time since their inception. The 16th-century Aztecs were culturally no further advanced than the Olmecs, who preceded them by 30 centuries. Like the Mayas and Toltecs, their societies were less unique than variations on a Mesoamerican theme common to them all. Perhaps the strangest quality of Mesoamerican civilization was the suddenness of its appearance. For at least 20,000 years, Middle America was populated by disjointed tribes of hunter-gatherers, whose material level of culture did not extend beyond the most primitive weapons and a few crude tools. Then, in 1500BC, a sophisticated, powerful civilization erupted into existence full blown on the Atlantic and Pacific coasts, spreading rapidly throughout much of Mexico.

Archaeologists refer to this first American civilization as

Olmec, although it is a name of scientific convenience only, as the real identity of these earliest culture-bearers is not known. Where before there had been savagery, the Olmecs introduced literacy, sculpture, monumental architecture, a complex religion, advanced textile production, astronomy, calendrics, commerce, social stratification, systems of weights and measures, divisions of labour, metallurgy, standardization of the crafts, government, and every aspect of a full-blown civilization. It did not develop in place slowly over centuries, but appeared all at once in its entirety, as though suddenly imported from somewhere outside Mexico.

This impression is heavily underscored by the numerous representations of persons from other parts of the world surviving in Olmec sculptural art. These unequivocally portray non-Amerindian faces, including bearded men with Near Eastern features and Asians bearing strong resemblances to modern Cambodians, together with West Africans depicted in colossal stone heads sculpted from black basalt.

Around 1200 BC, the Olmecs experienced an abrupt surge in population and reached the height of their influence. Thereafter they entered into a slow decline, eventually merging into the next stage of Mesoamerican civilization.

THE MAYA

The Mayas arose in the Lowland Yucatán about 400BC, and, although clearly derivative of the Olmecs before them, they developed their own distinctive culture of city-states. These were all built on a common general plan, but no two were alike, and styles varied enormously, resulting in a civilization of great colour and originality. Long assumed to have been a people of peaceful astronomer-priests more interested in the heavens than in mundane affairs, recent translation of the Mayan glyphs paints a completely different portrait.

The Maya city-states were entangled in ceaseless warfare with each other, and grabs for power were common. They also engaged in human mutilation and sacrifice, although not on the terrific scale achieved much later by the Aztecs. Despite their relentless battles for ascendancy, the Mayas achieved prodigious feats of astronomy, accurately computing, for example, the precise position of a certain star 1,000,000 years ago. Strangely, it was this advanced astronomy that was their undoing. The Mayas became so enamoured of science that they made it their religion. Although they worshipped a pantheon of various gods, they were all subordinate to the Great God of Time, who ruled the entire universe. Everything and everyone had to obey him, and no sacrifice was too great for his favour. So, when the astroncmer-priests determined that the Lord of Time desired the end of their civilization, the Mayas, as a whole people, dutifully abandoned all their cities en masse around AD900.

Of the daughters of Atlas – the seven Pleiades – one name is particularly evocative: Maia. Atlantologists find her philological identification with the ancient Maya of Yucatán irresistible. And well they should. Yucatán's first city, Mayapan – from which the people derived their name – was founded by Chumael-Ah-Canule, the 'First after the Flood', according to *The History of Zodzil*, a 16th-century collection of Maya oral traditions. He escaped the Hun Yecil – the 'Drowning of the Trees' – that engulfed Patulan, his kingdom on a large island across the Atlantic Ocean.

Another Maya source, the *Chilam Balam*, told of those who followed close behind him:

> … *the wise men, the Nahuales, the chiefs and leaders, called U Mamae (the Old Men), extending their sight over the four parts of the world and over all that is beneath the sky, and, finding no obstacle, came from the other part of the ocean, from where the sun rises, a place called Patulan.*
> *Together these tribes came from the other part of the sea, from the east, from Patulan.*

Resemblances between the Mayan Patulan and the Greek Atlantis, philological and otherwise, are self-evident.

CEREMONIAL CITIES OF THE MAYA

The story of the *Chilam Balam*'s Nahuales was graphically depicted on a sculpted temple frieze running around the top of the so-called Acropolis at the Guatemala ceremonial city of Tikal. The frieze was a portrayal of significant events in the history of the Maya up to the close of the ninth century, when the site was abandoned. The frieze began with the image of a man rowing his boat away from an island hurling its city into the sea during a volcanic eruption, while a corpse floats on the waters in between him and the doomed Patulan.

When Teobert Maler, the great Austrian archaeological photographer and explorer, found the Tikal frieze, he exclaimed, 'Until that moment, I dismissed Plato's Atlantis as nothing more than a Greek fantasy. But now I know he told the truth.' Given Maler's early 20th-century discovery and the event it depicts, correspondences between the Middle American Maya and the Atlantean Maia are as valid as they are enlightening.

Like the later Aztecs, who claimed ancestral descent from the lost volcanic island kingdom of Aztlan in the Atlantic

Ocean, the Maya spoke of a great flood that drowned most of the Bacabs. These were white-skinned rulers who (similar to the Atlantean kings described by Plato) held up the sky, as so many Atlases. Atlas representations of the Bacabs may still be seen at the famous Maya ceremonial centre in Yucatán. Chichen Itza, where the sculpted relief profile of a full-bearded man with Near Eastern facial features appears at the far western end of the great ball court. On the walls inside the shrine atop Chichen Itza's Pyramid of the Feathered Serpent are the likenesses of four bearded Bacabs signifying the four cardinal directions, as they support the sky. They wear a large conch shell on their back, identifying their maritime origins, and offer a more European profile.

Around the year AD900 the Mayas abandoned their cities in Yucatán en masse because their strict adherence to a ritual calendar, which literally ran their lives, informed them through their astronomer-priests that the moment had come to disperse. Theories in the form of self-destructive agricultural practices, earthquakes, wars, etc., to fathom the abrupt closure of the Mayas' city-states, have always been inadequate explanations for their universal collapse and disbursement, which was actually brought about by themselves in obedience to their deified science.

What became of the Mayas is more enigmatic than why they lost their civilization. Most fanned out into the jungle, where they regressed into primitivism. Another contingent of Mayas journeyed northwards along the coast of the Gulf of Mexico, up the Mississippi river, until they came to what is now Collinsville, Illinois, on the shores opposite St Louis, Missouri. Still others moved into northern and northeastern Mexico, where subsequent generations called themselves 'Toltecs', and evolved a distinct, highly militaristic culture that flourished into the early 14th century.

The Maya that ended up on the shores opposite present-day St Louis established a great population centre that archaeologists have named Cahokia after a local historic tribe. Trade goods flowed into Cahokia, including bear claws for ritual purposes from the Rocky Mountains in the west, to the shores of the Carolinas in the east for decorative mica; with copper from the Upper Peninsula of Michigan, and conch shells from Florida. These neo-Mayas brought with them the same all-commanding sacred calendar that continued to regulate their existence. After two centuries of prosperity, its interpreting priests ordered them to abandon Cahokia, just as they had previously relinquished their city-states in Yucatán.

FROM AZTALAN TO TENOCHITLAN

Cahokia's astronomer-priests sailed the Mississippi, Rock and Crawfish rivers into southern Wisconsin, where they built Aztalan – a 21-square-hectare ceremonial city – in AD1200. True to their abilities, this new city was a scaled-down virtual replica of Cahokia, and served as their home, an observatory and trade centre for the next two centuries.

Also known as the 'Place Near Water', Aztalan was complete with its own temple mounds surrounded by three enormous walls interspersed with two-storey watchtowers. The city was also an important hub of commerce that supplied all of Mesoamerica with copper mined from the Upper Great Lakes Region, from around AD1100 to 1300. Excavated from Aztalan were pottery shards decorated with the sacred spiral motif, the emblem of Chicomoztoc, which signified a newborn infant's spiral descent from the womb.

The Maya were only one of several peoples – all of whom venerated founding fathers from Atlantis – who at one time held sway from the Rio Grande in the north to the Isthmus of Panama in the south. The Aztecs who dominated Middle America long after Mayan power ebbed away and until the Spaniards arrived in the early 16th century claimed two separate origins: one recent; the other ancient.

Archaeologists believe they entered the valley of Mexico as a small tribe from the north around AD1320, a conclusion already preserved by the Aztecs themselves. This far northerly location was Chicomoztoc, or the 'Place of the Seven Caves'. The name also refers to high-grade copper and the eternal womb or navel of the world from which the seven clans that made up the Aztecs emerged. Both these elements are prominent features of Aztalan.

Five kilometres west of Aztalan lies Rock Lake with its stone pyramids lying at regular depths of 19, 12 and 7 metres beneath the surface of the water. Formerly a necropolis, or 'city of the dead', its 10 kilometres of shoreline are covered with innumerable burial mounds and effigy earthworks. Rock Lake was the Aztecs' more recent point of origin – Chicomoztoc.

Over many centuries, a powerful river running just north of Rock Lake – hardly more than a pond – spilled into its surrounding valley, raising water levels and drowning its man-made monuments. In the midst of a severe drought, both the ceremonial centre and its nearby sacred lake were abandoned. Exacerbating climate hardships was the sudden collapse of the copper trade, when sufficient deposits were discovered in Central Mexico by Toltec miners in the early 14th century. Thereafter, the Aztalaners lost their monopoly on this precious metal. Razing their ceremonial centre to the ground, these proto-Aztecs then made the long trek south to Mexico, where they built their city, Tenochitlan. Within a few generations, it had grown to become the capital of their empire and the ultimate ceremonial centre of Mesoamerican civilization.

With its surrounding man-made lake, bisecting canals and Atlas-like Temple of Ehecatl at its very centre, Tenochitlan was designed to impress upon everyone in ancient Mexico that the Aztecs were the direct descendants of the Feathered Serpent, who entrusted them with hereditary absolute power to govern Middle America. National capitals, then and now, were engineered chiefly for political reasons, foremost among them being the psychological subjugation of opponents. From Tenochitlan, the Aztecs followed the example set by their Atlantean forebears by launching imperialistic wars, which soon resulted in the empire they sought.

Just two centuries later, however, the Aztecs were themselves annihilated by the Spanish Conquest. How only 200 conquistadors could so thoroughly bring down an entire empire of millions cannot be explained merely by the superiority of European firearms. Long before the Spaniards set foot on Mexican shores, the Aztecs had been psychologically disarmed by millennial legends of a white-skinned, bearded visitor, who arrived over the sea from the east and, with his followers, founded Mesoamerican civilization. The Aztecs were never entirely sure if this man who called himself Hernán Cortés was not, in fact, the same, sacred culture hero, or his direct descendant. Paralysed by uncertainty, they were unable to effectively resist the invaders, despite their huge numerical advantage.

BETWEEN THE OCEANS

In this grand pattern of mass movements from south to north, and south again, we may perceive the ritual calendar at work, and the fundamental unity of all Mesoamerican cultures. In effect, and for all their individual differences, the Aztecs were the most recent development of the Toltecs and Mayas – indeed, of all the peoples which preceded them going back to the Olmecs 3,000 years earlier.

Long before these far-flung continental migrations over thousands of miles and many centuries, the Aztecs traced their deepest origins not to America, but to a vanished island across the Sunrise Sea, their name for the Atlantic Ocean. Their founding fathers were culture-bearers from far away Aztlan (not to be confused with the much-later Aztalan, although the name of the Wisconsin city may have derived from the older, ancestral location).

While Atlantis was the dominant formative influence in Middle America, it was also impacted by culture-bearers from Mu. Mexico's geographical location between the Atlantic and Pacific oceans made her a focal point for this other seaborne civilization. It seems credible, then, that they both played important roles in the early development of Mesoamerica, and even interacted with one another.

The Lemurians were already long-time residents on the American continent, where their less aggressive folk character worked perhaps more subtly, but no less effectively, transforming civilization into that curious, even bizarre mix of styles and elements peculiar to Mesoamerica, yet so suggestive of themes from both Asia and Europe. It was, in fact, this strange blend of sometimes inimical forces from both Atlantis and Mu with native cultures that resulted in a series of related societies that still mystify investigators today.

They wonder, for example, how this people could create a sophisticated astronomical computer, the famous Calendar Stone, or write poetry of high sensitivity, while conducting human sacrifice, in which 20,000 human victims at a time had beating hearts ripped from their chests. The perpetrators of such ritual atrocities were the Aztec elite, who used mass murder to overawe and thereby control the darker-skinned masses of labourers.

Mesoamerican histories recorded that human sacrifice had been outlawed by the bearded Feathered Serpent, but the practice was reinstated after his overthrow. Chichen Itza's Temple of the Warriors, the scene of so many gruesome acts, is decorated with a sculpted line of bearded Atlantean figures – all representing Kukulcan, the Feathered Serpent – supporting a representation of the sky. Atlas, the central mythic image from whom Atlantis derived its very name, was portrayed in Greek art as a bearded titan supporting the sky on his shoulders. The Feathered Serpent was also portrayed in temple art wearing a large conch shell, emblematic of his unparalleled sailing ability.

On the other side of the world, the *uraeus* was a badge of authority worn by ancient Egyptian royalty; it comprised the image of a cobra combined with the features of a vulture – literally, a feathered serpent. Although the *uraeus* signified the unity of Upper and Lower Nile in the person of the Pharaoh, the Egyptians themselves claimed that all their sacred regalia had been handed down from the gods after they left Sekhret-Aaru sinking in the Distant West.

The Aztecs claimed ancestry from Aztlan, portrayed in their birch-bark illustrations as a volcanic island to the east. It is apparent that the Egyptian Sekhret-Aaru and the Aztec Aztlan both refer to Plato's Atlantis, and the migration of her peoples, east and west. Thus understood, the supposedly 'Near Eastern' faces depicted in Olmec art are really the portraits of Atlanteans who established a large colony in Mexico. So, too, the 'Cambodian' features of other Olmec sculpture actually belong to Lemurians who exerted an important but less imperial influence on early Mesoamerica.

Indeed, the impact made by visitors from Lemuria, though still visible in the cultural and archaeological landscape, was neither as profound nor as widespread as changes made by their Atlantic Ocean cousins. That Mexico, with its geographical halfway position between Atlantis and Mu, was touched by both these maritime civilizations is hardly surprising.

A BLENDING OF RACES

The seafaring skills of the ancients combined with ocean currents acting as maritime highways to render America a meeting ground of diverse peoples long before the arrival of 16th-century Spaniards. Although Atlanteans were the first and formative of the civilized races to impact the American continents, they were followed by visitors from Bronze Age and Classical Europe, medieval North Africa and the Near East, Asia and India – centuries, even millennia, before Columbus. For example, Vada F. Carlson, author of *The Great Migration*, writes that:

> *Siguenza y Gongora, a Mexican of the 17th century, may have been correct when he made the statement that all Indians of the New World were descendants of Poseidon (ruler of Atlantis) and that Poseidon was a great-grandson of Noah.*

One wonders what led Siguenza y Gongora to conclude that the natives of Mexico were descendants of Atlantis. It is conceivable that he heard oral traditions of Aztlan recited by native shamans.

Such ancestral traditions were, in fact, still being recounted in the 17th century by the last Aztec survivors of the Spanish Conquest. Siguenza y Gongora quoted local Indian accounts to the effect that they had white-skinned people living among them thousands of years before the Spaniards set foot on the beach at Mexico. This would seem to contradict James Churchward, who wrote that prehistoric Mexico was the recipient of a brown-skinned race from the 'lost continent'. But there is no fundamental disagreement between Siguenza y Gongora and Churchward because white-skinned Atlantean culture-bearers represented only a fraction of all the pre-Columbian peoples, comprising, as they did, the ruling aristocracy of early Mesoamerican Civilization, known in Maya times as the Pilli. Even the conquistador leader Hernán Cortés remarked on the lighter complexion and auburn hair of the Aztec Emperor Moctezuma II and his imperial family members.

Some of the brown-skinned residents were possibly Lemurians, but the vast majority of natives who supplied the manual labor were certainly Amerindians. They developed their own racial identity over at least 20,000 years following migration out of Mongolia, across a long-since collapsed (or engulfed) land bridge spanning the Bering Strait.

FOUR CATASTROPHIC EPOCHS

Perhaps the best-known Aztec image belongs to one of their foremost scientific achievements. The so-called – and misnamed – Calendar Stone is not a 'calendar', but an astrological almanac erected on public display near the centre of the capital city, Tenochitlan, to forecast propitious and unfavourable days for specific activities. It simultaneously embodied the destructive aspect of time in the divine personification of Tonatihuh, the solar god depicted at its centre. The four major epochs, or 'Suns', which divided the past and preceded the present age, were all world-class disasters. They surround Tonatihuh, each in their own square, containing identifying images.

Paralleling the Bronze Age's four global cataclysms identified by scientists in 1997 at the Fitzwilliam College symposium, the Aztecs likewise believed in a quartet of worldwide catastrophes that pushed humanity to the brink of extinction before the present age, or 'Sun'. The first of these involved a deadly confrontation with the animal kingdom, which was only narrowly defeated with the loss of most human beings. This first Sun, known as 4-Ocelotl, or 'Jaguar', was commemorated in its own symbolic square on the famous Calendar Stone, and depicts a ferocious cat. Although the Aztecs flourished until the 16th century, their belief in 4-Ocelotl was undoubtedly a traditional concept understood by previous cultures, including the Toltecs and Mayas, if not the Olmecs, and, like the sophisticated astronomy that went into creating the Calendar Stone, went back to the origins of Mesoamerican civilization.

Also featured on the same Stone is 4-Atl, or 'Water', a Great Flood, from which the yellow-bearded founding father,

Quetzalcoatl, or the 'Feathered Serpent', arrived to initiate civilization in Middle America. This most recent epoch appears on the Calendar Stone as a pyramid being engulfed by a deluge of water falling from an overturned bucket. It was from this last catastrophe that Quetzalcoatl arrived.

These disastrous former epochs were presented to remind the Aztecs that, should they fail to live in accordance with the will of heaven, they could expect another exterminating cataclysm. The ancient European civilizations had already vanished 2,800, 1,400 and 1,000 years before the Aztecs came into existence. The Aztecs had been quick-frozen in an ancient past, and were culturally unchanged since their Olmec progenitors of 30 centuries before.

EHECATL AS THE GOD ATLAS

Tenochitlan's Temple of Ehecatl constituted wonderful evidence for the Atlantean heritage of Mesoamerican civilization perpetuated by the Aztecs at their chief city. As a manifestation of the Feathered Serpent culture-bearer, Ehecatl's temple in Tenochitlan was supposed to be a re-creation of the original he left behind at the volcanic Atlantic island of Aztlan. The Aztec version was a pyramid of five concentric steps, painted red, white and black, and situated at the absolute centre of the city, indicating its primal significance. Inside was enshrined a statue of the god envisioned as a man supporting the sky on his shoulders. In Plato's description of Atlantis in his *Kritias*, the city was designed in concentric rings, in which five was incorporated in Atlantean architecture as a sacred number. He reports that the chief building materials were red, white and black stone, resulting in virtually the national colours of Atlantis.

As though all of this did not draw Ehecatl and Atlas closer together, both the Aztec and Greek immortals were revered as founders of astrology. There is even a philological comparison between Ehec*atl* and *Atl*as. That the Aztecs consecrated their ancestral origins from Atlantis at the most sacred site in their most important city seems clear. In truth, one of the entering conquistadors (Cieza de Leon) outwardly compared the Aztec capital to Atlantis!

LEMURIAN INFLUENCE ON MESOAMERICAN CIVILIZATION

If not as profound as Atlantean contributions, Lemurian influences on Mesoamerican cilivizations – the Olmec, Maya and Aztecs etc – were not without enduring effect, particularly in Zac-Mu-tul – literally, the '(White) Man of Mu-tul'.

According to the Maya, he founded the city of Mu-tul after arriving in the company of fellow 'magicians' over the sea from the west. Both his name and that of the city he built clearly express that these were culture-bearers from the Central Pacific motherland, which was almost identically remembered as Mu-tu in Tahiti and Mu-tu-hei throughout the Marquesas. The Mayas' Mu-tul not only exhibits an important connection stretching thousands of kilometres westwards into Polynesia, but also suggests that Zac-Mu-tul named the city after his Pacific homeland.

Sometimes cited with Churchward on the subject of Mu in Mexico, August Le Plongeon was certainly the outstanding Mayanist of his day (the late 19th century). Unfortunately, however, subsequent research has found him incorrect in many of his basic translations and suppositions, especially as presented in his book, *Queen Moo and the Egyptian Sphinx*. The most fundamental of these was his misinterpretation of the Troano codex as an historical chronicle. It is, in fact, a treatise on the mystical interpretation of signs or portents. Dr Le Plongeon was nonetheless correct in detecting at least a few elements of ancient catastophism described in the document, which do indeed refer in passing to the Halach-Unicob – 'Lords', 'True Men', the 'Lineage of the Land', 'Great Men', or 'Priest-Rulers' – ancestors of the Maya, who landed at Yucatán from Tutulxiu, a radiant kingdom far across the Atlantic Ocean, long since swallowed by the sea.

THE TURQUOISE LORD AND LADY

More certain connections between Mu and pre-Columbian Mexico are found in Xiuhtecuhtli, the 'Turquoise Lord', also known as Huehueteotl, the 'Old God', in Nahuatl, when he assumed his incarnation as the Aztecs' oldest deity. A ubiquitous figure encountered throughout Mesoamerica, he was portrayed in numerous statues and figurines as an aged man seated in a lotus position, while wearing headgear stylized to mimic an incense burner. In this, he greatly resembled other immortals 5,313 kilometres southwest across the Pacific Ocean from the coast of Oaxaca, where this fire god's earliest known shrines were located.

Like the *moai*, or colossal statues of tiny Easter Island – originally known as Te-Pito-te-Henua, the 'Navel of the World' – representations of Xiuhtecuhtli emphasize his extended navel. A pre-Hispanic manuscript, the codex *Fejérváry-Mayer*, states that Xiuhtecuhtli 'dwells in the centre of world', a position reaffirmed by the emblems adorning his hat: crosses with circular mid points. So, too,

Easter Island's *moai* are topped with *pukao*, great turbans fashioned from red volcanic rock: tufa.

Usually depicted with a red or yellow face, Xiuhtecuhtli wears a chin beard, a curious anomaly for the god of a beardless people. His untypical head suggests foreign origins, as does his wife, Chalchiuhtlicue, the Aztec 'Lady of the Turquoise Skirt'. A sea goddess from 'watery Aztlan', she was portrayed in temple art seated on a throne, around which men and women were shown drowning in huge whirlpools. The *Florentine* codex identifies her husband with sunlight and resurrection, the same theme encountered among the protruding bellies of Easter Island's monumental statues, some of which were engraved with solar symbols. Perhaps the union of Xiuhtecuhtli with Chalchiuhtlicue signified the 'marriage' of spiritual concepts in Mesoamerica, respectively, from Mu and Atlantis.

BASALT COLUMNS

Another Pacific relationship found in ancient Mexico was uncovered in its first city. Founded around 1600BC – coincidental with the third and penultimate cometary catastrophe of the Bronze Age – the Olmec capital at Vera Cruz was partially built with columns averaging 9,000 kilograms each from basalt quarried at Punta Roca Partida, on the Gulf coast north of the San Andres Tuxtla volcano more than 80 kilometres away. How so much stone was moved successfully over challenging terrain baffles conventional scholars, convinced that the Olmec were ignorant of the wheel and possessed only primitive tools. The ancient construction engineers nonetheless shaped the basalt into numerous flawless pillars for their most important sacred architecture in an archaeological zone referred to today as 'Complex A', where the Olmec's 30-metre-high pyramid and other foremost structures are located.

The only other city in the world made of basalt columns lies 11,270 kilometres across the Pacific Ocean, off the small Caroline Island of Pohnpei. Built in the water over a submerged coral reef, Nan Madol originally comprised 250 million tons of prismatic basalt. According to today's Micronesian residents, this astounding site was constructed during the ancient past by a pair of twin sorcerers from Kanamwayso, a splendid kingdom, whose people very long ago exercised great 'magical' powers, and sailed throughout the Pacific. Falling stars and earthquakes set Kanamwayso aflame and sank it to the bottom of the ocean, where it is still inhabited by the spirits of those who perished in the cataclysm, and preside over the ghosts of all persons who perish at sea.

Clearly, this Western Pacific tradition of Kanamwayso is the folk memory of cataclysmic events that afflicted Lemuria during the late 17th century BC, when some of its intellectual elite sailed away from the natural disaster to make landfall along the Mexican shores of Oaxaca, where they initiated Mesoamerican civilization. Only such a conclusion can account for the remarkable, even unique similarity between basalt city construction at Vera Cruz and Nan Madol, separated as they are by nearly half the globe.

The arrival of these transoceanic culture-bearers who replanted their arts and sciences, politics and religions from both Atlantis and Mu/Lemuria may explain how, when and why civilization suddenly sprouted from nothing in Mexico. To be sure, the resultant growth was a hybrid of introduced novelty and native influence, featuring elements of both in a unique synthesis – the same process that formed Egyptian civilization (see chapter 7). But the materially advanced newcomers formed a governing aristocracy not only of the Olmecs, but also of every subsequent Middle American society, including the Mayas, Toltecs and Aztecs, as witnessed by the bearded, and decidedly un-Amerindian physical characteristics of Moctezuma II, the last Aztec emperor, who proudly traced his lineage directly back to the Feathered Serpent.

Over time, the ruling elite endeavoured to preserve its distinct identity, despite inevitable crossings with native peoples. Only this original racial disparity can account for the significant differences that existed between the Indian masses and their monarchs. All pre-Columbian civilizations were a mix of outside forces from the Atlantic and Pacific upon native cultures, a mixture of influences made all the more varied by much later, occasional visitors, either shipwrecked or deliberate, from Carthage, Rome, West Africa, Ireland, China and Japan.

CHAPTER 11

FROM ATLANTIS AND LEMURIA TO SOUTH AMERICA

'THE PARAGUAYAN AND BRAZILIAN
GUARANYS POSSESS A CYCLE OF LEGENDS
CONCERNING THEIR NATIONAL HERO,
TAMANDUARE, WHO, WITH HIS FAMILY,
WAS THE ONLY SURVIVOR SPARED BY THE
CATASTROPHE WHICH DESTROYED "THE CITY OF
THE SHINING ROOFS".'

ALEXANDER BRAGHINE, *THE SHADOW OF ATLANTIS*

Musaeus was the fifth monarch of Atlantis listed by Plato. Although we learn nothing further about the king, his name has long intrigued investigators, who believe it hints of an Atlantean colony in Colombia. 'On the common interpretation of mythic traditions,' observed the late 19th-century British writer J.S. Blackett, 'these Atlantides ought to be provinces or places in South America.' His suspicions were not unfounded, as native tradition indicates.

BOCHICA – SUPPORTER OF THE SKY

Occupying the high valleys surrounding Bogotá and Neiva at the time of the Spanish Conquest, the Chibchans were an indigenous people who revered the memory of their founding father, Muyscas-Zuhe – so much so, that they additionally referred to themselves as the Muysca in his honour. They believed that he was born in the 'Gilded One', a prosperous kingdom situated on an island far out into the Atlantic Ocean, where Bochica, a fair-skinned giant with a long beard, supported the sky on his shoulders. Growing tired of this burden, Bochica accidentally dropped it one day, causing the Earth to be consumed in flames, then deluged after a great flood.

In the midst of this worldwide cataclysm, Muyscas-Zuhe escaped from his homeland before it was engulfed by the sea, eventually landing on the shores of Colombia. There, he shared the high wisdom of his lost birthplace with the Chibchans, who knew him as the 'Civilizer', and the 'White One'. After teaching the Indians how to live in an organized society, Muyscas-Zuhe departed for the distant Andes Mountains to bring similar enlightenment to the Incas' ancestors. Before leaving, he appointed a quartet of select chiefs to govern through his authority and example. According to the Chibchan-Muyscas, after the global fire and flood, Bochica reassumed his burden of the heavens, which he continues to support, but still causes earthquakes whenever he shifts the weight on his shoulders.

That Muyscas-Zuhe's story could only be the Colombian Indian version of Atlantis is made transparently clear in the numerous fundamentals it shares with Plato's account. Bochica is self-evidently the first king of Atlantis, Atlas, depicted in Greek myth as a bearded titan holding up the sky. Aside from this conspicuous comparison, it seems otherwise impossible for a dark-skinned, beardless people isolated from the outside world to have imagined a bearded, white giant causing a global conflagration. The event Bochica unleashed was the same cometary disaster that triggered the Atlantean Deluge, just as Muyscas-Zuhe's oceanic kingdom was identically overwhelmed.

THE 'GILDED ONE'

This natural catastrophe was, in fact, commemorated by the Chibchans in their most important ceremony. Their Catena-ma-noa meant, literally, the 'Water of Noa', with a striking resemblance to the Old Testament flood hero, Noah. To demonstrate his lineage from Muyscas-Zuhe during the Catena-ma-noa, each newly installed Zipa – the Chibchan chief – personified the sunken homeland by entirely coating his naked body in gold dust applied with sticky resin. He then jumped into the waters of Guatavita, a sacred lake outside Bogotá. The trailing gold dust that washed off during his dive signified the riches of the 'Gilded One' lost at sea. The Zipa was then mantled in a blue robe, recalling the azure raiment worn by the kings of Atlantis, as described in Plato's dialogue.

These overtly Atlantean details associated with Guatavita are reinforced by the site itself. The lake is an astrobleme, a crater caused by a meteor fall, since filled with water. Although the geological date of its formation is uncertain, the impact that created Guatavita is concurrent with cometary events responsible for the destruction of Atlantis, as mirrored in the Chibchan's Catena-ma-noa and story of the Gilded One. In other words, the Indians recognized the crater-lake as a result of the same celestial catastrophe memorialized in their 'Water of Noa' ritual.

Muyscas-Zuhe's arrival on Colombian shores signifies the civilizing mission of flood survivors to the 'Opposite Continent', a conclusion underscored by the very names of the players involved: in the Chibchan language, the honorary tribal name chosen by the Indians was Muysca, or the 'Musical Ones', just as Plato's Atlantean king Musaeus, in Greek, means 'Of the Muses': divine patrons of the arts, from which our word 'music' derives.

OTHER SOUTH AMERICAN FLOOD HEROES

The native Colombians were not alone in their celebration of Atlantean influences. Venezuela's Orinoco Indians told 16th-century Spanish friars that Shikiemona, the sky god, long ago caused the 'Great Water', a worldwide flood, to

249

drown the first humans, who had transgressed his sacred laws. Sharing pre-Columbian Venezuela with the Orinoco were the Carib Indians. They recalled the story of Amaicaca, their own deluge hero who escaped the natural catastrophe in a 'big canoe'. It settled at the top of Mount Tamancu after the floodwaters receded.

Along Brazilian coasts, the Ge-speaking Indians spoke of Mai-Ra, the 'Walker', or 'Maker', the last and former king of the 'Land without Evil'. Because its inhabitants had not lived up to his high standards of morality, he set the island on fire, then sank it beneath the sea. As these calamities were transpiring, Mai-Ra departed the doomed 'Land Without Evil' with a small fleet of survivors, chosen for their unpolluted virtue. Eventually, they landed on the Atlantic shores of South America, where they interbred with native peoples to sire the present Indian races, who learned the arts of medicine, agriculture and magic from Mai-Ra.

In the Mataco flood myth, Argentine Indians of the Gran Chaco describe 'a black cloud at the time of the flood that covered the whole sky. Lightning struck and thunder was heard. Yet the drops that fell were not like rain. They fell as fire.'

Among the Maidu Indians of the eastern Sacramento Valley and foothills in northeastern California, and Pomo

Indians residing on the California coast north of the greater San Francisco Bay area, Kuksu was the creator of the world, who long ago set it afire with celestial flames in response to the wickedness of mankind. Before the entire earth was reduced to a burnt-out cinder, he extinguished the conflagration with an awful deluge.

The Paraguayan Indian version of the Feathered Serpent (see chapter 10) – the fair-haired, bearded leader of fellow survivors from the 'Place of the Sunrise' who brought civilization to the peoples of Mexico – was known as Zume, with whom we return full circle to Colombia. Zume's obvious philological and narrative resemblance to the Chibchans' Muyscas-Zuhe demonstrates the broad scope of the impact made on pre-Columbian South America by what must have been immense waves of immigration from Atlantis. But their greatest influences were among the continent's most famous people – the Incas.

THE WHITE MAN OF THE SEA FOAM

Like Mexico's Aztecs, the Incas were the last manifestation of a culture that preceded them by thousands of years and under different appellations. Although the term today is generally accepted as the name of a specific people and characterizes a whole civilization, 'Inca' originally applied only to the ruling aristocracy of blood-related individuals belonging to the same royal family that ruled Peru in the 15th and 16th centuries AD. In his conversations with the Spaniards, Emperor Atahualpa made a clear distinction between his Inca elite and 'those Indians', the Peruvian masses.

Scholars have long wondered what could have caused such a profound racial cleavage among a pre-Spanish people. The Incas themselves offered a straightforward explanation. They claimed direct descent from a foreigner, At-ach-u-chu, who arrived in Bolivia long ago. He was described as a tall, red-haired, bearded fair-skinned traveller from the east who landed on the shores of Lake Titicaca after surviving some terrible deluge. His indigenous hosts called him the 'Teacher of all Things', who founded the arts of civilization in the Andes, including agriculture, religion, astronomy, weights and measures, social organization and government.

At-ach-u-chu was the oldest of five brothers, the Viracochas, or 'white men', and was himself more often referred to by his title, 'White Man of the Sea Foam', Con-tiki-Viracocha. 'Sea foam' appears to have been a poetic description of the wave at the bow of his ship that brought him over the sea following a disastrous flood that drowned his homeland. As archaeological support for this aspect of his myth, some investigators point to submerged structures high in the mountains of Bolivia. The ruins were found on the bottom of Lake Titicaca, 23 metres below the surface, just off the port city of Puerto Acosta. They comprise a long pier or jetty (perhaps 100 metres long), with stone columns and massive walls.

Lake Titicaca's underwater site was investigated by the famed oceanographer Jacques Cousteau during the late 1970s, when it was photographed for the first time, although little research has been conducted there since. The sunken structures are obviously very ancient, perhaps the oldest physical evidence for civilization in the Andes. The features may have been inundated when some major geological upheaval tilted Lake Titicaca in the same seismic disturbance that drained the shoreline away from Tiahuanaco, a nearby pre-Inca city.

HOLES FILLED WITH SACRED WATER

Intriguing as the underwater find may be, Andean culture indicated a different source. The name of the Inca progenitor, At-ach-u-chu, appears derivative of Atcha, a variant of Sekhret-Aaru's 'Field of Reeds' remembered by the ancient Egyptians as a far-off, splendid but vanished city echoing lost Atlantis. At-ach-u-chu could mean, then, the 'Man from Atcha (Atlantis)'. Indeed, At-ach-u-chu's myth places his birth in Yamquisapa, a rich and powerful island kingdom in the Atlantic Ocean sunk to the bottom of the sea after having been set on fire with a 'celestial flame' for the idolatry of its sinful inhabitants. This event was remembered as the *Unu-Pachacuti*, or 'World Over-Turned by Water', a natural catastrophe of global proportions. It was commemorated at the Ushnu, a deep hole formerly located at today's Plaza de Armas, the main plaza in Cuzco, Peru, the Incas' capital and own 'Navel of the World'. Offerings of water, milk, fermented cactus juice, beer and other precious liquids were poured down the Ushnu at the centre of a ceremonial area, the Haucaypata. It was into the Ushnu that the waters of the Unu-Pachacuti supposedly drained after the arrival of At-ach-u-chu. The hole was also regarded as an entrance to the sacred underworld.

The ancient Etruscans of western Italy attached an identical significance to holes dug into ground at the exact midpoints of their cities, such as Tarquinia and Populonia. Each hole was a *mundus*, where holy water commemorating the Deluge was ritually deposited. The same kind of subterranean offerings were made at the Greek Hydrophoria and by the Phoenicians at Hierapolis, in Syria. Among the Anasasi, Hopi and other native peoples of the American Southwest, ritual players in an ancestral ceremony were doused with water, as they tried to climb out of an underground chamber known as a *kiva*. They symbolized the 'emergence' of survivors from the Great Flood (see chapter 9).

The vast cultural and geographical differences separating the Inca, North American Indian, Etruscan, Greek and Phoenician participants in these sacred dramas contrast with their close similarity, which may be explained only in terms of an actual experience shared independently, but in common, by them all.

WAVES OF NEWCOMERS

The Incas' Unu-Pachacuti cited three global cataclysms separated by many centuries, and each one spawned migrating populations of newcomers to South America. First were the Ayar-manco-topa, flood survivors who landed on Peru's northern coast, where they built the earliest cities, raised the earliest pyramids and other monumental structures understood applied mathematics, cured illnesses with medicines and surgery, and instituted all the cultural features for which Andean civilization came to be known. The Ayar-manco-topa correspond to an epoch in

Andean archaeology known as the Salavarry period, when South American pyramidal platforms with rectangular courts appeared along the coastal regions of northern Peru, around 3000BC. This time frame coincides with the sudden appearance of other civilizations in the Nile valley, the Indus valley, Ireland's Boyne valley, Mesopotamia, and Asia Minor, all sparked by masses of displaced Atlanteans fleeing the ravages of a killer comet.

Long afterwards, a second wave of foreigners appeared in South America. These were the Ayar-chaki, or 'Wanderers', led by Manco Capac and his wife, Mama Ocllo. They established a 'Flowering Age' in the Andes, when these 'Master Craftsmen' built Tiahuanaco about 3,500 years ago. Indeed, radiocarbon testing at the Bolivian ceremonial centre yielded an early construction date of +/-1,600 BC.

The third and last wave of foreign immigration into prehistoric South America belonged to the Ayar-aucca, a 'Warlike People', veterans of failed military campaigns in the Eastern Mediterranean, and survivors from the final destruction of Atlantis, in 1198BC. Their Atlantean identity is confirmed by the Incas themselves. They described the original Ayar-aucca as four twin giants who held up the sky, just like the Greek Atlas. But they eventually grew tired of their exertions on behalf of an ungrateful humanity, and let it fall into the sea, creating a worldwide deluge that destroyed most of humankind. One of the Ayar-aucca arrived in Cuzco, where he transformed himself into a *huaca*, or sacred stone, but not before mating with a local woman to sire the first Inca. Henceforward, Cuzco, known as the 'Navel of the World', was the capital of the Inca empire. The Ayar-aucca is the self-evident Peruvian rendering of the Bronze Age Atlantis catastrophe incorporated into the Incas' imperial foundation myth.

Remarkably, the Incas' 'World Overturned by Water' appears to have had a connection to a European medieval manuscript. First published in the mid-19th century, the originally handwritten *Oera Linda Bok* was the venerable heirloom of a Frisian family compiled from a medieval oral tradition with roots in an even more remote period. Although sceptics dismissed it virtually sight unseen as a hoax, general condemnation of 'The Book of What Happened in the Old Days' was inspired more by a refusal to review its unusual contents than for the usual academic considerations.

The *Oera Linda Bok* tells of the origins of the Frisian peoples on a volcanic island, Atland, and their subsequent migrational history after its destruction. A brief passage mentions one of their leaders, who led his followers over the

Atlantic Ocean into the west, and was never heard of again. Some researchers conclude that this Frisian sailed to South America, eventually arriving at Lake Titicaca, where he established the Andean civilization that bore his name: Inka.

THE CHILDREN OF MU

While cultural evidence on both sides of the world affirms an Atlantean impact on the formation of Andean civilization, Lemurian influences played no less seminal a role, as might be expected, given Peru's Pacific coastline. In the Chimu version of the first flood migrants, for example, the Ayar-manco-topa were led by King Naymlap, who landed with his followers in 'a fleet of big canoes'. The Chimu were a pre-Inca people who raised a powerful civilization, Chimor, that dominated the Peruvian coast from c.AD900, until their defeat by the Incas during the late 15th century.

The capital, Chan-Chan, lies just north of Trujillo, and was founded, according to Chimu historians, by Taycana-mu. He had been sent on a culture-founding mission by his superior, 'a great lord from across the sea', who ruled a kingdom in the Pacific Ocean. Tayacana-mu founded the city of Chan-Chan.

The so-called 'Palace of the Governor' at Chan-Chan – the city founded by Tayacana-mu – features a wall decorated with a frieze depicting a sunken city: fish swimming over the tops of linked pyramids. Colonel James Churchward might have been directly referring to the Chan Chan mural when he wrote, 'there are existing ruins which, by their location and the symbols that decorate them, tell of the lost continent of Mu, Motherland of Man.'

The scene doubtlessly memorializes the drowned civilization of the Pacific, from which the ancestors of the Chimu – literally, the 'Children of Mu' – arrived on Peruvian shores after the 3100BC catastrophe. It was from Tayacana-mu's descendants that all subsequent Chimu monarchs traced their lineal descent. That this Native American site and foundation story represent Lemurian culture-bearers to Peru is self-evident.

Related Spanish accounts of the Peruvian natives held that the Chimu administrative centre of Pacatna-mu was named after its first ruler. At another archaeological site in the central highlands of the Andahuaylas valley, excavators found a 3,440-year-old stone bowl containing metalworking tools along with gold beaten into thin foil, the earliest evidence for precious metalworking in the Andes. The name of the site where this discovery was made is Muyu Moqo.

Pacata-Mu was a huge and important religious centre featuring a complex labyrinth the size of four football fields surrounded by high walls of mud-brick. The maze was apparently the scene of large-scale ritual activities, judging from the sacrificed remains of llamas and tiny, curious squares of exquisitely woven cloth of no apparent utilitarian value. Such squares are still used, however, by North American aboriginals of the south-western states to contain religious offerings of tobacco. Pacata-Mu's name and location in northern coastal Peru, on a promontory over-looking the Pacific Ocean, underscore its Lemurian origins.

SOUTH AMERICAN MEGALITHS

Taycana-mu, Pacatna-mu, Muyu Moqo, etc. embody in their character and very names the Lemurian source, shared with Atlantis, of Andean civilization. Michael E. Moseley, a specialist in Andean archaeology, writes of these culture-founding traditions, 'The lore clearly contains myth and allegory, but also mentions places and events identifiable in the archaeological record.' Among the most revealing of these is Silustani, a pre-Inca ceremonial area near the shores of Bolivia's Lake Titicaca. It features a skilfully laid-out circle of standing stones unlike anything comparable in South America, but strongly reminiscent of megalithic sites common in Western Europe.

More famous are the Chulpas of Silustani, enormous, well-constructed towers that archaeologists believe – on paltry evidence – were used exclusively for funerary purposes. The Chulpas bear an uncanny resemblance to equally massive stone towers standing under 30 metres of water in the Sea of Korea, off Japan's western coast, not far from the small island of Okinoshima. Connections between the submerged Okinoshima structures and those on land, near water, at Silustani are suggested through the lost intermediary civilization of Mu, although early Atlantean influences, as found in the anomalous stone circle, may also be present.

The Chimu were not the only pre-Columbian people to suggest Lemurian origins. In Venezuela, Ka-Mu was the Arawak Indians' founding father, who led their ancestors into a massive cave as a place of refuge from the cataclysm. After the flood retreated, they followed him back into the world, and were guided by the song of a bird. This bird motif recurs in several deluge traditions around the world, not only in the biblical Genesis. The Caribs recounted virtually the same tradition, in which their ancestral hero was known as Ta-Mu. In the Chibchan language, the 'Gilded One' – the sunken homeland from which Muyscas-Zuhe arrived on the shores of Colombia – was Amuru.

Abundant cultural and even archaeological evidence from the Inca and other peoples that preceded them comprises a powerful argument for the ancient arrival of travellers from both Atlantis and Lemuria, who became the early movers and shakers of Andean civilization. Their legacy has not been confined to the myths and oral traditions of native Indians, but concretized in the stone monuments of Peru and Bolivia, and made self-evident in the fair-haired mummies of Pacific coastal South America.

CHAPTER 12

HOW AND WHEN WERE ATLANTIS AND LEMURIA DESTROYED?

'SLEEP, WHICH HIDES THE MIND'S INNER TRUTH,
IS LIKE A SEA COVERING THE LOST LAND
OF OUR ANCESTORS.'
MALAYSIAN PROVERB

With the collapse of the Soviet Union and consequent end of the Cold War, hitherto secret US Navy surveys of the world's seafloor were declassified and made available to the general public for the first time. California's renowned Scripps Oceanographic Institute at La Jolla used this ex-military data to compile the most detailed and up-to-date series of such maps, graphically revealing more of what lay on the bottom of the Earth's oceans than ever before. The resulting charts revealed several startling features. Among the most compelling of these was a sunken archipelago identified as the so-called Nazca Ridge. It is a more or less contiguous group of former islands extending in a straight line for some 443 kilometres southwest from the Peruvian coast at the town of Nazca, south of the capital of Lima, and adjoining another group known as the Sala y Gomez Ridge.

The Nazca Ridge bends almost due west for another 564 kilometres in the direction of Easter Island. Both ridges were known before the new data was released, but what the Scripps' charts reveal is that they are part of a sunken archipelago that stood as dry land above the ocean in the recent geological past. In fact, part of the Nazca Ridge is in shallow water, its topmost sections only 30 metres or less beneath the water's surface. Oceanographers now believe that, at least until the close of the last Ice Age some 10,000 years ago, a large archipelago of closely connected islands stood not far from the shores of Peru into the Pacific for more than 1,130 kilometres. With the discharge of melting ice at the close of the Quaternary phase – the latest interval of geological time – sea levels suddenly rose, catastrophically inundating the entire archipelago.

This latest information shows, therefore, that Mu or Lemuria could not have been a continent in any strict geological sense. The prehistoric motherland was less a landmass than a people with a uniform culture spanning the south-central Pacific chains of islands and archipelagos. Some of these territories were denuded of all or most human life when a series of horrific tsunamis washed over them. Others collapsed beneath the waves during seismic violence generated by natural catastrophes. But Mu was certainly intercontinental in terms of the cultural influences that spread outwards from this primeval civilization to impact half the globe from Asia to the Americas.

PUSHING BACK THE START OF CIVILIZATION

Earth scientists believe that the seas of the world rose suddenly with the end of the last Ice Age, reaching levels sufficient, for example, to have drowned the stone ruins recently discovered near Okinawa and Yonaguni. If these structures are in fact remnants of Lemurian civilization – and it is difficult to imagine how else they might be explained – then their Quaternary inundation dovetails with Churchward's translation of Hindu monastery records that he was shown while in India. Mainstream scholars are certain, however, that nothing resembling a high culture existed before 5,000 years ago. Official explanations for the beginning of civilization assign it to Mesopotamia's Fertile Crescent around the turn of the fourth millennium BC.

Given the limitations of this time and place, however, mainstream scientists are hard pressed to account for the discovery of complex urban centres, such as Turkey's 9,000-year-old condominium communities at Chatal Hueyuek, or Jericho's 1.6-hectare citadel, with its 3-metre-thick masonry perimeter and stone tower featuring an internal spiral stairway more than 9 metres high, and completed 10,000 years ago – making it almost contemporaneous with the earliest dates for Mu and Atlantis. Sites such as Chatal Hueyuek and Jericho were not raised by primitive farmers. Nor were they the first of their kind, but the results of predecessors going back at least several centuries earlier.

Hindu monastery documents translated by Churchward dated the natural catastrophe that overwhelmed Mu to 10,000BC. This date was not meant to be taken literally, of course, but signifies rather a general time frame that nonetheless closely coincides with the same period Plato assigned for the destruction of Atlantis: 11,500 years before the present. Is it conceivable, then, that both civilizations perished more or less simultaneously in a global cataclysm that geophysicists know accompanied the close of the last Ice Age? If so, then Mu and Atlantis must have begun and flourished long before, thereby pushing the origins of human civilization even deeper into prehistory.

TIMELINE PROBLEMS

There are some disturbing contradictions to this apparently credible hypothesis, however. If culture-bearers surviving the Lemurian catastrophe arrived in coastal areas of Japan, Southeast Asia, Australia, Polynesia and the Americas when Churchward wrote that they did, their impact on these regions lagged improbably behind for another 7,000 years. The earliest glimmer of Andean civilization appeared in the

Salavarry period, 5,000 years ago. China's first urban centre, at Longshan, was not built until 2500BC. And while Lemurian structures at Nan Madol, Tonga, Easter Island and elsewhere throughout the Pacific are undoubtedly older than conventional archaeologists claim, their provenance cannot lie in the Ice Age. Not even the most fringe theorist can explain the lacuna between the alleged destruction of Mu at the end of the Quaternary phase and the beginning of civilization in Asia and the Americas seventy and more centuries later.

The dilemma is even more pronounced in the case of Atlantis. The balmy climate that Plato says prevailed there did not exist during the Ice Age. Nor did the Greek or Egyptian empires against which the Atlanteans made war. The agriculture, irrigation facilities, public works projects, temple building, government, imperialism, military organization, chariots, cavalry, ships, harbours, dyeing industry, animal domestication, city planning, metallurgy, and all the rest he ascribes to the Atlantean capital did not come into being until millennia after the 9,500BC date he assigned to the florescence of Atlantis. Such troubling discrepancies force sceptics to conclude that the lost civilization was nothing more than a philosopher's fantasy, at most an allegory for his notions of utopia.

But it is precisely these apparent inconsistencies that simultaneously affirm the former existence of Atlantis and provide a credible time frame for its place in history.

The citadel Plato describes in such detail typified the palace architecture, city layout and military organization of the Late Bronze Age (from the 16th to the 13 centuries bc). Because he would have known virtually nothing of that period, which preceded his own era by 800 years, his narrative could only have come from a Homeric Age source for material with which he would have not otherwise been acquainted. In other words, claiming that Atlantis flourished in post-glacial times is analogous to stating that the Soviet Union existed during medieval times.

More significantly, the Classical times in which Plato lived were antedated by a dark age that obliterated knowledge of all previous epochs. So deep was the prolonged obscurity that fell over the past that, by the fifth century bc, the Greek historian Thucydides spoke for his contemporaries when he stated that civilization began only 300 years before his time. In short, everything in Plato's story is identifiably confined entirely to a period running from the 16th to 13th centuries BC. Atlantis, in its final form at the zenith of its magnificence, was a transparently Late Bronze Age phenomenon.

A LUNAR-CALENDAR EXPLANATION

It is now known that the Egyptian priest Psonchis, cited by Plutarch as the narrator in Plato's *Timaeus*, did not use a solar calendar. If Plato (or Solon) in his translation of the Atlantis account likewise employed lunar years, then the 9500bc date mentioned in both of Plato's dialogues actually took place very much later, closer to 1200BC, at the end of the Late European Bronze Age. This would be a perfect fit for the otherwise out-of-place civilization described by Plato, and coeval with a natural catastrophe known to have occurred just at this time in the eastern Atlantic Ocean, thereby accounting for the destruction of Atlantis.

James Churchward's sources may also have abjured a solar calendar (in fact, Hindu religious historians often calculated time in lunar years), rendering their actual date for the destruction of Mu at about 1250BC, just two generations before the actual loss of Atlantis. This date is feasible not only because it occurs well within the context of other civilizations, but also because it coincides with a period of massive geological upheaval that took place around the world.

But if neither Atlantis nor Lemuria met its respective end at the close of the last Ice Age, what can account for their destruction in pre-Classical times?

A METEORIC COLLISION

G.R. Corli (1744–1806), a French astronomer, was the first researcher, to conclude, in 1785, that the fragment of a passing comet collided with the Earth to destroy Atlantis. The earliest thorough investigation of the Atlantis problem was begun nearly 100 years later by the father of Atlantology, Ignatius Donnelly. His second book on the subject, *Ragnarok, Age of Fire and Gravel* (1884), proposed that the island civilization had been annihilated by a comet's collision with the Earth. At a time when established scientists did not even recognize the existence of meteorites, his speculation was roundly dismissed as untenable fantasy. He was supported by only a few contemporary thinkers, such as the Russian physicist Sergi Basinsky (1831–89), who argued that a meteor impact with the Earth had been great enough for the simul-taneous destruction of Atlantis and the rise of Australia.

But in the 1920s and 1930s, Donnelly's theory was revived and supported by the German physicist Hans Hoerbiger (1860–1931), whose controversial 'Cosmic Ice' paradigm included the Atlantean catastrophe as the result of Earth's impact with a cometary fragment of frozen debris. His British contemporary, the influential publisher Comyns Beaumont, had already come to the same conclusion independently. During the post-Second World War era, Hoerbiger was championed by another well-known Austrian researcher, H.S. Bellamy (1901–82). Meanwhile, Beaumont's work was taken over entirely by Immanuel Velikovsky (1895–1979) in his famous *Worlds in Collision* (1950), which elaborated on the possibility of a celestial impact as responsible for the sudden extinction of a pre-Flood civilization.

Intriguing or even as plausible as these catastrophists argued, their proofs were largely inferential. But the extraterrestrial theory began to find persuasive material evidence in 1964, when a German rocket engineer, Otto Muck, announced his findings of twin deep-sea holes in the ocean floor. They were caused by a small asteroid that split in half and set off a chain reaction of geological violence along the length of the Mid-Atlantic Ridge, a line of subsurface volcanoes, to which the island of Atlantis was connected.

In the late 1980s and early 1990s, astronomers Victor Clube and Bill Napier affirmed an asteroidal or meteoric explanation for the destruction of Atlantis. They demonstrated, however, the greater likelihood of a virtual Earth-bombardment of 'fire from heaven', as our planet passed through or near a cloud of large debris that showered down dozens or even hundreds of meteoritic materials, as opposed to Muck's single collision.

Particularly since the publication of Muck's convincing

evidence, leading scholars, such as the world's foremost authority on Halley's Comet, Dr M.M. Kamiensky (member of the Polish Academy of Sciences), Professor N. Bonev (Bulgarian astronomer at the University of Sofia) and Edgerton Sykes (the most important Atlantologist of the post-Second World War era) believed the final destruction of Atlantis was caused by an extraterrestrial impact or series of impacts. Preceding these scientific investigations by thousands of years are the numerous traditions of a Great Deluge caused by some celestial event, recounted in societies on both sides of the Atlantic Ocean. Many if not most of these worldwide folk memories invariably link a heaven-sent cataclysm with the Flood.

EVIDENCE FROM LITERATURE AND FOLK MEMORY

Beginning with the first complete account of Atlantis, Plato's *Timaeus*, the fall of an extraterrestrial object foreshadows the island's destruction, when Psonchis, the Egyptian narrator of the story, tells Solon, the visiting Greek statesman, about 'a declination of the bodies moving around the Earth and in the heavens, and a great conflagration of things upon the Earth recurring at long intervals of time'.

Inscriptions on the walls of Medinet Habu (Upper Nile valley) – the Victory Temple of Pharaoh Ramses III – tell how the Atlantean invaders of Egypt were destroyed: 'The shooting star was terrible in pursuit of them', before their island went under the sea. Ibrahim ben Ebn Wauff Shah, Abu Zeyd el Balkhy and other Arab historians used the story of Surid, the ruler of an antediluvian kingdom, to explain that the Great Flood was caused when a 'planet' collided with the Earth.

In North America, the Cherokee Indians remembered Unadatsug, a 'group' of stars – the Pleiades – one of whom, 'creating a fiery tail, fell to Earth. Where it landed, a palm tree grew up, and the fallen star itself transformed into an old man, who warned of coming floods.' As the modern commentator James Jobes has written of Unadatsug, 'The fall of one star may be connected with a Deluge story; possibly the fall of a Taurid meteor is echoed here.' A complementary version occurs in the Jewish Talmud:

'When the Holy One, blessed be He, wished to bring the Deluge upon the world, He took two stars out of the Pleiades.'

Similar accounts may be found among the Quiche Maya of the Lowland Yucatán, the Muysica of Colombia, the Arawak Indians of Venezuela, the Aztecs at Cholula, the Greeks of Classical times, and so on.

MODERN SUPPORT FOR THE METEOR THEORY

These enduring folk traditions and early investigations were dramatically borne out in July 1997 at an international symposium entitled 'Natural Catastrophes During Bronze Age Civilizations: Archaeological, Geological, Astronomical and Cultural Perspectives'. Scientists of various disciplines from around the world assembled at Fitzwilliam College, in Cambridge, England, to compare their evidence for a particularly stunning possibility; namely, that civilized man had been pushed to the brink of extinction on four separate occasions during pre-Classical times. Their consensus of opinion, published in Oxford the following year, held that a comet or multiple comets made dangerously close passes to the Earth around the years 3100, 2200, 1632 and 1198BC, with the first and especially the last event having caused the most serious damage. These cometary close calls caused barrages of meteoric materials, including asteroid-size bodies, which rained on the Earth, resulting in mass death and the fundamental disruption of civilization.

In the late fourth millennium BC episode, for example, a comet collided with the asteroid belt between Mars and Jupiter to produce the Stohl Meteor Streams, from which emerged the Taurid meteors responsible for Bronze Age cataclysms. One of the symposium's lecturers, Duncan Steel, said of the Taurid meteors:

> *Thus the night sky around 3000BC, and*
> *for a period of at least one or two millennia*
> *after it, was disturbed, contained one or a few*
> *major comets recurring annually, coupled with*
> *epochs (set by orbital precession) when the*
> *annual meteor storm reached prodigious levels.*

In their 1999 book *Uriel's Machine*, authors Christopher Knight and Robert Lomas point out that the direction of Earth's magnetic field was abruptly changed around 3150BC, when a comet struck the Mediterranean Sea. A so-called 'dust veil event', indicating the abrupt appearance of massive ash in the atmosphere, was documented through tree rings in Ireland and England. Increased cosmic dust input was coincident with widespread burning throughout various northern European bogs. And the Dead Sea abruptly rose an astounding 92 metres.

MULTIPLE IMPACTS
Other impacts directly devastated Atlantis, as indicated by contemporaneous volcanic eruptions that rippled from

Iceland to the Azores. Severe earthquakes sparked by meteoric material colliding with the geologically unstable Mid-Atlantic Ridge shattered much of the Atlantean capital, while 60-metre-high waves travelling at 200 kilometres per hour smashed into the island's coastal regions. Loss of life and personal injuries ran into the tens of thousands. Perhaps half of society's cultural infrastructure lay in ruins.

Although most survivors stayed on to rebuild society, large-scale migration to other parts of the world got under way, as indicated by the otherwise unaccountable birth of civilization in many parts of the world – Egypt's first dynasty; the founding of Troy; the Indus valley city-states; Britain's foremost megalithic sites at Stonehenge, the Stones of Stenness, Maes Howe, the Ring of Brodgar and Skara Brae in the Orkney Islands; China's first dynasty led by Emperor Fu Hsi; Mesoamerica's Maya calendar beginning on 12 August 3113BC; the Early Formative Period of the New World high cultures beginning in coastal Peru; and so on.

Less than a thousand years later, the killer comets returned with a vengeance. Plato himself wrote in *The Laws* that the 'famous Deluge' of Ogyges occurred less than 2,000 years before his time; i.e., around 2300BC. The renowned Roman scholar Varo stated that it took place about 2136BC.

William Whiston, the 17th-century successor to Isaac

Newton at Cambridge, stated that the Great Flood of 2349BC was caused by the near miss of a large comet. His conclusion was supported by a 20th-century environmental archaeologist with the US Air Force, W. Bruce Masse, who found that 'the period 2350–2000bc witnessed at least four cosmic impacts (c.2345, 2240, 2188 and 2000BC) and perhaps a fifth (c.2297–2265BC).' One of them, a 359-megaton asteroid, exploded over Argentina, creating a series of craters across the Rio Cuarto area.

REPERCUSSIONS AROUND THE WORLD

An extensive land bridge connecting Malta with the nearby island of Filfla collapsed to generate waves so potent they flooded the entire archipelago and extinguished neolithic civilization on Malta. According to Maltese researcher Anton Mifsud traces of major faulting in the submarine Pantelleria Rift upon which both islands sit have been dated to 2200BC. Meanwhile, Iceland's Hekla volcano staged a major eruption, and the productive farmlands and numerous cities of the Habur Plains in northern Syria were abandoned en masse. Glaciers were on the move again from Lapland and Sweden to the Himalayas.

As the Akkadian empire in northern Mesopotamia collapsed, a contemporary epic, *The Curse of Akkad*, told of 'heavy clouds that did not rain', 'large fields which produce no grain', and 'flaming potsherds that fall from the sky'. In Syria, the archaeologist Marie-Agnes Courty has recovered collections of petroglyphs suggesting humans witnessed a celestial impact c.2350BC.

In China, ten 'suns' fell from the sky after having been shot by a divine archer, an allegory in myth of the celestial chaos during this period. Using royal chronologies, Florida Atlantologist Kenneth Caroli has dated the 'ten suns' incident to around 2141BC. Emperor Shun wrote of a huge fireball he observed to fall from the sky and strike the Earth in 2240BC, an incident that he believed triggered the Great Flood:

The whole world was submerged and all the world was an
endless ocean. People floated on the treacherous waters,
searching out caves and trees on high mountains.
The crops were ruined and survivors vied with fierce birds for
places to live. Thousands died each day.

In Peru, the Auar-chaki, or 'Wanderers', arrived on the coast in large numbers from an awful deluge.

The Frisian *Ore Linda Bok* states that 'Atland' was wracked by cataclysmic upheavals in 2193BC. Indeed, Atlantis suffered extensive geological violence that shook its ceremonial and residential centres into ruins. Crops were incinerated by intense volcanism, as tsunamis ravaged coastal populations. The death toll rose, prompting a second wave of migration to the Americas, North Africa and Western Europe, and across the Mediterranean Sea to the Near East. But most Atlanteans remained behind to undertake again the rebuilding of their society.

The penultimate global catastrophe was longer in coming. Pre-Columbian Mexicans remembered it as 4-Quihuitl – literally, 'the Fire from Heaven' – depicted in its own square on the Aztec Calendar Stone as a sheet of descending flame. To the south, in Peru, the flood hero Thonapa arrived with his people after the Unu-Pachacuti, 'the World Overturned by Water'.

The priest-historian Manetho recorded that a 'blast of God' prostrated Egypt, destroying large metropolitan centres such as Ithtaw ('Residence City') and Hetepsenusret. Dendrochronologist Michael Baillie has suggested that the biblical plagues of Egypt and Exodus were brought about by a severe climate regression due to volcanic ash filling the atmosphere and the effects of a comet's pass near the Earth, citing German, British, Irish and North American tree rings as evidence of prodigious ash fall.

Although less devastated than on the two previous occasions, Atlantis nevertheless suffered significant damage to its cultural infrastructure, primarily through the earthquakes and tsunamis of 1628BC. This 17th-century BC date, as mentioned in chapter 4, matches almost exactly the end of the Age of Taurus and coincides simultaneously with the close of the Middle Bronze Age.

THE FINAL IMPACT

Reconstruction proceeded immediately, resulting in the capital's most opulent phase. But it was not to last. Human beings probably never witnessed a more potent natural catastrophe than the final cataclysm that doomed Atlantis and shut down the entire Bronze Age in 1198BC. Swedish geologists Thomas B. Larsson and Lars Franzen:

> ... *take the liberty to suggest that relatively large extraterrestrial bodies hit somewhere in the eastern North Atlantic, probably on the shelf of the Atlantic coast of North Africa or southern Europe around 1000 to 950BC, mainly affecting the Mediterranean parts of Africa and Europe, but also globally.*

There was, of course, the possibility that the island

of Atlantis itself was struck by one of these 'large extraterrestrial bodies'.

W. Bruce Masse cited a 'locally catastrophic terrestrial impact around 1000BC' which occurred in the badlands of northern Montana. West of Broken Bow, Nebraska, lies a mile-wide impact crater created approximately 3,000 years ago by a meteor which exploded with the equivalent force of a 120-megaton nuclear blast. Greenland's Camp Century ice-cores reveal that a global disaster threw several thousand cubic kilometres of ash into the atmosphere about 1170BC.

There was at the same time a global surge in lake levels. Flooding was so great – perhaps unequalled before or since in history or prehistory – that new lakes formed in Germany near Memmingen, Munich, Ravensburg and Toelz. In the German Rhineland, a vast majority of oak trunks show clear signs of massive flooding around 1000BC. Lakes, such as Loughbashade, overflowed throughout Northern Ireland. The largest soda lake on earth, Turkey's Lake Van, rose 77 metres in two years. Climatologists calculated that such an increase would have required approximately 381 centimetres of rainfall. In North America, Utah's Great Salt Lake and Canada's Waldsea Basin reached abnormally high levels. So did South America's Lake Titicaca in the Bolivian Andes and Lago Cardiel in western Argentina.

Geologist Robert Hewitt described the end of the Bronze Age as a 'catastrophe which was one of the worst in world history'. Larsson and Franzen felt compelled by the geological evidence to 'propose that cosmic activity could offer an explanation for the observed changes. We even suggest that relatively large asteroids or comets (about 0.5 kilometres in diameter) hit somewhere in the eastern Atlantic.'

The targeted victim was Atlantis. During early November – when the Day of the Dead is still venerated around the world in hundreds of culturally diffuse commemorations of the Great Flood – the night skies of the northern hemisphere blazed with the unholy light of a cometary dragon spitting flaming boulders at Earth and sea. The global catastrophe of 1198BC resonated in the racial memories of all humankind. At the close of Egypt's XX Dynasty (c.1197BC), Pharaoh Seti II described Sekhmet as a 'circling star' that spat flames throughout the known world. The *Ipuwer Papyrus* recorded fiery destruction all across Egypt. The *Harris Papyrus* documented immense clouds of ash overwhelming the Nile valley from the west at the time of Ramses III's coronation in 1198BC. Soon after, he defended Egypt from an invasion of the 'Sea Peoples', who told his scribes that a 'shooting star' burned their homeland before it sank into the sea.

A baked clay text from the port city of Ugarit described Anat as a star that fell on 'the Syrian land, setting it afire, and confusing the two twilights'. The last Shang emperor, Chou Hsin, lost a decisive battle to Wu Wang, founder of the succeeding Chou Dynasty, in 1122BC. Chinese myth recounted that simultaneous with this military confrontation a cosmic battle took place between comets in the sky. In the Aztec calendar, 4-Atl signified the worldwide deluge that destroyed a former 'Sun' or age. The Aztec Haiyococab was the 'Water-over-Earth', from which 'the Earth-upholding gods escaped when the world was destroyed by the Deluge'.

VOLCANOES AND TSUNAMIS

Vulcanism around the world peaked at the close of the 13th century BC. Italy's Mount Vesuvius exploded on three separate occasions after 1200BC over the next 100 years. Outstanding eruptions occurred in Arabia; Russia's Avachinsky and Sheveluch volcanoes near the Pacific Ocean on the Kamchatka Peninsula; the Japanese Atami-san; North America's Mount Saint Helens; California's Mount Shasta; Oregon's Newberry and Belknap volcanoes; and Central America's San Salvador volcano. Atlantic Ocean vulcanism was widespread, with events in Iceland (Hekla),

Ascension Island, Candlemas, the Azores (Mount Furnas), the Canaries (Gran Canaria, Fuerteventura and Lanzarote).

Development of Stonehenge suddenly terminated and the site was abandoned, while Bavaria's Black Forest went up in flames. Across Scandinavia, most coastal regions were evacuated. Catastrophic flooding deluged a vast area of low-lying land where several large rivers converged, totally submerging the Hungarian Plain. Massive coastal floods surged over the southeastern regions of North America. This truly catastrophic inundation was triggered by meteor and asteroid falls in the Atlantic Ocean, as indicated by a long pattern of impact craters, or 'bays', in South Carolina. Major earthquake damage and fire decimated Athens, Mycenae, Tiryns, Knossos, Troy, Urgarit and Cyprus. The imperial capital of the Hittite Empire, Hattusas, was consumed by conflagration. Many important and most secondary Bronze Age sites in Asia Minor were burned.

The ultimate destruction took place when Mount Atlas detonated, scoured and hollowed itself out with ferocious eruptions, then collapsed into the sea. 'In a single day and a night', according to Plato, Atlantis was obliterated. While most of its million-plus inhabitants perished, many thousands of survivors fled to various parts of the world. The migrations were captured in the mythic traditions of other peoples who hosted their survival.

THE DESTRUCTION OF LEMURIA

The global catastrophe of 1628BC dramatically impacted Polynesia. In a native version of *Haumaka's Vision* recounted by local authority, Arturo Teao, the god of earthquakes struck Mare Renga, the 'Land of the Sun', a magnificent kingdom, upending great stretches of territory into the sea. The narrative relates, 'Uvoke lifted the land with his crowbar. The waves uprose, the country became small.' Earth, sea and sky were contorted by violence. According to Teao, 'the waves broke, the wind blew, rain fell, thunder roared, meteorites fell on the island. The king (Haumaka) saw that the land had sunk in the sea. As the sea rose, the land sank. Families died, men died, women, children and old people' – *Ku emu a*, 'The Earth is drowned'. Hotu Matua, leader of survivors to Easter Island, lamented, 'The sea has come up and drowned all people in Marae Renga.'

Haumaka's Vision appears to reflect the far-flung geological upheavals that beset the whole Pacific realm during the late 17th century BC. Japan's Mount Sanbe, in southern Honsu, experienced a major caldera eruption at the same moment Alaska's Akiachak detonated on the opposite side of the ocean in a terrific event, spewing 80 cubic kilometres of ash, 20 cubic kilometres more than the contemporaneous blast at Thera, around the globe, in the Aegean Sea.

In between mounts Sanbe and Akiachak, the South Pacific island of Rabaul and Hawaii's Mauna Kea exploded with extraordinary violence, but they were outstripped by New Zealand's Taupo valley centre. More powerful than two hundred 50-megaton atomic bombs, it generated a 60-metre-high wall of water travelling several hundred kilometres per hour like an all-encompassing shock wave throughout the entire Pacific. Islands standing in its way were overwhelmed and utterly swept clean of every obstruction. Whole archipelagos vanished or were depopulated. Others abruptly sank beneath the surface of the ocean in accompanying earthquakes. These terrible cataclysms were sparked by and part of the broader cometary catastrophe that snuffed out Lemurian civilization in 1629BC.

AND SO BACK TO THE BEGINNING ...

Although we may conclude with a fair degree of certainty that Atlantis was destroyed in 1198BC, and the island arcs of Lemuria were obliterated by the 17th century BC mega-tsunamis, just when these civilizations were born is far more difficult to extrapolate from these events.

The only source material which may define Atlantean beginnings lies among the historical annals of ancient Persia. They record that the Great Flood took place in 3103BC, a date that conforms remarkably well with current scientific understanding of a global catastrophe that occurred near the close of the fourth millennium BC. The Persian annals go on to document 72 dynasties alleged to have ruled the world before the Deluge.

That same number appears in Egyptian accounts of the cataclysm. Another Egyptian source, *The Tale of the Shipwrecked Sailor*, a kind of Old Kingdom odyssey, relates that 72 'serpent-kings' ruled a distant island before it succumbed to 'a fire from heaven' and sank into the sea. According to the Hebrew cabbalah, 72 angels had sovereignty over the earth before the Flood. This figure appears to be the number of dynasties that governed Atlantis until the first cometary catastrophe it suffered around 3100BC. If so, then we may trace back the Atlanteans' royal lineage 72 dynasties from that time.

Dynasties have been known to vary greatly in longevity, from Tsarist Russia's 300-year-old Romanov rule to obscure houses that die with their founder. Nile valley civilization was made up of 31 dynasties in as many centuries. Applying ancient Egypt as a temporal standard of measurement to the question of Atlantean origins, deducting 72 dynastic centuries from the Persians' 3103BC brings the birth of Atlantis to 10,900BC. Yet again, we are met with an Ice Age date, and 1,400 years before Atlantis was destroyed in a literal reading of Plato's two dialogues.

If, when Plato wrote of Atlantis, he did indeed describe it in the context of solar and not lunar years, then he may be telling us that this civilization was born during post-glacial times after all, but persisted into and suffered its demise in the Late Bronze Age, as his description of its culture indicates. Uncertainty in this matter is generated by his failure to complete the more detailed of his two Atlantis dialogues, the *Kritias* – to say nothing of the notorious indifference with which he and his fellow Classical scholars regarded chronologies of any kind. As his modern English translator Desmond Lee, observes, 'The Greeks had a bad sense of time....' And though the Greeks, both philosophers and others, were interested in origins, they seem to have been curiously lacking in their sense of the time-dimension.

STONE AGE ORIGINS FOR ATLANTIS?
Plato nonetheless hints at Stone Age (c.10,000 years ago) origins for Atlantis. Before its kings convened every fifth or

six year on matters of imperial policy, they engaged in a bull hunt, 'using clubs and nooses, but no metal weapon'. This ritual activity was a re-enactment of some period in remote antiquity prior to the invention of metallurgy, when their royal forefathers were responsible for rounding up food and sacrifices. (The earliest known copper-smelting works goes back to Turkey's Chatal Hueyuek, c.6500BC.) The Atlanteans' ceremonial bull hunt recalled their origins in the seventh millennium BC, perhaps earlier, at a time when metalworking had not yet been invented.

In *Kritias*, Plato told how a pre-civilized people dwelt for time out of mind on the island, before the sea god Poseidon arrived to excavate a sacred site configured into concentric rings of alternating moats and islets, with a holy-of-holies at the absolute centre. This imagery calls to mind the megalithic stone circles found throughout Western Europe, particularly in the British Isles, where Stonehenge mirrors the physical embodiment of Atlantis on a smaller scale. After completing his landscaping project, Poseidon lay with a local woman (Kleito) to sire five male twins, thereby founding the first Atlantean dynasty, named after their first son, Atlas.

The sea god's arrival and his subsequent children by an indigenous female have been interpreted by

Atlantologists to mean that the original islanders were visited sometime during the Stone Age by more culturally advanced megalithic-builders, who interbred with the natives to produce the Atlantean race, while building a Neolithic site with its typically concentric pattern for the future development of the city of Atlantis. Taking the interpretation further, other investigators wonder if the newcomers signified by Poseidon were themselves mariners from an older, more advanced society on the other side of the world. Throughout the Pacific, the Polynesian sea god was Tangaroa, anomalously blond, so much so that, when Mangaians of the Cook Islands first saw modern Europeans, they regarded the foreigners as his children.

Tangaroa fathered deities 'of the fish class', including Te Pouna-Mu, in whom may be glimpsed the motherland's own name. Some researchers suspect that the Poseidon-creator of Atlantis was a mythic metaphor for none other than culture-bearers from the older civilization of Mu in their circumnavigation of the world as missionaries spreading the Lemurian gospel. If so, then the roots of that Pacific homeland may indeed stretch back into the last Ice Age. Interestingly, the 10,950BC high date for those concrete cylinders at Kurie – suggestive of Lemurian technology –

coincides with ancient Persian chronology for the first antediluvian dynasty. Another pertinent time parameter is the sudden emergence of the advanced Lapita potters, who spread throughout the Pacific around the beginning of the 16th century BC. Their abrupt florescence resembled a dispersal or forced migration in large numbers prompted perhaps by the penultimate cometary cataclysm that befell the Earth in 1628BC.

CHAPTER 13
DISCOVERING ATLANTIS

'I AM YESTERDAY, AND I KNOW TOMORROW. I
AM ABLE TO BE BORN AGAIN.'
THE RITUAL STATEMENT OF OSIRIS IN THE TURIN PAPYRUS, C.1900BC

'PROVING THE FORMER EXISTENCE OF ATLANTIS
IS LIKE TRYING TO BRING A MURDER CASE TO
COURT, DESPITE AN ABUNDANCE OF CREDIBLE
EVIDENCE, WITHOUT A CORPSE.'
JACQUES COUSTEAU, *THE MIRACLE OF THE SEA*

With so much persuasive evidence for the former existence of Atlantis, why hasn't it been found? The question seems obvious to anyone who imagines that the sunken city is sitting on the bottom of the sea waiting for someone passing by in a submarine at the proper moment, merely to look out through a glass porthole. Unfortunately, there are several significant obstacles to so easy a discovery. The first is the most obvious: no one has been looking in the right place.

THE EASTERN MEDITERRANEAN
In 2004, a Persian-American architect Robert Sarmast founded the world's premier scientific expedition to look for Atlantis. That same year, his First Source Enterprises undertook a sonar search using state-of-the-art instruments

aboard a professionally staffed research vessel to examine a site 1,500 metres deep in the Mediterranean Sea between Cyprus and Syria. Sarmast's personal investigations over the previous 15 years convinced him that Plato's lost city was the capital of an Aegean civilization. Although an initial study of the targeted area seemed promising, upon closer scrutiny in 2006, geologists determined that sea-floor sediment had been shifted into the general appearance of man-made structures millions of years before human arrival in the eastern Mediterranean. Atlantis expeditions in that part of the world before Sarmast had also come to naught.

During the 1970s, the famed oceanographer Jacques Cousteau conducted numerous underwater probes into the collapsed caldera of Santorini, believed by some conventional scholars to have been the island described in Plato's *Timaeus* and *Kritias*. Anciently known as Thera, it was a small outpost of the Minoan thallasocracy, until its volcano exploded in 1628BC. Ten years before Cousteau arrived at Santorini, advocates of an Aegean Atlantis indicated the presence three or four city-wide circles in the bay, suggesting the concentric arrangement Plato said characterized the sunken capital.

But Dorothy B. Vitaliano, a prominent geologist specializing in vulcanology with the US Geological Survey, pointed out that the sub-surface topography at Santorini:

> ... *was not in existence before the Bronze Age eruption of the volcano; it has been created by subsequent activity which built up the Kameni Islands in the middle of the bay, to which a substantial amount of land was added as recently as 1926. Any traces of the pre-collapse topography would long since have been buried beneath the pile of lava whose highest portions emerge to form these islands.*

Cousteau's deep-water dives in the waters surrounding Santorini revealed no trace of a sunken civilization, Minoan or otherwise. If anything, he proved that Atlantis was not in the eastern Mediterranean.

THE HORSESHOE SEAMOUNTS

The million dollars plus that Robert Sarmast spent on his two expeditions around Cyprus might have been better put to use at the Horseshoe Seamounts, a circle of sunken mountains due west from Gibraltar, where Soviet scientists aboard the *Academician Petrovsky* may have found archaeological traces of Atlantis in March 1974 that match Plato's description.

Unlike any other site on earth, the Horseshoe Seamounts fit the basic criteria for Atlantis set out in Plato's two dialogues: they comprise a ring of high mountains lying outside the Straits of Gibraltar; their foremost peak, Mount Ampere, stands to the south – the same position assumed by Mount Atlas Mount Ampere stood above sea level as an island until it collapsed beneath the surface within the past 10,000 years; the final destruction of Atlantis took place 3,200 years ago. The bones of numerous elephants have been dredged up from the area, corroborating Plato's observation that these creatures inhabited the island of Atlantis. Beach sand and algae have also been retrieved, proving that that region of the ocean was dry land in the recent geological past.

Clearly, the Horseshoe Seamounts generally and Mount Ampere specifically are prime targets worthy of serious investigation. But merely lowering an underwater television camera into the vicinity will probably not reveal Atlantis. Even if the city is relatively well preserved at several thousand fathoms deep, it will not be covered by water only. Thirty-two centuries of unremitting deposition have veiled whatever man-made structures or objects might have survived the cataclysm, burying them under what might be dozens or even hundreds of metres of mud and silt.

Worse, whatever ruins or artefacts might have survived the initial catastrophe might very well have been overwhelmed by rivers of lava, given the volcanic nature of most Atlantic islands. If so, the remains of Atlantis are triple-sealed under silt and mud, and encased in hardened lava rock. No device possessed by modern deep-sea geology is capable of penetrating such thickly layered obstacles. As Sarmast's Wikipedia biographer points out, 'There is currently no way of using current technologies (underwater research is still in its formative years)' to distinguish artificial from natural targets under deposited cover. 'There are no sonar devices that can "x-ray" large areas in order to find geometrical structures that have rested under mud for thousands of years.'

WOULD ANY REMAINS HAVE SURVIVED THE CATACLYSM?

The likelihood, however, of ruins of any kind waiting to be found by some future technology is dubious at best. The precise nature of the destruction of Atlantis is unknown, but any cataclysm powerful enough to have sunk an entire island the size suggested by the Horseshoe Seamounts, or even the much smaller dimensions of Mount Ampere, 'in a single day and a night', would have left very little in the way of cultural evidence.

Swedish geologists Thomas B. Larsson and Lars Franzen showed that a meteoric bombardment, perhaps including two asteroids, impacted the eastern Atlantic Ocean in 1198BC, just when Atlantis was destroyed. The kinetic energy released by such events at the geologically unstable Mid-Atlantic Ridge would have been sufficient to wreak terrible havoc on all related territories. But if Atlantis itself was unfortunate enough to have suffered a direct hit by either an asteroid or large meteor – something the research of Larsson and Franzen has made feasible – then the island's sudden obliteration becomes entirely realistic. While it is true that such a fate might explain a geological mechanism for the disaster, it would also account for the absence of any ruins.

Although these suppositions are based on current scientific understanding of catastrophism and its geological consequences at sea, possibilities for the survival of any archaeological materials from Atlantis are unknown. Until a professional expedition to the Horseshoe Seamounts and their environs is undertaken using today's state-of-the-art research, or the advent of more sophisticated instrumentation renders concealing mud, silt and lava rock transparent in some future investigation, what ruins or man-made objects from lost Atlantis there are will remain undiscovered.

COULD ATLANTIS BE IN THE BAHAMAS?

The small island of Bimini lies in the Bahamas, 90 kilometres east of Miami. Some 12 kilometres long and no greater than 2 kilometres at its widest point, this small sliver of dry territory has many claims to fame. The last scene of Anthony Hopkins' film *The Silence of the Lambs* was shot outside its seaplane dock. Towards the end of his life, Ernest Hemingway lived on Bimini, which early Spanish explorers believed was the location of the Fountain of Youth. But the feature for which the island is best known today is the so-called 'Bimini Road'.

This structure – only 6 metres beneath the ocean surface – suggested a paved highway to early investigators, who observed its huge, square-cut blocks running in two straight lines, diverging across the sea bottom for about 635 metres. Prevailing scientific opinion at the time dismissed it as nothing more than a natural arrangement of beach rock. Its limestones were the result of wave action 17,000 years ago, and were no different from other natural formations of the kind known all over the world, according to famous science writers such as Arthur C. Clark. Geologists point out, however, that, during the close of the Pleistocene epoch (from 1,808,000 to 11,550 years before the present), no waves could have reached the Bimini Road because it stood too high above sea level. The feature was not covered by the Atlantic until approximately 2800BC, and arose again about 1,300 years later until c.960BC.

A MAN-MADE STRUCTURE

Had the Bimini Road been found anywhere else – on dry land in Peru, Bolivia or Mexico, for example – the university-trained debunkers would have readily accepted its man-made identity. But because they have a visceral reaction to such structures popping up in places outside the parameters of conventional archaeology – especially if they happen to occur underwater – the site was dismissed out of hand as 'natural'. Even though their supposition was invalidated by core drillings of the site as long ago as the mid-1980s, sceptics choose to ignore anything that post dates their pronouncement, and continue to define the 'road' as a work of nature, not man.

But subsequent core samples revealed fragments of micrite, which do not occur in beach rock, and, during 1995, divers at the Bimini Road found granite, which is not native to the Bahamas; the state of Georgia in the United States is the closest source, hundreds of kilometres away. Moreover, adjacent stones in the road sometimes contain different geological components, such as aragonite in one and calcite in its next nearest neighbour, unlike the chemical uniformity of naturally occurring beach rock.

As even a casual visitor snorkelling around the island will observe, the stones that make up the Bimini Road are not the same as the very real beach rock in shallow waters off the island's western shore. The stones in the road are massive square-cut pillow-like blocks fitted together, sometimes placed one atop another, and terminate in a completely unnatural J-shape. About 3 or so kilometres away, the beach rock is formed into roughly squarish flakes by no means nicely fitted together nor stacked on top of each other, but often overlapping at their edges like a set of bad teeth, as they curve parallel to the shore. The demonstrable fact that the road runs diagonal to Bimini's former ancient shoreline is really all the evidence needed to prove its artificial identity beyond question, as it would have been impossible for such an orientation to have formed in situ under natural conditions.

ARCHITECTURAL SIMILARITIES

Beach rock comprises a single layer, compared to the three and four layers of stone in the road. The former is only a few centimetres thick, while the road's blocks are almost a metre thick. Comparison between the beach rock and the road leaves no doubt that they were not created by the same forces. The road also contains several angular 'keystones' with notches to fit into tenons, a prehistoric building style encountered in the Andean walls of Cuzco, Sacsahuaman and Machu Picchu. Sacsahuaman is a skilful arrangement of several thousand colossal blocks rising to 20 metres in three tiers outside the city of Cuzco. Many of the finely cut, meticulously fitted stones weigh about 100 tons each. The largest single block is 3 metres thick, 3.5 metres wide and 7 metres tall, with an estimated weight of nearly 200 tons.

According to conventional archaeological dogma, Sacsahuaman was raised as a fortress around AD1438 by the Incas. But they occupied the site only long after it was built by an earlier people remembered as the Ayar-aucca, a race of 'giants' who arrived in Peru as refugees from a cataclysmic flood. Sacsahuaman was used as a quarry by the Spanish throughout the 16th century to furnish construction material for churches and colonial palaces, so its original appearance and actual, not surmised, purposes were obscured. Even some mainstream archaeologists believe that the intentions of its creators were less military than ceremonial or spiritual.

The superb workmanship shown at Sacsahuaman is matched by the daunting tonnage of its blocks. Even with the aid of modern machinery, positioning them with equal precision and finesse would present severe challenges. Their cutting, moving, lifting and fitting during pre-Columbian times seems far beyond the capabilities of any pre-industrial people. Modern experiments to replicate construction using the primitive tools and means supposedly available before the Europeans arrived invariably produce ludicrous results. Clearly, some unimaginable lost technology was used by the ancient Peruvians. Their Atlantean identity in the Ayaraucca is underscored by Sacsahuaman's uncanny similarity to the Bimini Road.

Indeed, the Bimini Road's resemblance to Sacsahuaman and kindred Andean structures in some respects is remarkable. The Inca builders of these monumental works believed that their civilization had been founded by Con-tiki-Viracocha, 'Sea Foam', a red-haired, fair-skinned man who appeared in the Andes from the east following a terrible flood – the clear folk recollection of an Atlantean culture-bearer arriving in South America after the destruction of Atlantis.

The Bimini Road also resembles the massive walls of Lixus facing the Bahamas on the opposite shore of the Atlantic Ocean, in Morocco. South of Tangier, perched on the Atlantic coast, lie the ruins of a Roman city complete with theatre, mosaic pavements, temples, barracks, stables and public buildings. Before the Romans took it away from the Phoenicians, it was known as Maquom Semes, the City of Light. But it was not originally Phoenician. Beneath the Romans ruins and the earlier Punic storehouses the visitor may still see an even older wall of massive proportions – colossal blocks of square unmortared stone perfectly fitted together and constructed on the same monumental scale Plato described as typical Atlantean architecture.

An ancient people did indeed inhabit coastal Morocco well into Classical times. They called themselves 'Atlantes', according to the Greek geographer of the first century BC Diodorus Siculus. Four centuries earlier, the Greek historian Herodotus told of the 'Atlantioi' living along its North African shores. Plato, in the *Kritias*, cited the Atlantean kingdom of Autothchon, and, indeed, a people calling themselves the 'Autochthones' still occupied Morocco into early Roman times. Could all these similar sites – from Lixus on the Atlantic shores of North Africa to Bimini on the other side of the ocean and the Inca stonework in South America – have derived from a single source once located in between them all?

ANCIENT INHABITANTS OF BIMINI
The Lucayan Indians were a branch of the Arawaks who inhabited Bimini before the Spaniards arrived in the 16th

century to supplant the native population with African slaves. The Lucayans referred to their island as the 'Place of the Walls'. No wall-like structures of any kind were found on shore, so the ancient name is highly suggestive of the massive stone formation that does indeed lie hidden under water just off shore. They also claimed that the Bahamas anciently formed a much larger landmass that was subsequently overcome by 'the arms of the sea'.

The Lucayans additionally knew Bimini as the 'Place of the Wreath (or Crown)', which may refer to the Bimini Road's originally circular configuration. Their name for the island, in their tongue, was Guanahani. Although its specific meaning in Lucayan has been lost, the name handily translates into 'Island of Man (or Men)' in the language of the Guanches, the aboriginal inhabitants of the Canary Islands almost directly across the Atlantic Ocean from the Bahamas. The philological origins of 'Bimini' are likewise obscure. Some historians speculate that it may be the contraction of 16th-century Spanish slang, *bi*, for 'half'.

Curiously, 'Bimini' also translates into perfect Egyptian, as Baminini, or 'Homage to (*ini*) the soul of (*ba*) Min (Min)'. Min was the ancient Egyptian god of travellers, who appealed to him for guidance and protection whenever they set out on long journeys. Appropriately, Min was also the divine patron of roads. Could the island have been known to the Egyptian seafarers, their first landfall after long transatlantic voyages from the Near East?

We are told that dynastic civilization began in 3100BC. While the Bimini Road stood above water at that time, only 300 years later it was submerged. The Egyptians were certainly capable of building such a structure. But if they didn't, then who did? The structure is not actually a road, but possibly the remains of a quay, mooring breakwater or harbour facility of some kind, originally in the configuration of an elongated oval. Such an interpretation is lent some support by the feature's position at the extreme northern end of Bimini. A ship casting off from that location could sail directly into the North American current that would take it along the eastern seaboard as far north as the Gulf of Maine, then swing sharply east to bring the vessel on a heading due east for Europe, directly for the Azores.

AN ATLANTEAN OUTPOST

According to the 'Sleeping Prophet' Edgar Cayce (see chapter 5), the present island of Bimini anciently belonged to the western portion of the Atlantean empire known as Poseidia, named after the sea god described by Plato, and the mythic founder of Atlantis. In 1933, he described it as '... the sunken portion of Atlantis, or Poseidia, where a portion of the temples may yet be discovered under the slime of ages of sea-water ... near what is known as Bimini, off the coast of Florida'. Eight years passed before he mentioned Bimini for the last time: 'Poseidia will be among the first portion of Atlantis to rise again. Expect it in '68 and '69. Not so far away.'

Until he spoke of Bimini, and even long after some of his life-readings were published, no researchers bothered to consider that tiny island as a possible remnant of Atlantean civilization. Then, in 1968, a civilian pilot flying to Miami observed for the first time what he took for 'a road' underwater off Bimini's northernmost point. The discovery had been made just where and when Edgar Cayce said it would.

Much of what we know today about Bimini is the result of the work undertaken by William Donato, a Californian archaeologist and foremost authority on the Bimini Road. After more than 20 years of on-site and subsurface investigations – with everything from scuba dives and sonar to underwater cameras and submarines – he is certain that the lost civilization has been found. 'I not only believe that Bimini was Atlantis,' Donato says, 'I bet my life it was Atlantis.'

His conviction appeared borne out during a November

2006 dive off the north shore of the island, where he found a self-evidently artificial construction 30 metres beneath the surface of the sea. Dr Greg Little – his colleague and discoverer of the Andros Platform 161 kilometres to the south – reported that:

> ... the rectangular forms consist of elevated stone on the bottom that has been covered by thick layers of coral. Several of the photos clearly show what seem to be building blocks, some of which are embedded vertically into the bottom. In short, these forms appear, at face value, to be building foundations of some kind. These rectangular forms lie uniformly on a ridge running for at least a mile [1.6093 kilometres], and a 10-foot [more than 3-metre] drop-off is adjacent to them. This drop-off leads to a narrow, flat area that then descends quickly.

Dr Little adds that Donato's find occurred 'about 10 feet [more than 3 metres] above the 10,000 BC shoreline', which would place the structure near the close of the fourth millennium BC. This rough dating persuades some Atlantologists that the underwater ruins uncovered by Donato and Little rightfully belong to the early Bronze Age, an era of extensive seafaring, when Atlantis approached the zenith of its power and influence.

Despite these dramatic discoveries, the western Atlantic is an unlikely location for the capital of the lost civilization Plato described as mountainous, uncommonly fertile, seismically unstable, populated by elephants and geopolitically situated to invade the Mediterranean World – important characteristics absent in the Bahamas. They are, more probably, the remains of western outposts of the Atlantean empire. The ongoing investigations undertaken by Donato and Little represent one of the great scientific adventures of our time. And if Bimini is not exactly Atlantis, it may nonetheless be the first example of Atlantean civilization found and recognized as such since its disappearance.

If Atlantis has not yet been found, it is because the technological means to do so have not been invented whereby the geological obstacles that stand between the city and its discovery can be overcome. Developments in underwater research are advancing at a dynamic pace. So much so, that forthcoming technologies may some day make possible the greatest discovery of its kind ever made.

CHAPTER 14
HAS LEMURIA BEEN FOUND?

'AFTER MANY CENTURIES, A TIME WILL COME
WHEN THE OCEAN MUST TEAR THE CHAINS
WHICH BIND THIS WORLD, AND BARE A GREAT,
LOST LAND. THEN THE SEA-GODDESS WILL
DISCLOSE A NEW EMPIRE, AND NO MYSTERIOUS
PLACE WILL ANY LONGER BE UNKNOWN ON
EARTH.'

EURIPIDES, *MEDEA* 400BC

D uring their extensive preparations to invade the island of Okinawa in 1945, US Navy planners issued detailed maps to the commanders of their landing craft, showing the optimum areas for quickly and safely disembarking their troops. In the course of the invasion, contrary to the open water they expected to find, some deep-draught warships, which provided close support for the LSDs and approached the coast to engage enemy shore batteries, scraped their keels along underwater obstructions that should not have been there.

After the battle, so-called 'hard-hat divers' wearing copper helmets pumped with air supplied by their shipmates above went over the side to investigate, expecting to find some secret enemy installation. Instead, they were surprised to see a massive stone platform with broad steps. The divers' brief report, made just when Japan surrendered, did not characterize the curious obstruction as a modern structure. To them, it appeared to be the remains of an ancient stone building. Their report may still repose somewhere in the US military archives, but whatever impact it might have made on the outside world was entirely overlooked in the midst of the Allies' euphoria on VJ Day.

OKINAWA'S DROWNED ENIGMA

Forty-one years after the US Navy divers' discovery was made and almost as quickly forgotten, the battleground for the final land campaign of the Second World War was about to become the scene of another kind of drama. In 1985, a Japanese scuba instructor dove in the waters off Yonaguni, among the Okinawa or Ryukyu chain of islands. As he glided through unvisited depths some 13 metres beneath the clear, blue Pacific, the diver was suddenly confronted by what appeared to be a great stone building heavily encrusted with coral.

Approaching closer, he could see that the colossal structure was black and gaunt, a sunken arrangement of monolithic blocks, their original configuration obscured by the oceanic accretion of time. After circling the monument several times and photographing it with his underwater camera, he rose to the surface, reoriented himself and kicked to shore. Next day, the photographs he took appeared in Japan's leading newspapers.

The structure sparked instant controversy and drew crowds of diving archaeologists, media people and curious amateurs, none of whom was able to ascertain its identity. They could not even agree if it was man-made, let alone ancient or modern. Was it the remnant of some forgotten military coastal defence installation from the war? Or could it date back to something entirely different and far older? Already there were whispers of the lost culture of Mu, preserved in legend as the vanished motherland of humankind, which perished at sea long before the beginning of recorded time. But although Yonaguni's drowned enigma appeared entirely man-made, it was hermetically locked within a thick encrustation. Nature sometimes made her own forms seem artificial. Popular and scientific debate concerning the structure's origins raged.

Then, in late summer of the following year, another diver in Ryukyu waters was shocked to behold a massive arch or gateway of huge stone blocks beautifully fitted together in the manner of prehistoric masonry found among Inca cities on the other side of the Pacific Ocean, high in South

America's Andean mountains of Peru and Bolivia. This time there was no doubt. Thanks to swift currents in the area, coral had been unable to gain any foothold on the structure, leaving it unobscured in the 30-metre visibility of the crystal-clear waters. It was certainly man-made, very old, and seemed nothing short of miraculous – an unbelievable vision standing in apparently pristine condition on the ocean floor.

YONAGUNI

But its discovery was only the first of that summer's undersea revelations. Fired by the possibility of more sunken monuments in the area, teams of expert divers fanned out from the south coast of Okinawa using standard grid-search patterns. Their professional efforts were soon rewarded. Before the onset of autumn, they found five more sub-surface archaeological sites near three offshore Japanese islands. Their locations vary at depths from 30 to only 6 metres, but all seem stylistically linked, despite their great variety of architectural details.

They comprise paved streets and crossroads, huge altar-like formations, grand staircases leading to broad plazas, and processional ways surmounted by pairs of towering features resembling pylons. The sunken buildings are known to cover the ocean bottom (although not continuously) from the small island of Yonaguni in the southwest, to Okinawa and its neighbouring islands, Kerama and Aguni – some 500 kilometres of underwater terrain. If ongoing exploration does indeed reveal more structures linking Yonaguni with Okinawa, the individual sites may be separate components of a large island lying at the bottom of the Pacific.

The single largest structure so far discovered lies near the eastern shore of Yonaguni, 30 metres down. It is approximately 74 metres long, 30 metres across and 14 metres high. All the monuments, including the Yonaguni structure, appear to have been built from a granitic sandstone, although no internal passages or chambers have been found. To a degree, the underwater features resemble ancient buildings on Okinawa itself, such as Nakagusuku Castle. More of a ceremonial edifice than a military installation, Nakagusuku dates back to the early centuries of the first millennium AD, although its identity as a religious habitation site is lost to prehistory. Its builders and the culture it originally expressed are unknown, and the precinct is still regarded with a superstitious awe by local Okinawans.

Other parallels with Okinawa's oldest sacred buildings are found near Noro, where burial vaults designed in the same rectilinear style continue to be venerated as hallowed repositories for the islanders' ancestral dead. Very remarkably, the Okinawan term for these vaults is *moai*, the same word Polynesians of Easter Island, more than 9,657 kilometres away, used to describe the famous large-headed, long-eared statues dedicated to their ancestors.

Possible connections far across the Pacific may be more than philological. Some of the sunken features bear even closer comparison to *heiau* found in the distant Hawaiian islands. These are linear temples of long stone ramparts leading to great staircases surmounted by broad plazas, where wooden shrines and carved idols were placed. Many *heiau* still exist and continue to be venerated by native Hawaiians. In terms of construction, the Okinawan examples comprise enormous single blocks, while the *heiau* are made up of far more numerous, smaller stones. They were first built, according to Hawaiian tradition, by the Menehune, a yellow-haired race of master masons who occupied the islands long before the arrival of the Polynesians. The original inhabitants fled, unwilling to intermarry with the newcomers.

OTHER PACIFIC PARALLELS

Okinawa's drowned structures find possible counterparts at the eastern limits of the Pacific Ocean, along coastal

Peru. The most striking similarities occur at ancient Pachacamac, a sprawling religious centre a few kilometres south of the modern capital at Lima. Although still functioning into Inca times as late as the 16th century, it predated the Incas by at least 1,500 years and was the seat of South America's foremost oracle. Pilgrims visited Pachacamac from all over the Tiauantisuyu, or Inca empire, until it was sacked and desecrated by the conquistadors under Francisco Pizarro's high-spirited brother, Hernando, with 22 heavily armed men. Enough of the sun-dried, mud-brick city remains, with its sweeping staircases and broad plazas, to suggest parallels with the sunken buildings around Okinawa.

Another pre-Inca site in the north, just outside Trujillo, likewise shares some elements in common with the overseas undersea structures. The so-called 'Temple of the Sun' is a terraced pyramid built 2,000 years ago by a people known as the Moche. More than 30 metres high and 208 metres long, the irregularly stepped platform of unfired adobe bricks was formerly the colossal centrepiece of a city sheltering 30,000 inhabitants. Its resemblance to the structure found at Yonaguni is remarkable.

On the other side of the Pacific, the first emperor of Japan was remembered as Jimmu, whose immediate descendant was Kamu, one of the 'legendary' founders of Japanese civilization. Another ancestral emperor was Temmu, who was said to have committed to memory the *Kojiki*, or 'Records of Ancient Matters', and the *Nihongi*, 'Chronicles of Japan'. In northern Japan, 'mu' means 'that which does not exist or no longer exists', as it does in Korean. Does this word hark back to a land that 'no longer exists'?

THAILAND'S LEMURIAN ORIGINS

This supposition seems borne out in Thailand's most sacred shrine. The Lak Mu-ang is a pillar venerated in its own small shrine at the spiritual centre of Thailand, in the capital city of Bangkok. It is a copy of the original brought to Southeast Asia by the Thens from their drowned homeland in the Pacific Ocean. In Thai folk tradition, the Thens were an ancestral people who fled over the sea from their sinking kingdom during the ancient past. All they managed to salvage from the rising waters was a single column of their chief temple. It was set up at the centre of their new city in Southeast Asia, where the Thens blended Lemurian mysticism and technology with that of native cultures. They carried away just one column that belonged to the most important temple in Lemuria before the entire structure was engulfed by the sea. Arriving on the shores of what much later became Thailand, the Thens set up the Lak Mu-ang at the centre of their new capital, Aiyudiya. During centuries of subsequent strife, the city was sacked and its sacred souvenir lost, but memory of it persisted with the relocation of various Thai capital cities, each one erecting a simulacrum of the original pillar.

In 1782 King Rama I – who traced his royal descent from the lost motherland of Mu – erected a ceremonial column at the precise centre of the capital city. The original Lak Mu-ang was so ancient, however, no efforts succeeded in preserving it against decay, and it was eventually replaced with a replica by Rama VI. Today's Bangkok Lak Mu-ang is continually decorated with gold leaf by anyone wishing to pay homage to their country's sacred centre. The shrine itself is decorated with symbols and images of the Lemurian homeland from which the column was brought so long ago, such as stylized swastikas and scenes of a tropical island, suggestive of the land of Mu itself. The small shrine in which it stands is an elaborate pavilion with intricate gold-inlay doors, and is set, untypically, below ground level in a sunken court, suggesting the undersea condition of the civilization from which the pillar was taken.

The name recurs at important monumental sites in Thailand: Mu-ang Fa Daet, Ban Mu-an Fai, Mu-ang Semay, and Mu-ang Bon, where the original Lak Mu-ang may have been installed by immigrants from Mu.

LEMURIAN RITUALS IN PRESENT-DAY JAPAN

In ancient Rome, the Lemuria was a festival celebrated beginning every 9 May. The Romans revered it as the oldest ceremony associated with the origins of their civilization, when Romulus ritually appeased the spirit of his murdered brother. Here, too, we encounter 'mu' in relation to the founding of a civilization, as the brothers were honoured as the progenitors of Rome. In Latin, their names are pronounced with the accent, in both cases, on the second syllable: Ro-*mu*-lus and Re-*mu*-s.

Part of the Roman Lemuria demanded that at midnight the head of the household walk backwards through each room, casting black beans behind him as he said nine times, 'These I give and with these I redeem myself and my family.' The beans were symbolic gifts to the *lemures*, or demonic ghosts, who were supposed to have been sufficiently pacified by this humble offering to return to their underwater home, at least for a year. On 15 May the Lemuria concluded, significantly enough when the images of men, women and children – symbolizing the troubled spirits – were cast into the River Tiber to commemorate the sunken kingdom of the dead and perhaps the natural catastrophe that long before overwhelmed it.

Although Rome was separated from Lemuria by more than a thousand years and several thousand more kilometres, it should come as no surprise that so specific a reference was made to the Pacific civilization in ancient Italy. Seminal events indelibly stamp their names on the early development of cultures, such as Atlantean impact made on Mesoamerican history in the form of Aztlan, remembered into the 16th century by the Aztecs as their ancestral homeland. Modern parallels are found in the eastern United States, still referred to by Americans as 'New England'.

This most ancient of Roman ceremonies is remarkably similar to an annual New Year's Eve ritual still performed throughout Japan. At midnight, the head of the household dons his finest clothes, then goes barefoot into each of the rooms, throwing beans, while saying 'Out, demons! In, luck!' Only a Lemurian connection (or, less likely, a Roman one) that separately influenced both Japan and Rome seems capable of explaining the otherwise inexplicable resemblance of these two ancient, geographically divergent rituals.

THE MU MUSEUM

An obvious Lemurian impact on the Japanese people continues to be venerated, even institutionalized. In the aftermath of the Second World War, Reikiyo Umemto, a young monk, while engaged in deep meditation at the south-eastern shores of Japan, experienced a powerful vision of the ancient land of Mu. More than some archaeological flashback, it transcended his traditional Buddhist thinking with the sunken realm's lost mystery-cult, which he refounded as the 'World's Great Equality' in Hiroshima prefecture.

For the next 20 years, he lived and shared its principles with a few chosen followers, until some wealthy backers put themselves at his disposal. With their support, he built a 5-hectare temple-museum with surrounding landscaped grounds closely patterned after structures and designs recalled from his postwar vision.

Work on the red-and-white complex adorned with life-size statues of elephants and lively, if esoteric murals was undertaken at a selected site in Kagoshima prefecture because of the area's strong physical resemblance to Mu and the location's particular geo-spiritual energies. Construction was completed by the mid-1960s.

A large, professionally staffed institute with modern facilities for display and laboratory research, the Mu Museum is unique for its authentic artefacts and well-made re-creations associated with the lost civilization that bears its name. Although the institute is open to the general public, spiritual services at its temple are restricted to initiates. Reikiyo Umemto passed away in 2002 at 91 years of age.

THE WARRIOR WAVE

In the early 19th century, when English biologists were in the process of mammal classification, they applied the ancient term 'lemur' to describe primitive tree primates first found in Madagascar because the creatures possessed large glaring eyes, just like the ghostly *lemures* described in the Roman Lemuria. When the animals were discovered outside Africa, in such widely separated locations as South India and Malaysia, scientists theorized that a continent in the Indian Ocean may have once touched all these lands before it sank beneath the waves. Oceanographers have since established that no such continent ever existed.

But collectors of oral traditions throughout the island peoples of the Pacific were perplexed by recurring themes of a vanished motherland from which culture-bearers arrived to replant the seeds of society. On Kaua'i, the Polynesians told of the Mu (also known among Hawaiians as the Menehune), who arrived in the dim past from a 'floating island'. The most important ancestral chant to mention this place was the Kumulipo, which recounts a terrifying flood that destroyed it long ago. The chant's concluding lines evoke some natural catastrophe:

> *Born the roaring, advancing and receding waves, the*
> *rumbling sound, the earthquake. The sea rages, rises*
> *over the beach, rises to the inhabited places, rises*
> *gradually up over the land. Ended is the line of the first*
> *chief of the dim past dwelling in cold uplands. Dead is*
> *the current sweeping in from the navel of the world.*
> *That was a warrior wave. Many who came vanished,*
> *lost in the passing night.*

A survivor who escaped the 'warrior wave' was called Kuamu.

OCEANOGRAPHIC RESEARCH

Despite an abundance of folk traditions spanning the Pacific, all describing a sunken homeland, the first accurate sonar-generated maps of the ocean bottom reveal nothing resembling a lost continent. The latest Scripps Institute charts nonetheless show areas of the Pacific that were dry land until recent epochs. The Archipel des Tuamotu is a

325

massive collection of presently shallow features running northwest to southeast about 33 kilometres north and east of Tahiti. And there is the Emperor Seamount Chain, extending almost perfectly from north to south in the western Pacific. Add to these formerly above-water collections similar formations such as the Caroline Seamounts and the Shatsky Rise, and we have a radically different prehistoric panorama of extensive territories in the Pacific than ever before imagined.

Of particular interest, the Scripps' chart clearly shows a sometimes very shallow and long, relatively thin ridge of subsurface islands running in a chain from the southern tip of Japan and connected to Taiwan, including the Ryukyu chain, where the sunken monuments were found at Okinawa, Yonaguni and other islands. While not continental, these once-dry lands comprised vast territories over which Lemurian civilization spread, almost literally across the Pacific Ocean.

Indeed, archaeological enigmas supporting the Polynesian myths still exist at such remote corners of the Pacific as tiny Malden Island, where a road of paved stones leads directly into and under the sea. The uninhabited island is also home to some 40 pyramidal platforms.

THE SACRED GATEWAY

Another provocative architectural theme linking South America with Japan through Polynesia and suggesting a lost intermediary culture is the sacred gateway. The aesthetic focus of Tiahuanaco, a great ceremonial city high in the Bolivian Andes near Lake Titicaca, comprises two ritual gates. One above the sunken court at the entrance dramatically frames the 4-metre-tall statue of a god or man, while the other, at the far end of the complex, is the famous Gateway to the Sun, oriented to various solar phenomena.

Out across the Pacific, on the Polynesian island of Tonga, stands the Haamonga-a-Maui, the 'Burden of Maui', a 5-metre-high stone gate weighing some 109 tons, and aligned with the sunrise of the winter solstice. Japan is covered by many thousands of such gates, most of them made of wood, but all used to define a sacred space. They are known as *torii*; the same word appears in ancient Indo-European languages, and survives in the German word for 'gate': *Tor*. An outstanding feature of Japan's sunken structures in the vicinity of Okinawa is an unconnected gate not unlike Andean stonework. The Lemuria-celebrating Romans ornamented their Empire with freestanding ceremonial gates.

These intriguing parallels, combined with a wealth of

archaeological evidence and descriptive native traditions, convince investigators that some powerful, centrally located 'X culture' indeed existed in the Pacific, from which civilizing influences spread in all directions. Their conclusion seems borne out by recent discoveries among the Ryukyu Islands, where architectural features of the underwater structures bear telltale affinities to pre-Inca structures in Peru and ancestral burial vaults on Okinawa.

CEREMONIAL PURPOSES

The sunken buildings provoke more questions than they answer. How old are they? Why are they underwater? Who built them? For what purpose?

The evidence gathered so far indicates that the Japanese sites did not succumb to a sudden geological catastrophe. Aside from one or two monuments leaning at irregular angles, none of them displays any structural damage, and there are few cracks or fallen stones. Instead, they appear in unruined condition. They were either overwhelmed by rising sea levels or sank with a gradually collapsing landmass, or some combination of both. Most researchers opt for the last scenario, as oceanographers tell us that sea levels rose from 30 metres to present worldwide sea levels about 1.7 million years ago. Even so, the Japanese sites must be very old in human terms. They are constantly being swept clean by strong currents, so radiocarbon-dating material is not available.

The purposes for which these structures were made appear less difficult to guess. Their strong resemblance to Hawaiian *heiau* implies that they were mostly ceremonial in nature. Their expansive staircases lead up to presently barren platforms, where wooden shrines and idols were probably erected for religious dramas, just as they were throughout the Hawaiian Islands into historic times. Just who built and worshipped the original *heiau* suggests a word most professional American archaeologists are unwilling to pronounce. But, in view of the numerous accounts from dozens of cultures around the Pacific testifying to a flood that destroyed some former civilization, if Yonaguni's sunken city is not part of lost Lemuria, then what is it?

To offer at least a partial answer to this enigma, the American geologist Dr Robert Schoch travelled to the subsurface structure at Yonaguni. He observed that the massive platform appears to have been deliberately laid out in a specific east–west orientation to the daily passage of the sun, perhaps an important clue to its man-made provenance. Dr Schoch is more famous for his work at the Great Sphinx of Egypt's Giza Plateau. The professional geologist used his expertise to convincingly demonstrate that the sculpted mystery crouching in the Lower Nile valley is thousands of years older than establishment academics believe, even predating by millennia the officially posited beginnings of Pharaonic civilization itself 5,000 years ago. Proof lay in the abundant evidence of severe water damage suffered by the Sphinx at a time when Egypt's climate was radically different, with seasonally heavy rainfalls. In other words, the monument must have already existed some 7,000 or more years ago, not as recently as the 2600BC date insisted upon by conventional scholars.

Dr Schoch personally dove on the sunken feature at Yonaguni several times, beginning in 1997. He found it mostly composed of very fine sandstones and mudstones belonging to the Lower Miocene Yaeyama group. These rocks, which feature parallel bedding planes allowing even separation into layers, naturally fracture into strata to create a patterned arrangement resembling the Yonaguni structure, and are common at the island. Perhaps it was a natural formation after all. On closer inspection, however, he felt inclined to accept that it may have been at least partially artificial – perhaps altered in the ancient past before its inundation. He speculated that the structure perhaps served originally as part of some harbour facility for a seafaring people, and noticed the close resemblance of Yonaguni's prehistoric tombs cut directly from bedrock to the feature standing underwater just offshore.

Dr Schoch's terra-formed interpretation of the sunken monument seems credible. But he investigated only one of the seven or eight Japanese underwater sites. Most are found in the general vicinity of Okinawa, and do not appear to have been terra-formed. Their human origins are underscored by native folk memories, which still recount a time in the remote past when great tracts of land supposedly stood above sea level. According to Britain's Quest magazine, 'The local traditions tell of a great island in the south that vanished in a flood. It was from this legendary island that the gods came to Okinawa.'

SPIRAL STAIRCASE AT OKINOSHIMA

The parameters of Japan's underwater discoveries suddenly expanded in the spring of 1998, when divers encountered yet another stupendous ruin a full 1,125 kilometres from Okinawa. This most recent find is located near the uninhabited islet of Okinoshima in the Tsushima Kaiko, otherwise known as the Korean Strait, about 40 kilometres northwest of the larger island of Iki, and 45 kilometres off the mainland at Kyushu. Okinoshima has for time out of mind been revered as a sacred island associated with the three daughters of Japan's most important deity, the sun goddess, Amaterasu. The trio of deified sisters – Ichikishima, Tagitsu and Tagori – had a shrine built for them on Okinoshima, where they were worshipped as the divine patronesses of sailors. Even today, the island is still referred to as Oiwazu-sama, or 'Never Speak of It', emphasizing its enduring sacrosanct character.

Okinoshima was supposed to have been home to the Munakata – aggressive, prehistoric mariners in the service of the first emperor, Jimmu. The Munakata may have been the same dynamic sea people who built and used the stone monuments since sunk to their present locations at the bottom of the ocean around Japan.

At first sight, Shun-Ichiroh Moriyama, a local fisherman, observed what appeared to be a row of huge pillars standing more than 30 metres beneath the surface about a quarter of a mile off the northeastern shore of Okinoshima. He counted four of them, each one an enormous 7 to 10 metres across and almost 30 metres tall.

On closer inspection, divers realized that they were not pillars, but round stone towers, one of which featured a colossal spiral staircase winding around its exterior. This tower particularly brought to mind the Aboriginal

Australian tradition of the drowned 'Land of Perfection', with its great 'crystal cone' tower entwined with a spiralling 'snake'.

News of Mr Moriyama's discovery made the front pages of Japan's major newspapers, and Fuji Television twice broadcast a documentary 'special report' about the Okinoshima find, with underwater video coverage of the peculiar sunken structures. Even in the clear waters of the Korean Strait they were not easily photographed, however, owing to their great size. Subsurface visibility of more than 30 metres (conditions which do not exist around Okinoshima, with its 13- to 16-metre maximum clarity) is needed to see the monuments in their entirety. But the grand staircase spiralling around the tower furthest to the east was photographed. Divers from the university at Fukuoaka carefully measured its steps, and found them to be uniformly cut to a depth of 40 centimetres, with a varying width of 150 to 180 centimetres.

The area of the immediate sea bottom is very dissimilar from the structures. Boulders and smaller rocks irregularly shaped by the natural forces of subsurface erosion are scattered about in large, random heaps. According to Professor Nobuhiro Yoshida, President of Kitakyushu's Japan Petroglyph Society:

*Comparing these linear steps, so perfectly suited to
anyone climbing them, with the immediate subsurface
environment, we notice at once that the sea bottom
is otherwise composed exclusively of irregular, round
boulders and smaller rocks, and therefore in sharp
contrast to the vertical columns and rising staircase.*

In such an undersea environment, the quartet of towers
stands like an impossible anomaly. Yet, they are not without
parallel in the Pacific.

AN OCEANWIDE CIVILIZATION

On the other side of the ocean, tiny Easter Island once
included, among the mute colossi and massive altars of some
former age, stone towers whose dimensions approximated,
if not matched, the submerged monuments of Okinoshima,
save for the exterior spiral staircase.

Scattered across the Indian Ocean and Polynesia, even
to the west coast of California, variations of Lemuria
may still be found where we might expect the inundated
civilization to have left some impression on the cultures of
other indigenous peoples. In the Maldives, a string of tiny
islands dangling north–south from the southernmost tip
of the Indian subcontinent, Laamu is associated in native

tradition with pre-Hindu foreign red-haired seafarers, who raised pyramidal monuments throughout the Maldives in the forgotten past.

In Hawaiian dialects, *limu* is a general term for life in the depths of the ocean, particularly seaweed, defined in local myth as the tresses of a goddess who reigns over a pre-Polynesian kingdom beneath the sea. Before Nicholas Island, off the coast of Santa Barbara, received its current name, it was venerated by the Chumash Indians of southern California as a sacred place they called 'Lemu'.

Are these names from the Indian Ocean to Hawaii and California traces of a vanished civilization common to such widely separated locations? Are the bizarre monuments found under the waters near Okinawa, Yonaguni and Okinoshima the remnants of lost Lemuria? If so, we may be witnesses to the recovery of our most ancient origins as a civilized species.

Both underwater discoveries in the Korean Sea and off Yonaguni have counterparts on dry land throughout the Pacific. Although not as tall as the Okinoshima towers, similar specimens formerly existed on Easter Island, and may still be found on the shores of Bolivia's Lake Titicaca – the pre-Inca *chulpas* featured in chapter 11.

Yonaguni's sunken edifice finds its corresponding likeness

closer to home, near the Okinawa capital of Noro, where the sepulchres hewn from rock possess the same style of monumental architecture in evidence beneath the waves at Iseki Point. Oversized 'steps', broad plazas and extended walls are shared in common with the subsurface building.

Archaeologists have given scant attention to the Noro tombs, which cannot be attributed to any known culture, although they may date back to less than 2,000 years ago. However, they also appear to have been built and rebuilt within the same design parameters over unknown generations, so much so that the sepulchres as they now stand are but the latest in a long series of repair and reconstruction that could stretch back much further in time, perhaps even into the early Jomon period. If so, that would place them in the 10th millennium BC, contemporaneous with the underwater structure at Yonaguni they so resemble.

The Noro 'tombs' are actually less burial centres than ceremonial buildings, where the followers of the Shinto religion still pay regular homage to ancestral spirits of the deep past.

Close correspondence between ancient structures at Okinawa and elsewhere with those older versions found at the bottom of the Pacific Ocean not only define architectural and archaeological relationships, but also clearly demonstrate a continuous legacy from what is now the sea floor to the dry land. Tracing back that legacy to its underwater origins leads us to the lost motherland of Lemuria.

CHAPTER 15
KINDRED LOST CIVILIZATIONS

'HUMAN HISTORY IS NOT LINEAR. WE ARE NOT
THE DIRECT, LOGICAL RESULT AND EPITOME
OF EVERYTHING THAT HAS COME BEFORE US.
RATHER, THE PAST IS CYCLICAL. THE STAGE
THROUGH WHICH WE NOW PASS HAS BEEN
REACHED MANY TIMES BY NUMEROUS OTHER,
LOST CIVILIZATIONS. THEREIN LIES THE GREAT
ADMONITION OF OUR TIME – OF ALL TIME.'

OSWALD SPENGLER, *THE DECLINE OF THE WEST*

'A NATION LOSES THE PLACE WHICH IT ONCE
HELD IN THE WORLD'S HISTORY WHEN MONEY
BECOMES MORE PRECIOUS TO THE SOULS OF
ITS PEOPLE THAN HONESTY AND LABOUR. A
UNIVERSAL, WIDESPREAD GREED OF GAIN IS
THE FOREWARNING OF SOME UPHEAVAL AND
DISASTER. CIVILIZATIONS HAVE BEEN BORN AND
COMPLETED, AND THEN FORGOTTEN, AGAIN
AND AGAIN.'

COLONEL JAMES CHURCHWARD, *THE LOST CONTINENT OF MU*

Although Atlantis and Mu are humankind's most famous lost civilizations, they are not the only phantom kingdoms adrift in the spheres of myth. Many of these other vanished realms, however, are little more than different recollections of the Atlantean or Lemurian experience as it impacted various peoples throughout the Ancient World.

PRESERVED IN WORLD MYTHOLOGY

Mu appears in the Fiji islanders' Burotu – known as Buloto in distant Tonga and Samoa, or Baralku to Australian Aborigines; other representations are the Burmese Rutas; the Japanese Horai; China's Chien-Mu; Sri Lanka's Kaveripumpattinam; the Hindu Dwarka, or 'Island of Jewels'; the Sumerian Har-Sag-Mu, or 'Mu of the Mountain Range'; the Incas' 'Holy City' of Pacaritambo; Easter Island's Marae renga, the 'Land of Light'; the Polynesian Hiva, Haiviki, Kahiki Mutuhei; the Micronesian Kanamwayso; the Hawaiian Helani; and so on. The various traditions describing these different names all tell the same story of a large island kingdom, splendid beyond compare and inhabited by powerful magicians very long ago, and located in the Central Pacific before it was overwhelmed by a natural catastrophe from which survivors escaped to become the forebears of the Japanese, Chinese, Samoans and other Pacific peoples.

So, too, Atlantis is preserved in the folk traditions of the Basque 'Green Isle', Belesb-At; the Aztecs' Aztlan; the Egyptian Etelenty, also known as Aalu or Sekhret-Aaru; Dimlahamid or Dzilke of Canada's We'suwet'en and Gitksan tribes in northern British Columbia; the Cherokee Indians' Elohi-Mona; the Irish Falias; the Greek Fortunate

Isles, or Islands of the Blessed; Britain's Lyonesse; the Welsh Avalon; the Mayas' Valum; and so forth.

The Celtic Hy-Breasail is a case in point. Some Atlantean veterans of their empire's wars of foreign aggression were said to have returned to Hy-Breasail in Old Irish folk tradition, where they are known as the Tuatha de Danann, 'Followers of the Goddess Danu', an earth mother deity. As late as the 17th century, Hy-Breasail was still indicated on Irish sea charts of the mid-Atlantic. According to encyclopedist Anna Franklin, 'maps have even existed which usually depict it as round, divided in the centre by a river, leading to comparisons with Atlantis'. She goes on to relate that, in Irish myth, 'a red-hot arrow was fired' into Hy-Breasail before it was dragged to the bottom of the ocean by the sea god Manannan. This variation of the legend suggests the comet or meteor fall that brought about the final Atlantean destruction, an implication re-emphasized by Manannan, the Celtic counterpart of Poseidon.

'There are still families with that name (Breasail) living in Clare and Galway counties even today,' writes Irish historian Dr Bob Curran. Contrary to popular misconception, the modern South American country of Brazil derived its name from the abundance of brasa trees found there, not from any pre-Flood civilization.

THE QUEST FOR TREASURE

Taken collectively, ancestral islands such as Hy-Breasail combine for powerful evidence on behalf of the Atlantean capital's former existence. Its impact on the native consciousness of America's indigenous peoples was so profound that invading Spaniards in the early 16th century mistook traditional descriptions of opulent, long-vanished Atlantis for surviving cities of gold. Their ambitions thus whetted by the prospect of untold wealth, the rapacious conquistadors began chasing after greedy fantasies – actually tribal traditions confused by Spanish gold fever.

Foremost among these sometimes tragic misconceptions was El Dorado. As cited in chapter 11, Colombia's Chibchan Indians practised the Guatavita ceremony known as the Catena-ma-noa, or 'Water of Noa', a ritualistic celebration of their forefathers' island. The avaricious foreigners, failing to realize that the 'Gilded One' had already been lying at the bottom of the sea for some 1,700 years, convinced themselves it still existed somewhere in the Colombian interior, and spent the next several centuries in a fruitless search. Explorers continued to hunt for El Dorado until 1850, when the renowned German anthropologist Alexander von Humboldt proved that the 'Gilded One' no longer existed.

While the conquistadors were searching for El Dorado

across Colombia, their comrades in North America marched after the Seven Cities of Gold. Sometimes collectively referred to as Quivira or Cíbola, their story predated the Spanish Conquest by 350 years. It began in AD1150, as seven bishops and their congregations fled Spain by ship, carrying away certain religious relics before the Moors could seize the city of Mérida.

Although the refugees were never heard from again, it was rumoured that they crossed the Atlantic Ocean to land on another continent, where they set up seven cities, one for each bishop, soon growing rich in gold and precious stones. The legend persisted over the centuries, but abruptly swelled to hysterical proportions with the Spanish Conquest of Mexico.

CITIES OF GOLD, MOUNTAINS OF SILVER

The legend was reinforced in 1519, when Emperor Moctezuma II told Hernán Cortés that, prior to their occupation of Tenochtitlan, the Aztecs dwelt north of the imperial capital at a place called Chicomoztoc. Hearing its translation as the 'Place of the Seven Caves', the Spanish concluded that the Aztecs' former residence could have been none other than Cíbola's Seven Cities of Gold. In reality, Chicomoztoc was either Rock Lake in faraway Wisconsin or a large if relatively humble settlement built around a height near the present-day town of San Isidro Culhuacan, 100 kilometres northeast of the Valley of Mexico. In either case, there was no gold to be found in Rock Lake or San Isidro Culhuacan.

Spurred on by inflated traditions of Chicomoztoc and other local tales describing far-off cities overflowing with riches, Viceroy Antonio de Mendoza dispatched an expedition led by Marcos de Niza, a Franciscan monk, in search of Cíbola and Quivira. After ten months, de Niza returned to claim that he had visited a populous urban centre where its residents ate from dishes of gold and silver, decorated their houses with turquoise and adorned themselves with enormous pearls, emeralds and other stunning gems. Sure that the Seven Cities of Gold were to be had for the taking, de Mendoza ordered a large military contingent to conquer the famous Cíbola and Quivira. The expedition was led by Francisco Vásquez de Coronado, who set out at the head of the Viceroy's well-equipped army from Culiacán on 22 April 1540. But by the time he reached the Arizona desert, Coronado realized that the Franciscan monk had lied.

In South America, Spanish invaders were lured into the interior with hopes of finding Sierra del Plata, the 'Mountain

Range of Silver'. Survivors of an early 16th-century shipwreck on the Argentine coast had received abundant gifts of silver from the natives, who spoke of several mountains rich in the metal. Soon after, the Spaniards discovered the estuary of the Uruguay and Paraná rivers, which they called the Río de la Plata, the 'River of Silver', known in English as the River Plate, because they believed it led to Sierra del Plata. Although the Río de la Plata became a prosperous mining area, the 'Mountain Range of Silver' was never found. Nevertheless, as a demonstration of the power of myth, Argentina derived its name from the Latin word for 'silver', *argentum*.

FROM ANCIENT ROME TO SOUTH AMERICA

Sierra del Plata was not the only elusive source of untold riches said to exist at the bottom end of South America. For decades, the insatiable Spanish heard rumours of El Ciudad de los Césares, the 'City of the Caesars', also known as the 'City of the Patagonia'. Said to have been founded by ancient Roman sailors fleeing civil unrest after Julius Caesar's assassination and later shipwrecked at the Straits of Magellan, the city was supposed to be awash in gold, silver and diamonds received from grateful Indians for Roman expertise in building the Incas' extensive network of roads. Interestingly, an Inca aqueduct at Rodadero, Peru, 'employs two tiers of rounded, stone arches often referred to as "true arches"', according to American archaeologist Gunnar Thompson, Ph.D. 'This style of architecture was a characteristic of the ancient Mediterranean. Consequently, the Rodadero aqueduct represents a strong argument for Greco-Roman cultural diffusion.'

While El Ciudad de los Césares has not been not found, nor is it ever likely to be, it may nevertheless echo other discoveries of an ancient presence on America's eastern shores, such as a Roman shipwreck investigated by underwater archaeologist Robert Marx, off Rio de Janeiro, in 1976. Amphorae he retrieved from the vessel were scientifically analysed by Elizabeth Will, a professor in Classical Greek History at the University of Massachusetts. She positively identified them as part of a cargo from the Mediterranean port of Zilis, c.AD250. Marx went on to find a bronze fibula – a garment clasp – in Brazil's Guanabarra Bay.

Further north, near the Mexican Gulf Coast, bricks that went into building the Maya city of Comalcalco were stamped with second-century Roman mason marks, while its terracotta plumbing – unique in all Mesoamerica – was identical to contemporary pipes found in Israel. These and similar finds – such as the ceramic representation of a bearded European with Roman-style haircut and wearing a typically Roman cap, retrieved during the excavation of a second-century pyramid at Caliztlahuaca, Mexico – suggest that accounts of the 'City of the Caesars' may have some basis in pre-Columbian contacts.

THE LOST LAND OF ANTILIA

Those contacts are likewise suggested by the lost lands of Antilia, from the Latin *anterior*, suggesting a place 'before' the western horizon. The earliest description of Antilia appeared in a biography of Quintus Sertorius written by the Roman historian Plutarch in AD74. Nearly 150 years earlier, the Roman military commander returned after campaigning in Mauretania (northwest Africa) to his consulship in Spain, where he 'met some sailors who had recently come back from the Atlantic islands, two in number separated by a very narrow strait and lie 10,000 furlongs from Africa':

> *They enjoy moderate rains and long intervals of winds*
> *which for the most part are soft, and precipitate dew,*
> *so that the islands not only have a rich soil excellent*
> *for ploughing and planting, but also produce a natural*
> *fruit that is plentiful and wholesome enough to feed,*
> *without toil or trouble, a leisured folk. An air that is*

> salubrious, owing to the climate and the moderate
> changes in the seasons, prevails on the islands. The
> north and east winds which blow out from our part of
> the world plunge into fathomless space and, owing to
> the distance, dissipate themselves and lose their power
> before they reach the islands, while the south and west
> winds that envelop the islands sometimes bring in their
> train soft and intermittent showers, but for the most
> part cool them with moist breezes and gently nourish
> the soil. Therefore a firm belief has made its way, even
> to the barbarians, that here are the Elysian Fields and
> the abode of the Blessed of which Homer sang.

With the universal collapse of Classical civilization, all knowledge of Antilia was lost. But the Renaissance and early voyages of discovery into the Atlantic Ocean rekindled interest in the island. The Portuguese Archbishop of Porto, together with six bishops and their parishioners, was said to have rediscovered Antilia and settled there to escape the Moorish conquest of Iberia. After their arrival, they supposedly founded the cities of Aira, Anhuib, Ansalli, Ansesseli, Anscdi, Ansolli and Con. Their story was repeated in 1492 by the Nuremberg geographer Martin Behaim, on his globe of the Earth, which featured an inscription to the effect that the crew of a Spanish vessel sighted Antilia in 1414, while Portuguese sailors allegedly landed there during the 1430s. Earlier, the Pizzigano Chart of 1424 included Antilia, which also appeared on the maps of the Genoese mapmaker Beccario II years later. The renowned Paul Toscanelli advised Christopher Columbus that Antilia was the principal landmark for measuring the distance between Lisbon and Zipangu (Japan).

Later, Antilia was identified with an island in the Azores. While San Miguel fairly matches the generalized distance from Morocco given by Plutarch (1,825 kilometres) for Antilia, its representation on Renaissance maps – in area, about the size of Portugal – does not fit the Azores' largest island. Moreover, Antilia was depicted as an almost perfect rectangle, its long axis running north–south, but with seven or eight trefoil bays between the east and west coasts. While this configuration is wholly unlike San Miguel, it does somewhat resemble Puerto Rico. The comparison led some geographers, including Peter Martyr d'Anghiera, to believe in 1493 that Puerto Rico was indeed Plutarch's Antilia. As a consequence of this conclusion, the Caribbean islands were henceforward known as the Antilles.

ANTILIA IN THE AZORES

Renaissance Portuguese mapmakers aside, the Azores island of San Miguel does bear some general resemblance to the outlines of Puerto Rico, which d'Anghiera and his fellow cartographers took for Antilia. Interestingly, Arab geographers even before his time independently identified Antilia as Jezirat al Tennyn, the 'Dragon's Isle', evoking an island of active volcanoes, a description that hardly fits Puerto Rico. San Miguel, however, boasts numerous volcanoes, one of which is still known as Sete Cidades, the 'Seven Cities'. Its caldera is about 5 kilometres across, with walls some 500 metres high. Sete Cidades has erupted at least eight times since 1444. An unnamed group of pyroclastic cones experienced a single, historic eruption in 1652, but Agua de Pau erupted for almost a month during 1563. Just offshore, the Monaco Bank submarine volcano blew up in 1907, and again four years later. San Miguel's largest, most dangerous volcano is Furnas. With a summit caldera about 6 kilometres in diameter and 300 to 400 metres deep, Furnas generated a week-long eruption in 1630, which claimed the lives of more than 200 people, mostly in swift boiling mud flows.

As such, San Miguel certainly matches Arabic descriptions of Antilia as the 'Dragon's Isle'. Moreover, the

Azores island's distance from Morocco is close enough to the 1,825-kilometre distance that Plutarch said lay between Antilia and the Atlantic coast of North Africa to persuasively argue that the Romans or someone before them sailed far beyond the limitations placed on ancient seamanship by mainstream historians. The Azores were uninhabited at the time of their discovery by the Portuguese in 1427, but inside a cave on Santa Maria they stumbled upon a stone altar adorned with serpentine designs. At Corvo, a small cask of Phoenician coins dated to the fifth century BC was found.

A more dramatic find was an equestrian statue atop a mountain at San Miguel itself. The 5-metre-tall bronze masterpiece comprised a stone pedestal with a badly weathered inscription, and surmounted by a magnificent horse, its rider stretching forth his right arm to point across the sea towards the west. When notified of the discovery, King John V ordered it removed to Portugal, but the statue slipped from its improvised halter and crashed down the side of the mountain. The rider's head, one arm and the horse's head and flank alone survived the fall. These fragments, together with an impression of the pedestal's inscription, were sent to the king.

They were preserved in his royal palace in Lisbon, where scholars were baffled by the 'archaic Latin', as they thought the inscription might have read, but were reasonably sure of deciphering a single word – cates. Its meaning or significance, however, eluded them. The word is close to *cati*, which means, appropriately enough, 'go that way' in Quechua, the language spoken by the Incas. Cattigara is the name of a Peruvian city, as indicated on a second-century AD Roman map, so a South American connection with the mysterious San Miguel statue is possible. Cattigara was probably Peru's Cajamarca, a deeply ancient pre-Inca site. The two city names are not even that dissimilar. In 1755, however, all the artefacts removed from San Miguel were lost during the great earthquake that destroyed most of Lisbon.

Santa Maria's altar, Corvo's Carthaginian coins and San Miguel's equestrian statue had all been left behind by ancient Old World voyagers to the Azores islands, while the bronze rider's gesture pointing towards the west suggested that more distant expeditions to the Americas were undertaken during Classical times, perhaps by Carthaginians or their precursors from Atlantis.

Antilia's mysterious allure persists into the 21st century. In 2007, Canadian architect and amateur archaeologist Paul Chiasson published his controversial book *Island of Seven Cities*, in which he identified Cape Breton Island, south of

Newfoundland, with Antilia. Unknown stone structures and peculiar oral traditions of seafaring foreigners among the local Micmac Indians led him to conclude that Chinese sailors, some of them Nestorsian Christians, rounded Africa and sailed up the Atlantic before Cape Breton was officially discovered by John Cabot in 1497. But a team of five Nova Scotian provincial archeologists visiting the ruins the summer before Chiasson's book was published refuted his claims.

HYPERBOREA – WHERE THE SUN NEVER SETS

A less identifiable Atlantic Ocean *terra incognita* was Hyperborea. 'Beyond Boreas', the North Wind, its name persuaded some investigators to place the island in the polar region, a conclusion bolstered by Greek myth, which described the sun shining 24 hours a day in Hyperborea, every day of the year, except one, when the sun rose and set just once. From the time of the vernal equinox to the time of the autumnal equinox above the Arctic Circle, the sun shines for 24 hours a day. At the northerly extreme, it rises and sets annually. This description alone proves that the ancient Greeks or their predecessors – 2,000 or more years before the advent of modern exploration – had visited the North Pole.

An Arctic location for the obscure island is underscored by Heracles, who sought the golden-antlered hind in Hyperborea: reindeer belong to the only deer species of which females bear horns. Even today, 'Hyperborean languages' is a term used by anthropologists to categorize all linguistically unrelated peoples residing in the northern polar regions.

Hyperborea was supposedly populated by a highly spiritualized people who lived long lives 'far from labour and battle', according to the poet Pindar (522–443BC) in his tenth Pythian Ode (498BC), and devoted all their time observing and venerating but one deity – Apollo, who spent his winters among them. Each year, on his feast day, the Hyperborean maidens – a religious sect – carried mysterious gifts packed in straw to the sun god's temple at Delos, his birthplace in the Aegean Sea. Modern tourists visiting Delos are still shown the bleached ruins of the Temple of the Hyperborean Maidens.

It is difficult, however, to reconcile a population of sun-worshippers living merrily near the Arctic Circle. The historian Hecataeus of Abdera clearly placed Hyperborea in Britain, as did the later Roman historian and geographer Strabo. Both described the Hyperboreans' chief temple there in language that strongly suggested Stonehenge, the solar alignments of which were only rediscovered by astronomer Gerald Hawkins in the 1960s. Classical Greek knowledge of a Druidic society attending sun orientations at Stonehenge probably melded with earlier, half-remembered Bronze Age voyages to the North Pole. The Roman geographer Avienus mentioned a Greek voyage to Hyperborea nearly a thousand years prior to his time, c.AD350. When Hecataeus wrote *On the Hyperboreans* during the fourth century BC, the builders of Stonehenge had already vanished a millennium before. Their long-abandoned megalithic site was only much later taken over by Druid priests, who were part of the Celtic invasion of Britain around 600BC.

THE ARCTIC REALM OF THULE

Yet another Arctic realm sometimes equated with Hyperborea was Thule, although the two were really quite different from each other. Thule's earliest written reference goes back to a Greek merchant, geographer and explorer, Pytheas, whose *On the Ocean* narrated his decade-long travels outside the Mediterranean Sea, beginning in 330BC. Officially, he had been dispatched on a fact-finding mission by the Greek colony of Massalia (today's Marseille, France) to learn more of certain trade goods, particularly tin and amber; unofficially, he was looking for remnants of

Atlantis, which Plato had spoken of for the first time just 20 years earlier, and which was still a subject of great interest throughout the Greek world.

Taking advantage of a temporary lapse in the Carthaginians' blockade of the Straits of Gibraltar, Pytheas embarked on a round-trip voyage from Massalia to Bordeaux, Nantes, Land's End, Plymouth, the Isle of Man, the Outer Hebrides, Orkney, Iceland, Great Britain's east coast, Kent and Helgoland. In Cornwall, he studied the production and processing of tin, then sailed around Great Britain, calculating its circumference to within 2.5 per cent of modern estimates. Next, he voyaged to Thule, 'a six-days' sail north of Britain, and is near the frozen sea', according to Strabo's *Geography* of 30BC. 'Thule, the most northerly of the Britannic Islands, is farthest north, and that there the circle of the summer tropic is the same as the Arctic Circle. Thule, of all the countries that are named, is set farthest north.'

Although some historians place Thule among the Orkney Islands or in Norway, fourth-century BC fishermen and their predecessors, going back to Neolithic times, routinely travelled between northern Great Britain, the Orkneys and the Norwegian coast. The Roman author Orosius (AD384–420) and the early ninth-century Irish monk Dicuil both place Thule north and west of Ireland and Britain. Dicuil stated that it lay beyond the Faroes, which means that Thule could only have been Iceland, a conclusion supported by the fifth-century Roman writer Claudian. In his *Against Rufinias*, he told of 'Thule lying icebound beneath the pole-star'. Earlier, Pliny the Elder's *Natural History* described Thule:

> ... *in which there be no nights at all, as we have declared, about mid-summer, namely when the Sun passes through the sign Cancer; and contrariwise no days in mid-winter: and each of these times they suppose, do last six months, all day, or all night.*

Pytheas was the first observer on record to document the midnight sun and the aurora. His report is also the earliest written record of polar ice, which he likened to mist-enshrouded 'marine lung' – literally, 'jellyfish' – a metaphor for the formation of 'pancake ice' at the edge of drift ice, where sea, slush and ice mix, often surrounded by fog. In addition to its texture, pancake ice often resembles waves of jellyfish.

But if Iceland really was Thule, who were the people Pytheas wrote were its inhabitants? He described Thule as an agricultural country, where they produced honey and mixed it with grain to make a special drink. They also enjoyed fruits and dairy products, and threshed grain inside barns, contrary to southern European practice. Yet, Iceland was not occupied until Norse settlers arrived in the late ninth century, some 1,200 years after Pytheas supposedly visited there. Either Thule was some other place, or the islanders he met were remnants of what archaeologists currently refer to as the Red Paint People, Neolithic seafarers who sailed the polar route from Scandinavia to Labrador 6,000 years ago. Some researchers believe faint traces of the Red Paint People's cultural impact on Iceland have been found. Could at least a small colony of them have survived into the fourth century BC? Their honey production and barns disqualify them as Inuit, who, in any case, never settled in Iceland.

Although Pytheas was unable to find Atlantis, he did venture further into the Arctic than any traveller during Classical times. The precise identity of Thule, however, remains unknown.

THE VOYAGE OF ST BRENDAN
Less elusive is the location of St Brendan's Isle, named after the founder of sixth-century Ireland's Clonfert monastery and monastic school. While evangelizing among the

residents of the offshore islands, together with 17 of his fellow monks, his sturdy currach – a capacious, tubby vessel made of stretched leather – was blown out to sea. They survived the long voyage to the other side of the ocean, where they landed on the shores of a new continent, the 'Land of Promise', but more often referred to as St Brendan's Isle. It was here that he shared communion with two dozen brethren in a monastic hideaway, previously stopping at an island with a trio of parish choirs. Three hundred years were to pass before their experience was transcribed in the *Navigatio Santi Brendani Abatis*, the 'Voyage of Saint Brendan the Abbot'. Marcos Martinez's *Planiferio de Ebstorf* of 1234 mentioned 'the lost island discovered by St Brendan, but nobody has found it since'. During 1976, Irish explorer Tim Severin re-created St Brendan's voyage in a leather currach built according to sixth-century methods. Scrupulously following the details laid out in *Navigatio Santi Brendani Abatis*, Severin made landfall at Newfoundland. 'Some scholars regard Brendan's description of a continental land as proof that the abbot's expedition reached America,' writes Dr Gunnar Thompson. 'The monk's sojourn at a monastic hideaway and the isle of the "three choirs" point to established Christian congregations in North America around AD565.'

SHANGRI-LA

But not all lost realms were encompassed by the Atlantic Ocean. Of these enigmas, Shangri-La is among the most famous. Its name is a variant of the Shambhala of Tibetan-Buddhist tradition used by the early 20th-century English author James Hilton, for the subject of his bestselling novel *Lost Horizon*. 'Shambhala' is a Sanskrit term meaning 'place of peace-tranquillity-happiness', and applied to an obscure kingdom in a deep valley surrounded by inaccessible mountains. All its inhabitants were enlightened beings who followed a purified form of Buddhism.

Shambhala has been located at various sacred sites in or near Tibet, and occasionally identified with Lhasa generally and the Potala specifically: the Tibetan capital and the former residence of the Dalai Lama. His Holiness the 14th Dalai Lama said of Shambhala during the 1985 Kalachakra initiation ceremonies in Bodhgaya:

Although those with special affiliation may actually be able to go there through their karmic connection, nevertheless it is not a physical place that we can actually find. We can only say that it is a pure land, a pure land in the human realm. And unless one has the merit and the actual karmic association, one cannot actually arrive there.

His description was in keeping with Tibetan-Buddhist 'outer', 'inner' and 'alternative' meanings for such a concept. Achieving perfect meditation or enlightenment signifies arrival at the 'perfect city', while the same sacred site may be simultaneously found in religious art. Shambhala's 'outer meaning' implies it actually exists (or existed) in material form. The most likely candidate was Hunza, an independent principality in northern Pakistan founded nearly a thousand years ago. 'A remote and extremely verdant river valley,' writes Dr Bob Curran, 'it was said to have boasted a predominantly Buddhist community, which spread its influence into nearby Kashmir ... for a good number of months, the Hunza can be cut off from the rest of the world by snowfalls in the mountains.'

In 1926, and again during 1928, the renowned mystical painter Nicholas Roerich and a Soviet agent Yakov Blumkin led two failed Tibetan expeditions to discover Shambhala, ignoring the Hunza valley as too insignificant for something allegedly so magnificent. Unable to successfully pursue the 'outer meaning' of the 'place of peace-tranquillity-happiness', they might have redirected their search for another Tibetan realm. Agartha is supposed to be an underground metropolis illuminated by its own subterranean sun, and populated with 4-metre-tall initiates who will one day fulfil an ancient prophecy by establishing their divine leader as the king of the world, thereby ushering in a golden age of universal enlightenment.

A great deal of nonsense has been written and said about Agartha, mostly by novelists and theosophists, who have associated its entrance with such places as Ecuador's 'Cave of the Oil Birds'; North America's Mammoth Cave in Kentucky; the North Pole; the South Pole; the Great Pyramid of Giza; and so on. Predating these unlikely locations, Agartha was originally identified with Lhasa, where an underground series of tunnels connecting chambers beneath the Potala is known to have existed up until the city was occupied by forces of the Chinese army in the 1950s. Doubtless, this subterranean network was conflated by imaginative outsiders into the subsurface paradise of Agartha.

LOST CITIES OF THE WICKED

Contrary to the refined spirituality of Shambhala and Agartha, Sodom and Gomorrah are still regarded as the wickedest cities that ever existed. Or did they? Their Old Testament story recounts that they were actually two of five urban centres, along with Admah, Zeboim and Bela (also called Zoar), known collectively as the 'Cities of the Plain', because they lay together on the plain of the River Jordan.

In the Tanach version, Yahweh determines to destroy Sodom for the iniquity of its residents, and dispatches a pair of angels to warn the city's only virtuous citizens, Lot, his wife and their children. Earlier, Paltith, his daughter, gave some bread to a poor man who had entered the city, for which she was burned alive by the Sodomites, as described in the Talmud and the Book of Jasher. Her unnamed friend they smeared with honey, then hung her from the city wall until she was entirely devoured by bees.

While the heavenly messengers were staying at Lot's house, a crowd outside called to him, "'Where are the men who came to you tonight? Bring them out to us, and let us know them." Lot refused to give the visiting angels to the inhabitants of Sodom. He offered them his two daughters instead, but the people refused.' His fellow townspeople must have been particularly degenerate for Yahweh to have singled him out as the city's only righteous man because Lot was not only willing to hand over his daughters to the mob, but also committed incest with them while drunk. It is hard to imagine the other Sodomites topping such depravity.

The Roman Era Jewish historian Flavius Josephus wrote that:

God accordingly resolved to chastise them for their

arrogance, and not only to uproot their city, but to
blast their land so completely that it should yield
neither plant nor fruit whatsoever from that
time forward.

But while Sodom and Gomorrah were bombarded with 'brimstone and fire from the Lord out of heaven', the angels instructed Lot and his family that in leaving Sodom they were to avert their gaze from its destruction. But Lot's wife, unable to control herself, looked back at the dying city, and was instantly transformed into a pillar of salt. In the Qur'an's version, she was deliberately left behind to perish along with the rest of the Sodomites because she refused to renounce polytheism.

FINDING SODOM AND GOMORRAH

The Old Testament specifically locates Sodom and Gomorrah near the Dead Sea in the southern limit of the lands held by the Canaanites on the River Jordan plain, a position affirmed by Strabo, who wrote that locals living near Moasada (probably Masada) reported 'there were once thirteen inhabited cities in that region of which Sodom was the metropolis'. Even so, archaeologists have never been able to identify the remains of either city. In 1850, the French antiquarian Ferdinand de Saulcy declared that a limestone and salt hill at the southwestern tip of the Dead Sea known as Jabal (Mount) Usdum and its nearby ruins of Kharbet Usdum were the traces of ancient Sodom, but excavations in the next century proved him wrong.

A volcanic eruption is often posited for the destruction of Sodom and Gomorrah because they sat along a major fault, the Jordan Rift Valley, the northernmost extension of the Great Rift Valley of the Red Sea and East Africa. Yet, geologists determined that no volcanic activity occurred there within the past 4,000 years. They have, however, confirmed that the area was catastrophically bombarded with meteoric debris generated by a passing comet in 1198BC, the same period that witnessed the final destruction of Bronze Age Atlantis – a parallel with special significance, as we will soon see.

A renowned scholar of ancient linguistics, Archibald Sayce, translated an early 12th-century-BC Akkadian poem memorializing a number of unnamed urban centres obliterated by a rain of fire from the sky. Written from the point of view of someone who escaped with his life, it obviously describes an eyewitness account of the historic cataclysm that may have claimed the biblical 'Cities of the Plain'. In 1973, archaeologists Walter E. Rast and R. Thomas

Schaub excavated Bronze Age ruins near the Dead Sea. Bab edh-Dhra, Numeira, es-Safi, Feifeh and Khanazir showed evidence of extensive burning and abrupt evacuation. Although these sites generally fit the profile of Admah, Bela, Zeboim, Sodom and Gomorrah, the biblical story may allude to something altogether different.

Three years later, however, an Italian archaeo-linguist, Giovanni Pettinato, found that a cuneiform tablet from the newly discovered library at Ebla contained the names of all five of the cities, listed in the same order as provided by Genesis. Pettinato discovered that the original name of Sodom was Si-da-Mu, while Gomorrah – I-ma-ar – is based on the root *gh m r*, which means to 'be deep', or 'copious (water)'. These indications suggest that the lost cities of Sodom and Gomorrah will never be found on the plain of the River Jordan, because they are instead under 'copious' fathoms of sea water. As such, Sodom and Gomorrah may be biblical allegories, respectively, for the vanished Pacific and Atlantic civilizations of Mu and Atlantis.

To be sure, comparisons with Plato's account are unavoidable: Zeus and Yahweh were alike determined to utterly destroy both cities for the degeneracy of their inhabitants with celestial fire. Although Atlantis was finally enveloped by the sea, Zeus was, after all, a sky god.

Meanwhile, Plato prefigured the destruction he described with talk of Phaeton, 'a mythical version of the truth that there is at long intervals a variation in the course of the heavenly bodies, and a consequent widespread destruction of fire of things on the Earth'.

If this interpretation of 'the Cities of the Plain' is correct, then our examination of lost lands – Lemurian, Atlantean and otherwise – has come full circle with the fate of Sodom and Gomorrah.

CONCLUSION – THE LESSONS OF ATLANTIS

Plato described the Atlanteans as an initially virtuous people. But in time they:

> ... became too diluted too often, and with too much
> of the mortal mixture, human nature got the upper
> hand. Then, they being unable to bear their fortune,
> became unseemly, and to him who had an eye to see
> they began to appear base, and had lost the fairest of
> their precious gifts. But to those who had no eye to see
> true happiness, they still appeared glorious and blessed
> at the time when they were filled with unrighteous
> avarice and power.

Plato reported that the island of Atlantis was swallowed up by the ocean after 'a single day and night' of exceptionally violent seismic activity, followed by an extraordinary degree of magmatic debris which pervaded the seas outside the Straits of Gibraltar for literally centuries thereafter. His description has led most investigators to conclude that the catastrophe was the outcome of a major volcanic event, wherein a part of the volcano (Mount Atlas) blew outwards laterally, allowing the sea to rush into its suddenly exposed interior, forcing the entire island to collapse. Such a scenario is well within the geological province of the seismically active Mid-Atlantic Ridge, where Atlantis was located.

But its final destruction may not be entirely understood in purely geological terms. With fascinating consistency, the cataclysm is linked to the spiritual decline of the Atlanteans from Plato to Cayce, beyond to the folkish traditions of Wisconsin's Winnebago Indians and the Basque in Spain. The precise relationship between social decay and physical annihilation is defined in none of these accounts, although they do provide a model for what might have occurred. Despite the apparently natural disaster that obliterated the oceanic civilization, Plato also argued that the Atlanteans brought about their own demise. Their sins against the very foundation of not only society but also life itself so offended the natural order of the universe that the keepers of that divine order, the gods, condemned them to oblivion.

The theme of an Atlantean judgement stated in Plato was repeated in faraway cultures he never dreamed existed, from the Hopi of the American Southwest to African tribes of the Ivory Coast. This world memory indelibly printed in the folkish consciousness of dozens of peoples, often separated by thousands of miles and as many years, substantiates the verity of lost Atlantis.

On another level, its resemblance to the present condition of world civilization is more than uncanny. Perhaps the ultimate significance and power of Atlantis to impact our time will be revealed when modern man realizes that he has allowed his own society to slip almost as far. The Atlanteans' exploitation of their environment – the misuse and abuse of natural forces – was the immediate cause of their annihilation. Here is preserved the great lesson of Atlantis for our own self-destructive civilization. We, too, are using our high technology to exploit the earth for material wealth. Perhaps the worldwide deterioration of our planet's biosphere, and the dreaded greenhouse effect, resulting in climate destabilization and global flooding (shades of Atlantis!) are all ecological warnings that we are repeating the same catastrophic mistakes made by our Atlantean ancestors.

The present-day planet-wide environmental crisis, international political upheavals on an unprecedented scale, and the emergence of the so-called 'New Age' popularization of unconventional spirituality are perhaps indications that the spirit of Atlantis is re-emerging in our time, while the despoilers of earth's rainforests or the industrial exploiters are the lost souls of reincarnated Atlanteans. Now, as the world again approaches a question of 'to be or not to be', their spirits are returning to work out once more the eternal dilemma of survival. Insatiable for unlimited material prosperity, all the previous values that made the Atlanteans great and powerful were discarded, even despised. They broadened their uncontrolled exploitation of the natural environment until Earth, pushed too far for too long, turned on them with overwhelming fury, annihilating them and all their works. 'In a single day and night', their wealth, technology and self-indulgent power were reduced to ashes floating on the sea.

The gods who combined against Atlantis at the close of Plato's account were for the Greeks mythic representatives, metaphors of the forces of nature. But the parallel stretches beyond Plato, no less powerfully, to us and our time. Is the Atlantis phenomenon a cycle of destruction through which we, too, must pass? Or is it the great warning we may recognize before Mother Earth turns on us, as she did against our Atlantean ancestors?

APPENDIX
A TIMELINE OF LOST WORLDS

40,000 Years Before Present – Sudden sea-level rises triggers migration from Mu around the world. The Pacific motherlanders settle on a large, fertile island about 380 kilometres due west from the Straits of Gibraltar. There, the newcomers merge with the native, Cro-Magnon inhabitants, resulting in a new, hybrid culture – Atlantis.

11,600 Years Before Present – Plato's literal date for the destruction of Atlantis coincides with the end of the last Ice Age which flooded extensive areas of Mu. Some flood-survivors seek refuge in distant Atlantis, swelling its population and significantly contributing to its civilized development.

3113BC – Specified by the Maya calendar as 'the beginning of time', in this same year the Comet Encke, in company with three other comets, makes a close pass to the earth, bombarding its northern hemisphere with meteoric material. Atlantis and Lemuria suffer widespread destruction, but survive the celestial onslaught, which prompts expansionism in the peoples of both lands. While Atlanteans begin copper-mining in North America's Upper Great Lakes Region, Lemurians construct the anti-typhoon weather station at Nan Madol.

2193BC – According to the Frisian *Oera Linda Bok*, in a period reinforced by contemporary geophysical and climate changes, the killer-comet returns to wreck havoc on the world, prompting new migrations from Mu and Atlantis.

1628BC – As revealed in drill-cores extracted from Greenland's icesheet, the Eastern Mediterranean island of Thera catastrophically erupts, as do numerous volcanos around the globe, triggered by the penultimate near-miss of Comet Encke. The geological upheavals it generates are too much for Lemuria, which is overwhelmed. Atlantis, far less effected, recovers at once, and rises toward the apogee of its imperial greatness.

1198BC – In its final, closest and most devastating pass, Comet Encke scores a number of meteoric hits along the

Mid-Atlantic Ridge and possibly on Atlantis itself, which perishes 'in a single day and night', according to Plato. The catastrophe is global, encompassing the destruction of the biblical Sodom and Gomorrah.

Beginning around 700BC – Apollo's sanctuary at the Aegean island of Delos begins receiving offerings brought by the Hyperborean Maidens, members of a Druidic sect, from Salisbury, the south of Britain.

330BC and 320BC – The Greek explorer Pytheas sails to Thule, known today as Iceland.

2nd Century BC – Greek mariners sail far out into the Atlantic Ocean to make land-fall at Antilia, known today as San Miguel in the Azores.

4th Century AD – Roman seafarers arrive along the Atlantic coasts of Mexico and South America, resulting in later legends describing the 'City of the Caesars'.

c.AD550 – 17 Irish monks land at St Brendan's Isle, since known as Labrador.

c.AD1100 – In northern Pakistan, the independent principality Hunza is founded, giving rise to legends of Shambhala or Shangri-La.

BIBLIOGRAPHY

ARMSTRONG, F.W., *Man, Myth and Magic,* NY: Prestigious Publishers, 1985.

BAILLIE, Michael, *Natural Catastrophes During Bronze Age Civilizations: Archaeological, Geological, Astronomical and Cultural Perspectives,* Oxford, England: Archaeo Press, 1998.

BJORKMAN, *The Search for Atlantis,* NY: Alfred A. Knopf, 1927.

BRAGHINE, Col. A., *The Shadow of Atlantis,* US: 60919: Adventures Unlimited Press, 1997 reprint of the 1940 release.

BRINTON, Dr. Daniel G., *Religions of Primitive Peoples,* NY and London: G.P. Putnam's Sons, 1897.

BROWN, J.M., *The Riddle of the Pacific,* US: Adventures Unlimited Press, 1997 reprint of the 1924 release.

BRUNDAGE, Burr Cartwright, *Fifth Sun, Aztec Gods, Aztec World,* US: University of Texas Press, 1983.

BRYANT, Alice, with Galde, Phyllis, *The Message of the Crystal Skull,* US: Llewellyn Publications, 1989.

BUDGE, E.A. Wallis, *The Egyptian Book of the Dead,* NY: Dover Publications, Inc., 1967.

BURLAND, C.A. and Foreman, Werner, *Feathered Serpent and Smoking Mirror,* NY: G.P. Putnam & Sons, 1975.

BUSHNELL, Geoffrey H., *Peru*, NY: Prager, Inc., 1963.

CARLSON, Vada F., *The Great Migration*, US: A.R.E. Press, 1970.

CERVE, W.S., *Lemuria, the Lost Continent of the Pacific*, US: AMORC Printing and Publishing Department, 1942.

CHIASSON, Paul, *The Island of Seven Cities*, NY: St. Martin's Press, 2007.

CHILDRESS, David Hatcher, *Lost Cities and Ancient Mysteries of South America*, US: Adventures Unlimited Press, 1986.

_____, *Lost Cities of Ancient Lemuria and the Pacific*, US: Adventures Unlimited Press, 1988.

_____, *Lost Cities of North and Central America*, US: Adventures Unlimited Press, 1992.

_____, *Vimana Aircraft of Ancient India and Atlantis*, US: Adventures Unlimited Press, 1994.

Chorvinksy, Mark, 'The Mitchell-Hedges Crystal Skull, Part 2: The Skull's Origin', US(MN) FATE 547, October 1995, pp. 22–4.

CHURCHWARD, Col. James, *The Lost Continent of Mu*, Albuquerque, US: Brotherhood of Life Publishing, 1988 reprint of the 1923 release.

_____, *The Children of Mu*, US: Brotherhood of Life Publishing, 1988 reprint of the 1925 release.

_____, *The Sacred Symbols of Mu*, US: Brotherhood of Life Publishing, 1988 reprint of the 1926 release.

_____, *The Books of the Golden Age – The Sacred and Inspired Writings of Mu*, US: Brotherhood of Life Publishing, 1997 reprint of the 1927 release.

_____, *The Cosmic Forces of Mu*, Volumes I and II, NY: Ives Washburn, 1931.

COLTRELL, Arthur C., *The MacMillan Illustrated Encyclopaedia of Myths and Legends*, NY, 1989.

COOPER, C.W., *Crystal Magic*, London: Faber and Faber, 1986.

CROW, Robert, *Crystal Handbook*, US: Hathaway Press, 1984.

CURRAN, Bob, *Lost Lands, Forgotten Realms*, US, NJ: New Page Books, 2007.

DANIEL, Glynn, The Illustrated Encyclopedia of Archaeology, NY: Crowell, 1977.

DEAL, David A., *Discovery of Ancient America*, US: Kherem La Yah Press, 1992

DONNELLY, Ignatius, *Atlantis, the Antediluvian World*, NY: Harper's, 1882.

DORLAND, Frank, *Holy Ice*, US: Galde Press, Inc., 1995.

DUNN, Christopher, *The Giza Power Plant, Technologies of Ancient Egypt*, US: Bear & Co., 1995.

FARRER, Louis, *The Modern Survival of Ancient Linguistics*, London: Regnal House Publishers, Ltd., 1922.

GADDIS, Vincent H., *Native American Myths and Mysteries*, McDonald, Ltd.,1902.

GARVIN, Richard, *The Crystal Skull*, NY: Doubleday and Co., 1971.

GOETZ, Delia and Morley, Sylvanus, *Popol Vuh* (trans. Adrian Recinos), Norman: University of Oklahoma Press, 1950.

HAUGHTON, Brian, Hidden History, Lost Civilizations, Secret Knowledge and Ancient Mysteries, US(NJ): New Page Books, 2007.

JOSEPH, Frank, *Opening the Ark of the Covenant*, US: New Page Books, 2007.

_____, *The Lost Civilization of Lemuria*, US: Bear & Company, 2006.

_____, *The Atlantis Encyclopedia*, US: New Page Books, 2005.

_____, *Survivors of Atlantis*, US: Bear & Company, 2004.

_____, *The Destruction of Atlantis*, US: Bear & Company, 2002.

_____, *Atlantis in Wisconsin*, US: Galde Press, 1995.

_____, *The Lost Pyramids of Rock Lake*, US: Galde Press, 1992.

DE JUBAINVILLE, Arbois, 'Irish Myths', in *The Encyclopaedia of World Mythology*, NY: Galahad Books, 1975.

KRAMER, Noah, *A Sumerian Lexicon*, University of New York Press, 1975.

LEICHT, Hermann, *Pre-Inca Art and Culture*, NY: Orion Press, 1960.

LEMESURIER, Paul, *The Secret of the Great Pyramid*, NY: Faber & Faber, 1975.

LE PLONGEON, August, *Queen Moo and the Egyptian Sphinx*, London: Kegan, Paul, Trench, Truebner, 1896.

LITTLE, Dr. Gregory, *Lost Civilization and the Bermuda Triangle*, (MT) US: Atlantis Rising, Nr. 66, November/December, 2007, p. 42.

MACCANA, Prosinas, *Celtic Mythology*, London: Hamlyn, 1970.

MARRIOTT, Alice and Rachlin, Carol K., *American Indian Mythology*, NY: New American Library, 1968.

MERCATANTE, Anthony S., *Who's Who in Egyptian Mythology*, NY: Clarkson N. Potter, Inc., 1978.

MERCER, Stanley, *The Canary Islands*, NY: Roland Press, Inc., 1962.

MILEWSKI, J.V. and Harford, V.L., (eds), *The Crystal Sourcebook*, Sedona, US: First Editions, 1987.

MOSELEY, Michael E., *The Incas and their Ancestors*, London: Thames &Hudson, 1992.

_____ *Civilization before the Incas*, NY: Parthenon Press, 1995.

NIETZSCHE, Friedrich, *Thus Spake Zarathustra*, NY, Penguin Classics, 1980.

O'KELLEY, Michael, *New Grange*, Cork, Ireland: Houston Printers, Ltd., 1984.

OPPELT, Norman T., *Guide to Prehistoric Ruins of the Southwest*, CO (US): Pruett Publishing, 1989.

POWELL, T.G.E., *The Celts*, NY: Praeger Press, 1959.

PRESCOTT, William H., *The Conquest of Peru*, reprint of 1847 original edition, NY: New American Library, 1961.

QUEST MAGAZINE, Chester (England), Vol.1, number 6, September, 1997.

RIVA, Anna, *Candle Burning Magic, A Spellbook of Rituals for Good and Evil*, US: International Imports, 1994.

SCOT-ELIOT, W., *The Lost Lemuria*, London: Theosophical Publishing House, 1925.

SMITH, William Ramsey, *Myths and Legends of the Australian Aboriginals*, London: George G. Harrap, 1930.

SPENCE, Lewis, *The History of Atlantis*, London: Rider & Co., 1924.

_____, *The Problem of Atlantis*, London: Rider & Co., 1924.

_____, *Atlantis in America*, NY: Brentano's Publishers, 1925.

_____, *The Occult Sciences in Atlantis*, London: Rider & Co., 1942.

Spengler, Oswald, *The Decline of the West*, translated by Lloyd Newhouse, London: Casteleton Publishers, Ltd., 1939.

STACY-JUDD, Robert B., *Atlantis, Mother of Empires*, US: DeVorss & Co., 1973.

SYKES, Edgerton, *Ancient Mythology*, NY: Rawlinson Publishers, 1959.

THOMPSON, Dr. Gunnar, *American Discovery, the Real Story*, US (Seattle): Argonauts Misty Isles Press, 1995.

TOZZER, Alfred, *The New Mayan Dictionary*, US: Dover, 1979 reprint.

UPCZAK, Patricia Rose, *Synchronicity, Signs and Symbols*, US: Synchronicity Publishing, 2001.

VAN OVER, R., Sun Songs, *Creation Myths from around the World*, NY: New American Library, 1980.

WATERS, Frank, *Book of the Hopi*, NY: Viking Press, 1963.

WILLIAMS, Mark R., *In Search of Lemuria, The Lost Pacific Continent in Legend, Myth and Imagination*, US: Golden Era Books, 2001.

YEOWARD, Eileen, *The Canary Islands*, US: Raffelson Press, 1979.

PICTURE CREDITS

Plate page 1, bottom: Bill Stoneham

Plate page 3, bottom: Topfoto

Plate page 4, top: Topfoto

All other images: Frank Joseph